POLITICS AND POLICY
IMPLEMENTATION IN THE
THIRD WORLD

Politics and
Policy Implementation in
the Third World

Politics and Policy Implementation in the Third World

Edited by
MERILEE S. GRINDLE

PRINCETON UNIVERSITY PRESS
PRINCETON, NEW JERSEY

Copyright © 1980 by Princeton University Press

Published by Princeton University Press, Princeton, New Jersey
In the United Kingdom: Princeton University Press, Guildford, Surrey

All Rights Reserved

Library of Congress Cataloging in Publication Data will be
found on the last printed page of this book

This book has been composed in Linotype Times Roman

Clothbound editions of Princeton University Press books
are printed on acid-free paper, and binding materials are
chosen for strength and durability

Printed in the United States of America by Princeton
University Press, Princeton, New Jersey

To Alexandra

Contents

Contents

List of Tables

List of Tables

List of Figures

List of Abbreviations

APRA	American Popular Revolutionary Alliance (Peru)
BNH	National Housing Bank (Brazil)
CAP	Agrarian Production Cooperative (Peru)
CENCIRA	National Center for Training and Investigation for the Agrarian Reform (Peru)
CDC	Commonwealth Development Corporation
CHISAM	Coordinating Agency for Housing in the Rio Area (Brazil)
CNA	National Agrarian Confederation (Peru)
CNC	National Peasants' Confederation (Mexico)
COHAB	Popular Housing Company (Brazil)
CONASUPO	National Staple Products Company (Mexico)
DAPC	District Agricultural Production Committees (India)
FAFEG	Federation of Associations of Favelas in the State of Guanabara (Brazil)
HFCK	Housing Finance Company of Kenya, Ltd.
IAS	Indian Administrative Service
ICS	Indian Civil Service
ICSM	Instant Corn-Soya-Milk
ICT	Territorial Credit Institute (Colombia)
Invicali	Cali Housing Institute (Colombia)
KANU	Kenya African National Union
KPU	Kenya People's Union
MNR	Revolutionary Nationalist Movement (Bolivia)
NCC	Nairobi City Council (Kenya)
NCCK	National Christian Council of Kenya
NHC	National Housing Corporation (Kenya)
PRI	Institutional Revolutionary Party (Mexico)
RE	Rural Electrification (India)
RSEB	Rajasthan State Electricity Board (India)
SAIS	Agrarian Social Interest Society (Peru)
SEB	State Electricity Board (India)
SINAMOS	National System for the Support of Social Mobilization (Peru)

List of Abbreviations

UNIP   United National Independence Party (Zambia)
USAID   United States Agency for International Development
VLW   Village Level Worker (India)

Acknowledgments

MANY individuals have helped this book along its way toward publication. Principal among these, of course, have been the contributors who have been enthusiastic about our shared concern with implementation and open to dialogue about their individual chapters. They deserve credit for the energy expended in field research and the insightfulness of their analyses. In addition, Norman Uphoff of Cornell and John Montgomery of Harvard made useful comments on a draft of the manuscript. Henry Dietz of the University of Texas read it with thoroughness and made numerous constructive suggestions. Cheryl Publicover of Wellesley College provided expert editorial assistance and Steven Grindle added his admirable good humor, his advice, and his understanding. At Princeton University Press, Sanford Thatcher and Marsha Shankman were consistently helpful. I would like to express my appreciation to these individuals for their support and encouragement. I am also grateful to Wellesley College for a faculty research grant that helped defray some of the costs involved in manuscript preparation.

Acknowledgment is given to the University of California Press for permission to reprint parts of the following books:

Bureaucrats, Politicians, and Peasants in Mexico: A Case Study in Public Policy, by Merilee S. Grindle

The Myth of Marginality: Urban Politics and Poverty in Rio de Janeiro, by Janice Perlman

Introduction

ONE · *Policy Content and Context in Implementation*

MERILEE S. GRINDLE

THE politics of policy implementation has recently emerged as a topic of interest for students of politics in both industrial and Third World countries. Implementation has captured their attention because it is evident that a wide variety of factors—from the availability of sufficient resources to the structure of intergovernmental relations, from the commitment of lower level officials to reporting mechanisms within the bureaucracy, from the political leverage of opponents of the policy to accidents of timing, luck, and seemingly unrelated events—can and do frequently intervene between the statement of policy goals and their actual achievement in the society. Such factors can account for the "often imperfect correspondence between policies adopted and services actually delivered."[1] Attempts to explain this divergence have led to the realization that implementation, even when successful, involves far more than a mechanical translation of goals into routine procedures; it involves fundamental questions about conflict, decision making, and "who gets what" in a society.[2]

It was during the late 1960s and early 1970s that a series of useful and provocative books and articles appeared in the United States dealing explicitly with the problems of implementation. Many of these were stimulated by the desire to explain why the programs of the Great Society of the Johnson Administration had

Note: I am indebted to Norman Uphoff of the Center for International Studies, Cornell University, for invaluable comments, suggestions, and insights into the problems of implementation in the Third World.

[1] D. Van Meter and C. Van Horn, "The Policy Implementation Process: A Conceptual Framework," *Administration and Society*, 6, No. 4 (February 1975), 446.

[2] The phrase is Harold Lasswell's. See his *Politics: Who Gets What, When, How* (New York: Meridian, 1958).

not achieved the results they predicted.[3] Each of these studies considered how the policy or program itself—its goals, implementing design, and availability of resources—helped shape the observed outcomes. In addition, however, the studies revealed other explanatory variables in the division of political power in the society and in the conflict and influences brought to bear on implementing decisions, factors that focused attention on the broader environment in which the programs were pursued. More recently, there have appeared several studies that have attempted to define the parameters of a general process of implementation by cataloguing the range of variables that intervene in it and by specifying some of the relationships among such variables.[4]

Explicit considerations of the frequent disparity between goals and outcomes in the implementation of public policy in the Third World, however, have tended to focus more narrowly on the administrative apparatus and procedures of implementing bureaucracies or on the characteristics of bureaucratic officials.[5] Until now,

[3] See, for examples of case studies of policy delivery, M. Derthick, *New Towns In-Town: Why a Federal Program Failed* (Washington, D.C.: The Urban Institute, 1972); M. Derthick, *Uncontrollable Spending for Social Services Grants* (Washington, D.C.: The Brookings Institution, 1975); A. Heidenheimer and M. Parkinson, "Equalizing Educational Opportunity in Britain and the United States: The Politics of Implementation," in W. Gwyn and G. Edwards, III, eds., *Perspectives on Public Policymaking*, 15 (New Orleans, La.: Tulane Studies in Political Science, 1975); P. Lermack, "Hookers, Judges, and Bail Forfeitures: The Importance of Internally Generated Demands on Policy Implementing Institutions," *Administration and Society*, 8, No. 4 (February 1977); J. Murphy, "The Education Bureaucracies Implement Novel Policy: The Politics of Title I of ESEA, 1965-1972," in A. P. Sindler, ed., *Policy and Politics in America: Six Case Studies* (Boston: Little, Brown & Co., 1973); G. Orfield, *The Reconstruction of Southern Education* (New York: John Wiley, 1969); J. Pressman and A. Wildavsky, *Implementation* (Berkeley: University of California Press, 1973).

[4] See E. Bardach, *The Implementation Game* (Cambridge, Mass.: MIT Press, 1977); E. Hargrove, *The Missing Link: The Study of the Implementation of Social Policy* (Washington, D.C.: The Urban Institute, 1975); T. B. Smith, "The Policy Implementation Process," *Policy Sciences*, 4, No. 2 (June 1973); Van Meter and Van Horn, "Policy Implementation Process"; D. Van Meter and C. Van Horn, "The Implementation of Intergovernmental Policy," in C. Jones and R. Thomas, eds., *Public Policy Making in a Federal System* (Beverly Hills, Calif.: Sage Publications, 1976); W. Williams, "Implementation Analysis and Assessment," *Policy Analysis* (Summer 1975).

[5] See R. Gurevich, "Teachers, Rural Development, and the Civil Service

there has been little attention given to linking characteristics of policies and programs to their subsequent implementation, to relating implementation problems to characteristics of the political regimes in which they are pursued, or to exploring the general nature of implementation in the Third World.[6] These are the interests that have stimulated the editing of this volume.

More specifically, this book is the result of a conviction held by its contributors that the implementation process is especially central to politics in the countries of Africa, Asia, and Latin America and is thus worthy of investigation and analysis. The chapters in this collection are addressed to two broad questions about implementation in general that are related by the authors to the specific conditions surrounding the execution of public programs in the Third World. First, the authors are concerned with the impact of *content*: What effect does the content of public policy have on its implementation? A second question, about *context*, is of equal concern to them: How does the political context of administrative action affect policy implementation? Such questions are of interest to these scholars because they share a common perspective about implementation itself. For them, it is an ongoing process of decision making by a variety of actors, the ultimate outcome of which is determined by the content of the program being pursued and by the interaction of the decision makers within a

---

in Thailand," *Asian Survey*, 15, No. 10 (October 1975); H. Hart, "The Village and Development Administration," in J. Heaphey, ed., *Spatial Dimensions of Development Administration* (Durham, N.C.: Duke University Press, 1971); S. Heginbotham, *Cultures in Conflict: The Four Faces of Indian Bureaucracy* (New York: Columbia University Press, 1975); J. Honey, *Toward Strategies for Public Administration Development in Latin America* (Syracuse, N.Y.: Syracuse University Press, 1968); M. Kriesberg, *Public Administration in Developing Countries* (Washington, D.C.: The Brookings Institution, 1965); A. Raper, *Rural Development in Action: The Comprehensive Experiment at Comilla, East Pakistan* (Ithaca, N.Y.: Cornell University Press, 1970); S. Wallman, *Take Out Hunger: Two Case Studies of Rural Development in Basutoland* (London: Athlone, 1970).

[6] Exceptions to this statement can be found in P. Cleaves, *Bureaucratic Politics and Administration in Chile* (Berkeley: University of California Press, 1974); R. Daland, *Brazilian Planning: Development Politics and Administration* (Chapel Hill, N.C.: University of North Carolina Press, 1967); L. Graham, *Civil Service Reform in Brazil* (Austin: University of Texas Press, 1968); M. Grindle, *Bureaucrats, Politicians, and Peasants in Mexico: A Case Study in Public Policy* (Berkeley: University of California Press, 1977); F. Riggs, *Administration in Developing Countries: The Theory of Prismatic Society* (Boston: Houghton Mifflin, 1964).

5

given politico-administrative context. The task the authors have set for themselves is to develop generalizations on the basis of case study material about how and why content and contextual variables intervene in the implementation process in the Third World. Before exploring in greater detail the contributions to this volume, however, it is useful to define more explicitly what is meant by implementation, content, and context, and to consider why the Third World has been singled out as a focus of the studies appearing here.

Implementation: From Policy to Program to Outcomes

In general, the task of implementation is to establish a link that allows the goals of public policies to be realized as outcomes of governmental activity. It involves, therefore, the creation of a "policy delivery system," in which specific means are designed and pursued in the expectation of arriving at particular ends.[7] Thus, public policies—broad statements of goals, objectives, and means —are translated into action programs that aim to achieve the ends stated in the policy. It is apparent, then, that a variety of programs may be developed in response to the same policy goals. Action programs themselves may be disaggregated into more specific projects to be administered. The intent of action programs and individual projects is to cause a change in the policy environment, a change that can be considered an outcome of the program.

The distinction made here between policy and program implies that policy implementation is a function of program implementation and is dependent upon its outcome. As a consequence, the study of the process of policy implementation almost necessarily involves investigation and analysis of concrete action programs that have been designed as a means of achieving broader policy goals. This is apparent in the studies collected here, for instance. Each discusses the general developmental objectives that a Third World government hoped to achieve—greater agricultural productivity, provision of low-income urban housing, slum eradication, rural development—and then analyzes a specific program aimed at achieving these goals. The successes and failures that are catalogued in the following chapters are the outcomes of specific programs but they also serve as partial measures of the success or failure of overall policy implementation.

Such a clear distinction between policy and program is difficult

[7] Van Meter and Van Horn, "Policy Implementation Process," p. 446.

to maintain in practice, however. It is to some degree obscured by the variety of levels at which the term "policy" is often used. For example, a policy may go through successive stages at which objectives are defined more precisely. A general statement that the agricultural policy of the government is to increase productivity may be translated into a policy of providing government aid to commercially oriented small farmers. This in turn may be translated into a policy of providing irrigation and transportation facilities to these indivduals. At this last phase of definition, the terms policy and program are frequently used interchangeably. In addition, because policy implementation is considered to depend on program outcomes, it is difficult to separate the fate of policies from that of their constituent programs. At what point, for example, do program failures signal the overall failure of the general policy? Moreover, to say that policy implementation depends upon program implementation assumes that the programs are in fact appropriately geared to achieving the goals of the policy, an assumption not always borne out in practice.[8]

In this volume we have tried to resolve this problem by considering implementation to be a general process of administrative action that can be investigated at the specific program level. Its success or failure can be evaluated in terms of the capacity actually to deliver programs as designed. In turn, overall policy implementation can be evaluated by measuring program outcomes against policy goals (see Figure 1-1). The general process of implementation thus can begin only when general goals and objectives have been specified, when action programs have been designed, and when funds have been allocated for the pursuit of the goals. These are basic conditions for the execution of any explicit public policy.[9] Theoretically, at this point the policy formulation process is super-

[8] See G. Benveniste, *Bureaucracy and National Planning: A Sociological Case Study in Mexico* (New York: Praeger, 1970); A. Gilbert, "Urban and Regional Development Policies in Colombia Since 1961," in W. Cornelius and F. Trueblood, eds., *Urbanization and Inequality: The Political Economy of Urban Development in Latin America* (Beverly Hills, Calif.: Sage, 1975); F. Levy, Jr., "Economic Planning in Venezuela," in C. Thurber and L. Graham, eds., *Development Administration in Latin America* (Durham, N.C.: Duke University Press, 1973); E. Lozano, "Housing the Urban Poor in Chile: Contrasting Approaches Under Christian Democracy and Unidad Popular," in Cornelius and Trueblood, *Urbanization and Inequality*; R. Packenham, *Liberal America and the Third World* (Princeton: Princeton University Press, 1973).

[9] We have not considered in this volume the implementation of implicit policy.

7

seded by the policy implementation process, and programs are activated. But the difference between formulation and implementation is also one difficult to maintain in practice, since feedback from implementation procedures may lead to modifications in policy goals and directions; or demands that rules and guidelines be interpreted or reinterpreted may lead to a considerable amount of policymaking at the site of implementation. More important in terms of the process of implementation is the fact that decisions made at the design or formulation stage have a considerable impact on how implementation proceeds. This is clear by considering, for example, the impact on subsequent implementation of the decision to allocate three million dollars to achieve policy goals rather than thirty or three hundred million. In addition, the process of implementation is greatly affected by the kinds of objectives that have been specified for it and by the manner in which the goals have been stated. That is, formulation decisions made—or not made—about the type of policy to be pursued and the shape of programs to be executed are integral factors in determining how successfully the programs themselves will be delivered.

The Content of Policy

Theodore Lowi has pointed out that the kind of policy being made will have considerable impact on the kind of political activity stimulated by the policymaking process.[10] This observation can be applied with equal validity to the implementation process, encouraging consideration of the "implementability" of various programs. For instance, to the extent that public actions seek to introduce changes in social, political, and economic relationships, they generally stimulate considerable opposition from those whose interests are threatened by them. Landowners who oppose agrarian reform measures, often violently, are evidence of this reaction. A distinction can also be made between programs providing collective benefits, which encourage categorical demand making, and those providing benefits that are divisible, which may mobilize more particularistic kinds of demands at the implementation stage. Thus, programs delivering collective goods such as the provision of light and water in urban slum neighborhoods may be readily implemented in the Third World because the compliance of groups or localities affected will tend to be forthcoming with a minimal

[10] See T. Lowi, "American Business, Public Policy, Case Studies, and Political Theory," *World Politics*, 16, No. 4 (July 1964).

amount of conflict or dissent.[11] Programs with divisible benefits such as housing, in contrast, may exacerbate conflict and competition among those seeking to benefit from them and may be more difficult to execute as intended.[12]

Differences in the degree of behavior change the program envisions for its intended beneficiaries is another way the content of policy affects its implementation. The introduction of new technologies for agricultural development is a commonly cited example of a program requiring considerable behavioral adaptation and participation on the part of recipients. In contrast, providing housing for low-income groups may require little in the way of changed behavior patterns. Moreover, programs that are designed to achieve long-range objectives may be more difficult to implement than those whose advantages are immediately apparent to the beneficiaries. As an example, the small amount of support and participation that preventive health programs are able to elicit from target populations in the Third World often stands in stark contrast to the receptiveness of potential recipients of land titles in urban squatter settlements. This is because the latter policy directly affects residents' economic situation and sense of security.[13]

The content of various policies also dictates the site of implementation. The activation of monetary policy, for instance, usually depends upon a limited number of key decision units in the national capital, such as high-level actors in the finance ministry and the central bank. Education policy, on the other hand, is executed by a large number of individual decision makers dispersed throughout an extensive geographic area but usually belonging to a single bureaucratic organization. Ultimately, each school director might be envisioned as an implementor of whatever programs are designed. Even more complicated is the case of housing or agricultural policy that depends upon a network of widely dispersed decision units whose responsibilities are also organizationally dispersed. Local and national level agents of the ministry of agriculture, the agrarian reform institute, the community development agency, the public works ministry, and the agricultural credit bank,

[11] See W. Cornelius, "Urbanization and Political Demand Making: Political Participation Among the Migrant Poor in Latin America," *American Political Science Review*, 68, No. 3 (September 1974); S. Hadden, Chap. 7 of this volume.

[12] See Irene Rothenberg, Chap. 6 of this volume.

[13] See Cornelius, "Urbanization and Political Demand Making."

for example, may all be implicated as implementors of a rural development policy in any given country. As the site of implementation becomes more dispersed, both geographically and organizationally, the task of executing a particular program becomes more difficult, given the increase in decisional units involved.[14] Accordingly, it might be expected that implementing a rural development program would be far more onerous than executing a new program for primary school instruction.

Decisions made during policy formulation may also indicate who is to be charged with executing various programs, and such decisions can affect how the policy is pursued. There may be, for example, differences in the capacity of various bureaucratic agencies to manage programs successfully. Some will have more active, expert, and dedicated personnel than others, some will enjoy greater support of political elites and have greater access to resources, and some will be more able to cope with the range of demands made upon them. In addition, the form in which policy goals themselves are stated may have a decided impact on implementation. Whether goals are stated clearly or ambiguously and whether political and administrative officials are in agreement about what the goals are will be shown to have been decisive for the implementation of specific programs in several of the case studies in this volume.

The Context of Policy

Clearly, then, the content of public programs and policies is an important factor in determining the outcome of implementation initiatives. But as many of the examples above indicate, and as is evident in Figure 1-1, policy or program content is often a critical factor because of the real or potential impact it may have on a given social, political, and economic setting. Therefore, it is necessary to consider the context or environment in which administrative action is pursued. We have conceived of implementation to be an ongoing process of decision making involving a variety of actors. In the process of administering any given program, many actors are called upon to make choices about specific allocations of public resources and many others may attempt to influence decisions. A brief listing of those who might be involved in the implementation of any particular program would include national level planners; national, regional, and local politicians; economic

---

[14] On this point, see Pressman and Wildavsky, *Implementation*, chap. 5.

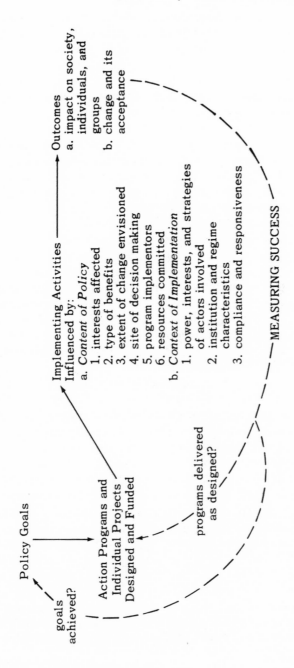

Figure 1-1. Implementation as a Political and Administrative Process

elite groups, especially at the local level; recipient groups; and bureaucratic implementors at middle and lower levels. These actors may be intensely or marginally involved in implementation, depending upon the content of the program and the form in which it is administered. Each may have a particular interest in the program, and each may seek to achieve it by making demands on allocation procedures. Frequently, the goals of the actors will be in direct conflict with each other and the outcome of this conflict and consequently, of who gets what, will be determined by the strategies, resources, and power positions of each of the actors involved. What is implemented may thus be the result of a political calculus of interests and groups competing for scarce resources, the response of implementing officials, and the actions of political elites, all interacting within given institutional contexts. Analysis of the implementation of specific programs therefore may imply assessing the "power capabilities" of the actors, their interests and the strategies for achieving them, and the characteristics of the regime in which they interact.[15] This in turn may facilitate assessing the potential for achieving policy and program goals.

In achieving such goals officials face two subordinate problems that highlight the interaction of program environment and program administration. First, officials must address the problem of how to achieve compliance with the ends enunciated in the policy.[16] They must, for example, acquire the support of political elites, and the compliance of implementing agencies, of bureaucrats charged with carrying out programs, of lower level political elites, and of intended beneficiaries. They must turn the opposition of those who may be harmed by the programs into acceptance of them, and they must keep those who are excluded, but who wish to acquire benefits, from subverting them. Eliciting this kind of compliance may mean much bargaining, much accommodation, and again, con-

[15] The term, "power capabilities," is taken from C. Anderson, "The Latin American Political System," in N. Uphoff and W. Ilchman, eds., *The Political Economy of Development* (Berkeley: University of California Press, 1972), p. 171.

[16] The general problem of compliance and control within bureaucracies is considered in A. Downs, *Inside Bureaucracy* (Boston: Little, Brown & Co., 1967), chaps. 11-12; and H. Kaufman, *Administrative Feedback: Monitoring Subordinates' Behavior* (Washington, D.C.: The Brookings Institution, 1973). The need to attain the compliance of extragovernmental groups is considered in the context of the Third World in W. Ilchman and N. Uphoff, *The Political Economy of Change* (Berkeley: University of California Press, 1969).

siderable conflict. But, if overall policy goals are to be realized, the resources traded to acquire compliance must not jeopardize the impact or focus of specific programs. Frequently, however, this is precisely what occurs.

The other side of the problem of achieving policy and program goals within a specific environment is that of responsiveness. Ideally, public institutions such as bureaucracies must be responsive to the needs of those they are intended to benefit in order to serve them most adequately. In addition, without a considerable amount of responsiveness during implementation, public officials are deprived of information to evaluate program achievement and of support crucial to its success. In many cases, however, responsiveness may mean that policy goals are not achieved because of the intervention of the same individuals or groups, either in order to acquire specific types of goods and services in greater amounts or to obstruct the accomplishment of particular programs that may not be accepted by them as beneficial. The problem for policy administrators is to ensure an adequate amount of responsiveness to provide flexibility, support, and feedback, while at the same time maintaining enough control over the distribution of resources to achieve the stated goals.[17] This is a delicate balance to attain, and one that requires considerable political acumen in the calculation of the probable response of the actors involved and their capacity to subvert program goals. To be effective, then, implementors must be skilled in the arts of politics and must understand well the environment in which they seek to realize public policies and programs.

[17] The question of responsiveness of public administrations in Third World countries is discussed in D. Emmerson, *The Bureaucracy in Indonesia* (Cambridge: MIT, Center for International Studies, 1974); M. Esman, "Administrative Doctrine and Developmental Needs," in E. Morgan, ed., *The Administration of Change in Africa* (New York: Dunellen, 1974); A. Guerreiro-Ramos, "The New Ignorance and the Future of Public Administration in Latin America," in Thurber and Graham, *Development Administration in Latin America*; J. Heaphey, "Spatial Aspects of Development Administration: Introduction," in Heaphey, *Spatial Dimensions*; J. Montgomery, *Technology and Civic Life: Making and Implementing Development Decisions* (Cambridge, Mass.: MIT Press, 1974); P. Raup, "Some Interrelationships Between Public Administration and Agricultural Development," in Uphoff and Ilchman, *The Political Economy of Development*; F. Riggs, *Administration in Developing Countries*, chap. 10. In this volume, the relationship of control and compliance is discussed by Susan Hadden in Chap. 7.

Related to this is a theme that emerges in a number of the case studies in this volume: the extent to which political regimes and administrative organizations have the power to implement policies they are committed to. Good intentions may count for little if those responsible for various policies or programs are unable to control their pursuit. At issue here may be the extent to which implementation activities should be decentralized or, on the other hand, controlled from the political or bureaucratic center of the country. Our studies suggest that political systems that do not concentrate extensive amounts of power at the center ought not to decentralize implementation authority or responsibility if they wish to see their objectives attained. They may fail because they have little control over the rewards or the penalties necessary to elicit compliance with program goals. Studies of implementation in the United States also suggest the possibility of subversion of program goals when power at the center is diffused widely. Yet, decentralization may be a viable strategy where central authorities retain the capacity to ensure that implementing activities remain within the boundaries of program objectives and structures.

This suggests that consideration of the context of administrative action also involves such variables as the structure of political institutions and the type of regime in which a policy or program is pursued. A number of studies of implementation in the United States, for example, have singled out the federal structure of American political institutions to be a contextual factor that shapes policy and program outcomes.[18] In this volume, several studies indicate that the process of implementation may vary considerably depending upon whether the political regime is an authoritarian one, or a more open system where elections impose a greater degree of responsiveness on both political and administrative officials and limit the capacity for imposed "solutions." Matters of ideology, culture, political alliances and payoffs, and international events are other environmental influences that may also have considerable impact on the administrative process. Moreover, programs are not implemented in isolation from other public policies; a program's success may easily be affected by the priorities of political officials or the outcome of other programs. These factors imply that programs identical in content may still be implemented differently if the context in which they are pursued differs substantially. This

[18] See Derthick, *Uncontrollable Spending*; Murphy, "The Education Bureaucracies"; Pressman and Wildavsky, *Implementation*.

consideration of the environment in which implementation occurs leads to the question of why we have chosen to devote a volume to the study of implementation and politics in the Third World, a question that can be answered best through a discussion of characteristic aspects of politics in the countries of Asia, Africa, and Latin America.

THE THIRD WORLD: POLITICS AND IMPLEMENTATION

To a much greater extent than in the political systems of the United States and Western Europe, the process of implementing public policies is a focus of political participation and competition in the countries of Asia, Africa, and Latin America. This is true because of characteristics of the political systems themselves, such as the remoteness and inaccessibility of the policymaking process to most individuals and the extensive competition engendered by widespread need and very scarce resources. Thus, while in the United States and Western Europe much political activity is focused on the input stage of the policy process, in the Third World a large portion of individual and collective demand making, the representation of interests, and the emergence and resolution of conflict occurs at the output stage.[19]

[19] Thus, for example, James Scott states, "A large proportion of individual demands, and even group demands, in developing nations reach the political system, not before laws are passed, but rather at the enforcement stage," and Myron Weiner indicates that "organized groups largely influence the administration rather than the formulation of policy." See J. Scott, "Corruption, Machine Politics and Political Change," *American Political Science Review*, 63, No. 4 (December 1969), 1142; and M. Weiner, *The Politics of Scarcity* (Chicago: University of Chicago Press, 1962), p. 217. In a wide-ranging discussion of administration in the Third World, Riggs concludes, "Since the clientele is unable to organize or exercise political influence to modify the rules, its primary strategy involves direct pressure upon the officials concerned with policy implementation, to secure a suspension of the rules or to speed the provision of authorized services." See F. Riggs, *Administration in Developing Countries*, p. 271. Studies indicating this characteristic of politics in Third World countries are found in J. Abueva, "Administrative Culture and Behavior and Middle Civil Servants in the Philippines," in E. W. Weidner, ed., *Development Administration in Asia* (Durham, N.C.: Duke University Press, 1970); Cornelius. "Urbanization and Political Demand Making"; N. Leff, *Economic Policy-Making and Development in Brazil, 1947-1964* (New York: John Wiley, 1968); J. Scott, *Comparative Political Corruption* (Englewood Cliffs, N.J.: Prentice Hall, 1972). The literature on corruption and machine politics in the Third World

15

This output stage acquires added significance because interest aggregating structures tend to be weak in the Third World. Political parties, for example, may be more important as mechanisms by which elites control mass followings than as means by which interests are articulated from below to government leadership. This is particularly true in regimes in which single or dominant parties direct the political stage.[20] Elsewhere, parties may be vehicles for the personal ambitions of individual politicians who are divorced from any real commitment to achieving goals beyond the acquisition of government jobs and their distribution to loyal followers.[21] In other countries, "technocratic" military regimes have abolished parties and declared them to be inappropriate for the society at its level of development.[22]

Interest groups may be similarly ineffective as structures for presenting collective demands to the political leadership. Interest associations frequently are captive organizations of ruling parties, exist only at the sufferance of the government, or, like parties, are formed for the single purpose of protecting the political interests of their leadership. Added to these problems may be other constraints on their aggregative capacities such as limited communication facilities, dispersed potential membership, and lack of education and experience. These characteristics mean that frequently there are few organizations in existence that are capable of representing the interests of broad categories of citizens and formulating policies responsive to their particular needs. Those few that are effective in this role tend to be the creatures of wealthy and powerful groups such as bankers, industrialists, and landowners.

---

has especially emphasized this aspect of the implementation process. See the articles in A. Heidenheimer, ed., *Political Corruption* (New York: Holt, Rinehart and Winston, 1970; and Scott, *Comparative Political Corruption*.

[20] See R. Hansen, *The Politics of Mexican Development* (Baltimore: Johns Hopkins University Press, 1971), for a description of the control function of the dominant party in Mexico.

[21] See D. Chalmers, "Parties and Society in Latin America," *Studies in Comparative International Development*, 7, No. 2 (Summer 1972); and C. Lande, "Networks and Groups in Southeast Asia: Some Observations on the Group Theory of Politics," *American Political Science Review*, 67, No. 1 (March 1973).

[22] See, for example, T. Skidmore, "Politics and Economic Policy Making in Authoritarian Brazil, 1937-1971," in A. Stepan, ed., *Authoritarian Brazil: Origins, Policies, and Future* (New Haven: Yale University Press, 1973). For a general commentary on military regimes, see E. Feit, *The Armed Bureaucrats* (Boston: Houghton Mifflin Co., 1973).

Related to the weakness of interest aggregating mechanisms in Third World countries is the frequently encountered attitude of leaders in both political and administrative positions that participation in policy formulation processes is illegitimate or inefficient.[23] Their concern for rapid development and the central role of the public sector in achieving economic and social goals may lead them to give policymaking responsibility to elite planning bodies in the national capital, and then to protect these organizations from the "parochial" pressures exerted by interest and clientele groups, and from the delays and conflict resulting from open debate, inputs from legislative bodies, and exposure to the mass media. Some political regimes have been particularly active in attempting to institute "technocratic" and "apolitical" approaches to policymaking. This attitude of political and administrative elites establishes major barriers between the rural and urban poor and the remote officials who generate plans for national development.

At the same time, the policies of a regime have great impact on the daily lives of citizens. Most Third World countries have extensive and active public sectors involved in many aspects of economic and social life, and state bureaucracies may be among the strongest institutions in the society.[24] Many of the most important policies established by political elites include distributive and redistributive measures. Agrarian reform, urban development, housing, social security, health, employment, and education all vitally concern the lives of individual citizens and, in a context of very scarce resources, who gets what and how much is likely to be of central concern to the populace. Moreover, governmental decisions such as where to focus regional development plans, where to locate government industries, who should receive government contracts, or who should be included in a preventive health program all highlight the potential for conflict and the predictable desire to influence such decisions. Thus, while participation is frequently limited to policymaking, there still exists a great desire among citizens to affect the outcome of governmental decision making because such outcomes affect them vitally and personally.

In order to have any impact on decision making, then, many in Third World countries have found the implementation phase of the

---

[23] See Grindle, *Bureaucrats, Politicians, and Peasants*; Leff, *Economic Policy Making*; Riggs, *Administration in Developing Countries*, p. 271.

[24] See, for example, Esman, "Administrative Doctrine and Developmental Needs."

policy process to be particularly suited to their needs. In attempts to acquire government goods and services, individuals and groups find it especially rewarding to focus their demand making efforts on officials and agencies empowered to distribute benefits, or on politicians who may have influence on individual allocations. The factions, patron-client linkages, ethnic ties, and personal coalitions that are often the basis of political activity are well suited to making individualized demands on the bureaucratic apparatus for the allocation of goods and services.[25] This kind of participation, which may have a great impact on whether and how national policy goals are achieved, frequently occurs at the local level, far beyond the purview of national administrators charged with program or policy responsibility. Thus, structures and relationships that impede effective demand making on an aggregative national level may be entirely functional for achieving particularistic and short-term goals at the local level where very specific groups and interests are affected. In fact, from the perspective of individual citizens, this may be the most effective and rational means to acquire what they want from the government.

Moreover, political elites, by choice or by inability to change the situation, may regard the implementation process as a political one in which a considerable amount of adjustment must occur. Flexibility in policy execution may even be part of a polity-wide accommodation and conflict resolution system used by political elites to maintain the often tenuous cohesion of the political community itself.[26] Additionally, constraints on communication between superiors and subordinates, often described in studies of Third World bureaucracies, may mean that national level plans are not adapted to the realities of physical, economic, or political conditions; adjustment of policies or programs to local conditions

[25] See, for examples of this kind of demand making, G. Heeger, "Bureaucracy, Political Parties, and Political Development," *World Politics*, 25, No. 4 (July 1973); Lande, "Networks and Groups"; N. Nicholson, "The Factional Model and the Study of Politics," *Comparative Political Studies*, 5, No. 3 (October 1972); R. Sandbrook, "Patrons, Clients, and Factions: New Dimensions of Conflict Analysis in Africa," *Canadian Journal of Political Science*, 5, No. 1 (March 1972); A. Valenzuela, "Political Constraints to the Establishment of Socialism in Chile," in A. Valenzuela and J. Valenzuela, eds., *Chile: Politics and Society* (New Brunswick, N.J.: Transaction Books, 1976).

[26] See Grindle, *Bureaucrats, Politicians, and Peasants*; M. Greenberg, *Bureaucracy and Development: A Mexican Case Study* (Lexington, Mass.: Heath Lexington Books, 1970), p. 81.

may be the responsibility of field agents of national or regional bureaucracies who, confronting difficulties in their daily routines, may employ considerable discretion in distributing public resources.[27] They, rather than national planners or politicians, may be the most logical and the most accessible individuals to contact in any attempts to make effective demands on the political system.

This means that the implementation process may be the major arena in which individuals and groups are able to pursue conflicting interests and compete for access to scarce resources. It may even be the principal nexus of the interaction between the government and the citizenry, between public officials and their constituents. Moreover, the outcome of this competition and interaction can determine both the content and the impact of programs established by government elites, and thus influence the course of a country's development. Given the concentration of political activity on the implementation process, it is likely that policies and programs will be even more difficult to manage and predict and even more subject to alteration in the Third World than elsewhere. Therefore, we think it both appropriate and useful to present a volume of studies that explores the process of implementation in the specific political context of the Third World.

THE CONTRIBUTIONS: STUDIES OF IMPLEMENTATION
CHOICE MAKING

The chapters appearing in this volume have been selected because they illuminate much about both the general process of implementation and the more specific parameters of political activity in the Third World. Nine are case studies of specific development programs that Third World governments have attempted to implement; concrete experiences from Brazil, Colombia, India, Kenya, Mexico, Peru, and Zambia are presented. Most of the studies report on field investigations undertaken after 1970. All of the contributions analyze the implementation of distributive or redistributive policies. Studies include cases of rural electrification, health care, and rural development in India; cooperative policy in

---

[27] See M. Hanson, "Organizational Bureaucracy in Latin America and the Legacy of Spanish Colonialism," *Journal of Inter-American Studies and World Affairs*, 16, No. 2 (May 1974); Heginbotham, *Cultures in Conflict*; L. Pye, *Politics, Personality and Nation Building* (New Haven: Yale University Press, 1962), chap. 15; Raup, "Some Interrelationships," p. 41.

Zambia; housing policy in Brazil, Colombia, and Kenya; agrarian reform in Peru; and agricultural development in Mexico. These programs involve the choice of how scarce resources will be allocated and who should be the beneficiaries of governmental programs. Especially in the case of redistributive policies, low-income and low-status recipient groups are involved; the studies provide important insight into the capacity of these generally powerless groups to elicit resources and response from their governments, frequently in the face of considerable opposition from those who are threatened by redistribution.

The case studies also attempt to analyze "what went wrong" with the program under consideration and several seek to suggest means of avoiding similar outcomes in other contexts. While each scholar has proposed unique solutions to his or her particular policy problem, there is much to be learned from the studies taken as a whole. From the perspective of implementation as an ongoing process of decision making influenced by both program content and environmental context, the contributions to this volume focus attention on the choices made by decision makers—how and why such choices are arrived at—and on the consequences of these choices for subsequent policy implementation.

The volume is organized into three parts, each of which addresses a crucial juncture where decisions are made that shape the range of choices available for subsequent implementation efforts and affect the outcome of those efforts. These important choices involve those made in defining policies and programs; those made about the strategy for implementation; and those concerning the beneficiaries of a given program. Figure 1-2 is a simple diagram of these decision points. The arrows between boxes suggest that decisions made at one point about the content of programs have important consequences for later decisions. The broken arrows suggest that decisional outcomes are influenced by the political and administrative environments in which they are made. This figure, then, presents a schematic of the organization of the volume and indicates major relationships among broad categories of the independent and dependent variables considered.

By emphasizing the importance of choice and decision making, we do not mean to suggest that the implementation process is entirely predictable and always capable of management, nor do we claim that we have considered all possible influences on it. As will be evident in many of the case studies, accidents of timing

20

Figure 1.2. Critical Choices in the Implementation Process

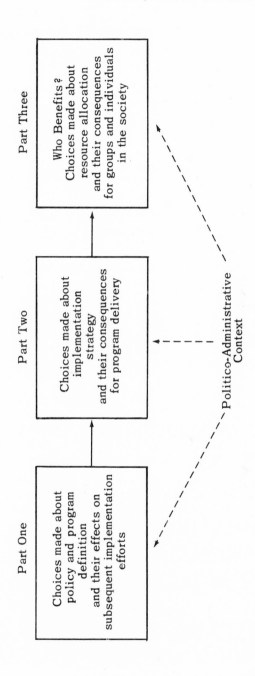

Part One

Choices made about
policy and program
definition
and their effects on
subsequent implementation
efforts

Part Two

Choices made about
implementation
strategy
and their consequences
for program delivery

Part Three

Who Benefits?
Choices made about
resource allocation
and their consequences
for groups and individuals
in the society

Politico-Administrative
Context

21

and happenstances seemingly unrelated to the program being considered—a change in political leadership, a war, a devaluation, an alteration in foreign policy—can have a decisive influence on even well planned and managed programs. That all possible variables have not been taken into consideration nor their ramifications explored is also evident. What we have tried to do is present a general explanation of the dynamics of implementation decision making in the Third World, indicating where we think important types of choices cluster in the process. We have not intended this to be a handbook on how to implement specific programs, nor on how to organize implementing agencies; we seek rather to consider the implementation process broadly, from the perspective of conscious choice making embedded within particular politico-administrative contexts. A brief preview of the studies may serve to indicate how we have attempted to achieve this.

Part One: From Formulation to Implementation

The two chapters in the first part of this volume consider the linkage between policy formulation and the implementation process. The chapters by Stephen Quick and Cynthia McClintock both deal with the overall goal structure of public policies and its consequences for the implementation of specific programs. In each case, aspects of the political environment—in the case of Zambia, the political impetus given to a program of agricultural cooperatives, in the case of Peru, the lack of agreement about the scope and rapidity of change in the society—influenced how programs were intially defined. In terms of our emphasis on choice making and its consequences, both studies suggest the extensive influence of nondecisions on the implementation process. The failure of political elites to specify priorities in Zambia and to agree on what priorities should be in Peru, were cases of nonchoice making with extensive ramifications for the capacity of administrative agencies to carry out program activities.

These chapters indicate that governments in Third World countries may be subject to special conditions that influence how program and policy goals are arrived at. Most are in a position of having to promise much to their citizens. The enormity of human and physical needs in poor countries, the desire to establish the legitimacy of the political regime by providing tangible evidence of improving conditions, the feeling that the deprivations of the colonial or neocolonial past must be obliterated, the commitment

22

to indigenous or "Third Way" ideologies, the need for rapid development—all create a situation in which political leaders are
likely to espouse policies that will lead to radical and rapid improvement in the conditions of life. Frequently such policies are
couched in ideological contexts that may cloud the actual problems involved in executing them.

In Chapter Two, Quick develops an arresting case against
policies that receive extensive political support and limelight at
the formulation stage. Using the example of cooperative policy in
Zambia, he demonstrates that such policies, when poorly defined
but extensively promoted, will result in a failure to achieve any
useful development advance. Instead, regime resources will be
expended in a futile attempt to prove that action is being taken
and results are being achieved in order to satisfy the political
leadership. Popularity, in terms of political support and exposure,
may therefore actually undermine attempts to implement programs.
Moreover, Quick suggests that the character of the policy itself may
predetermine receptivity to feedback information that might result
in a redefinition of program goals. The chain of choice and consequence and the cumulative impact of procedural and political decisions and nondecisions is clearly in evidence in this Zambian case
study. Quick indicates the need for political and administrative
leaders to establish unambiguous goals for programs with developmental objectives; political commitment and support is not a
sufficient condition for successful implementation and may even be
a liability. The specific content of the program to be implemented
must be given serious attention by its promoters.

In the following chapter, McClintock carries this argument one
step further by suggesting that goals of public programs must not
only be clear and unambiguous, they must also be agreed upon by
both political and administrative officials at all levels in the government hierarchy. Where this is not the case, she indicates, the
course of subsequent program implementation is difficult to manage and the capacity of the government to control its course may
rapidly disappear. In Peru, the agrarian reform of the military
government in power in the late 1960s and early 1970s was implemented in a context of uncertainty and conflict. McClintock
argues that while some of the implementation problems can be
traced to scarcity of resources and to communication problems,
the major source of the inability of the government to elicit compliance from reform beneficiaries was the failure of political

23

officials and bureaucratic implementors to agree on the specific content of the program of rural cooperative enterprises. This was largely a result of circumstances often faced by Third World governments that embark on reformist paths to development, and may correspond to a lack of power at the center of the political system.

Such a failure to agree on program goals during the formulation process had the interesting result of shifting power downward in the political system during the implementation stage of the policy process. This occurred because conflict over goals at national policy-making levels was translated into conflict between bureaucratic leaders and lower level implementors and between implementing agencies and their clienteles. As a consequence, government officials were unable to elicit compliance with the policy from low-income rural beneficiaries. Instead, peasants were able to seize the opportunity afforded by a reformist and redistributive agrarian reform to acquire resources from the government on their own terms, to manipulate the political system to their own benefit, and to foil the efforts of government officials to control their activities. This Peruvian case study would suggest, then, that implementation problems in Third World countries might frequently be traced to the failure of bureaucratic and political officials to agree on the basic parameters and intent of the policy itself, and that this failure in turn may be linked to the political conditions of elite interaction, especially in situations in which policies are proposed to bring about major changes in the societies.[28]

It is clear that there is an important nexus between policy-as-formulated and program-as-implemented. While this is a statement about the general process of policy implementation, and one that has been documented in the United States,[29] its importance may be especially vivid and its consequences especially grave in Third World countries where the political environment may increase the difficulties involved in policy formulation. Both Quick and Mc-Clintock suggest how political and bureaucratic leaders may attempt to ameliorate the problems resulting from poorly formu-

[28] For discussions of elite conflict and goal setting, see G. Heeger, *The Politics of Underdevelopment* (New York: St. Martin's Press, 1974); Ilchman and Uphoff, *The Political Economy of Change*; and S. Huntington and J. Nelson, *No Easy Choice: Political Participation in Developing Countries* (Cambridge: Harvard University Press, 1976).

[29] See Derthick, *Uncontrollable Spending*.

lated policies. Perhaps the most important lesson of these cases is that such problems might be anticipated and can best be managed, not during implementation, but at the outset of the policy process when goals are initially defined and established. Clearly, this requires sensitivity and openness on the part of public officials, characteristics that may be rare in the frequently isolated context of policymaking in the Third World. Moreover, as has been the experience in the United States, ambiguous or poorly formulated policies may be the result of political processes that emphasize coalition formation and compromise more than technically elegant planning. Nevertheless, extensive evidence of wasted resources, accumulated experience with failure, and the desire or pressure to accomplish more positive ends surely should encourage administrators and political elites to become more alert to the problems resulting from ill-defined policies and to ameliorate their worst impact before they become official policy. The failure to do so has evident political causes, but lack of awareness of the linkage between policy formulated and policy implemented should not be ignored in acounting for past failures. This book can do little to alter political conditions, but it may help to educate and sensitize those responsible for policymaking to other types of problems.

Part Two: Choice and Consequence of Implementing Strategies

Four chapters compose Part Two of this volume. They are concerned with how implementing strategies are chosen and the variables determining the success or failure of the strategy chosen to achieve program goals. Choices concerning how program goals will be pursued, which organization is to be responsible for implementation, the extent of program "coverage," the speed with which program results will be sought, and the mechanisms for establishing reporting and accountability within bureaucratic agencies are all aspects of strategic choices that must be made if programs are actually to be implemented. Such decisions, made consciously or by default, clearly affect the results attained from any given program. As will be clear in these chapters, choices about strategies are frequently made as a result of political reasoning or in response to political pressures.

Once again, while the importance of strategic choices is characteristic of the implementation process in all settings, it is deserving of special attention in Third World countries. The functions of public administrations, and thus the capacity to carry out program

25

activities, are characteristically not well institutionalzed in Third World countries.[30] This means there may be wide divergences in the capacities of different agencies to assume responsibility for implementation; the choice of which of them is to be made responsible may be crucial, especially when resources are scarce. An agency's commitment to one program rather than another, or its decision to expand the number of targeted beneficiaries without expanding the amount of resources available, may lead quickly to an inability to achieve program goals. Public officials may be especially subject to political pressures due to the competition surrounding resource allocation and the amount of demand making centered on the process. The fact that implementing decisions are made in the context of the Third World, then, makes the decisions themselves more likely to be affected by a wide variety of factors and may make the programs themselves more subject to failure.

Chapters Four and Five are directed at the general question of what determines the choice of action programs as implementing strategies. Both chapters are concerned with the pilot project and the decision about whether or not to replicate it as a regular government program, employing the lessons and insights provided by

[30] The study of development administration provides evidence of this. Heeger, "Bureaucracy, Political Parties, and Political Development," provides a general discussion of the literature of development administration. See also W. Ilchman, *Comparative Public Administration and "Conventional Wisdom"* (Beverly Hills, Calif.: Sage Professional Papers in Comparative Politics No. 01-021, 1971). The Comparative Administration Group of the American Society for Public Administration has published a series of volumes on various aspects of development administration. See R. Braibanti, ed., *Political and Administrative Development* (Durham, N.C.: Duke University Press, 1969); Heaphy, *Spatial Dimensions*; F. Riggs, ed., *Frontiers of Development Administration* (Durham, N.C.: Duke University Press, 1970); Thurber and Graham, *Development Administration in Latin America*; D. Waldo, ed., *Temporal Dimensions in Development Administration* (Durham, N.C.: Duke University Press, 1970); E. Weidner, ed., *Development Administration in Asia*. See also F. Heady and S. Stokes, eds., *Papers in Comparative Public Administration* (Ann Arbor: University of Michigan Press, 1962); J. Montgomery and W. Siffin, eds., *Approaches to Development: Politics, Administration, and Change* (New York: McGraw-Hill, 1966); and B. Schaffer, ed., *Administrative Training and Development: A Comparative Study of East Africa, Zambia, Pakistan, and India* (New York: Praeger, 1974). For a commentary, see J. Springer, "Empirical Methods and Theories of Development Administration: Prologues and Promise," paper prepared for delivery at the annual meeting of the American Political Science Association, San Francisco, Calif., Sept. 1-5, 1975.

26

the pilot experience to ensure greater implementability. In Chapter Four we are presented with a "perfect case" for pilot project replication. A program for community development was thoroughly tested in rural India in the late 1940s and early 1950s. In terms of its content—its specific goals, organization, and operational procedures—it was extremely successful in achieving the outcomes desired. It offered simple and useful guidelines for future replication on a broader scale, and had proven itself to be an economical way to achieve community development. Why was it, then, that Indian leaders, who were familiar with the pilot experience and much impressed by it, did not adopt it as a model? It may be because the guidelines it laid down and the goals it pursued were not necessarily those considered to be most relevant by the political and bureaucratic leadership.

This is the hypothesis posed by Gerald Sussman. He examines why the information about the considerable success of a pilot project for community development was not used to develop the same project of proven utility on a broader scale. Instead, the parameters of the pilot project were abandoned, and a program was pursued that in many respects ran directly counter to the lessons it provided and ultimately resulted in program failure. Political rationality, rather than potential program results, it seems, dictated the answer to the question, How should this policy be implemented? The design of the action program in this case was influenced by political needs for national integration and for mass support building. That these considerations seemed to dictate that ultimately the community development movement would suffer was not really relevant to the decision making process. Sussman's chapter might therefore suggest that policy planners consider not only the political acceptability of various programs, but also their political *attractiveness* to national decision makers.

David Pyle, in Chapter Five, poses the same question about how implementation strategies are chosen and he also concludes that the output in terms of project results has little to do with why a pilot project is accepted or rejected for replication. He explores the reasons why a state government in India was uninterested in adopting and expanding a nutrition program that had been tested through a pilot study. When the pilot project was completed and feedback information on it was available, a nondecision was made that allowed the program to expire, not because of the technical

27

content of the information, but because of a series of seemingly unimportant choices and strategies that were followed during the pilot project itself. Pyle reiterates the lessons of the first two case studies when he points to the importance of the way the goals of the pilot study were defined and agreed upon; but additionally he emphasizes choices about the agencies designated to manage and oversee the initial program, the way rural health centers were staffed, the type of food supplement that was utilized, and channels for funding and reporting. These were the variables that influenced the decision to abandon the program, and not the program's impact on the nutrition or health conditions of recipients. Many of these pilot project choices were made by default or without conscious consideration of their consequences for later expansion of the program. Using the example of the nutrition experience, Pyle suggests that the choices made at various stages of the implementation process should be made more carefully and consciously, with a view to the future of the program. He would agree with Sussman that the decision to replicate a pilot project ultimately is a political one, and he argues in addition that careful strategic thinking about the specific content of the program can enhance its political attractiveness.

The central focus of the next two chapters changes from how implementing strategies are chosen to what factors seem to influence the actual success or failure of the strategy chosen. Susan Hadden and Irene Rothenberg are both interested in the potential of administrative decentralization to improve program implementability. Both make suggestions about which factors ought to be taken into consideration in deciding whether a program should be decentralized or not. For Rothenberg, planners need to evaluate characteristics of the political system at local and national levels to determine if in fact decentralization would make program implementors more responsive. For Hadden, on the other hand, the determinants of whether a program can be successfully implemented through administrative decentralization have to do with characteristics of the policy itself and with the kind of decentralization scheme that is chosen.

Rothenberg's chapter deals with the failure of decentralization to address housing problems in a large city in Colombia. A decision to decentralize administration over the housing program encouraged political conflict over decisions such as staffing and site selection, which in turn led to a paralysis of implementation. The failure of the program led not only to an inability to provide low-income housing in the city, but also to the elimination of decentralization as an alternative considered by policymakers for subsequent program and project implementation. Rothenberg suggests that under conditions of fragmented political power, decentralization is not a useful strategy for achieving policy goals, and its failure may have consequences for its future as a strategy.

Susan Hadden also explores decentralization as a strategy but comes up with a more positive evaluation of its utility. What was missing from the Colombian case, and what is in evidence in Hadden's study of rural electrification in India, is control. Specifically, the design of the Indian program included both definite means for judging whether goals were being achieved and mechanisms of financial control to ensure that standards were adhered to. In determining whether this strategy of controlled decentralization will prove effective, Hadden advises that we evaluate the specific content of the program: Is it distributive? Does it have a technical aspect that makes it possible to develop criteria to measure whether it is being implemented? These conditions in fact may strengthen the hand of central authorities and allow them to permit extensive decentralized responsibility for implementation activities. Hadden also makes the useful suggestion that with certain types of programs, political inputs can be advantageous in achieving program goals.

In comparing the Colombian and Indian experiences, it might be suggested that the relative degree of success and the recommendations of each author about where to look to find the determinants of success or failure, were much influenced by the type of policy pursued. Rural electrification, for example, can be considered a collective good from the perspective of a rural village, and its implementation did not arouse great conflict; rather it seems to have encouraged cooperative political activity. Housing, on the other hand, is a more divisible good and may exacerbate demand making and conflict in the implementation process. This observation might lead us to suggest that the prospects for decentralization strategies could be anticipated by first exploring the type of political response that the specific program is likely to encourage and then judging whether the program contains the necessary control mechanisms for handling the conflict sufficiently so that implemen-

29

tation can proceed. If not, then administrative decentralization may not be a viable strategy for program implementation. Once again, this is a question of the capacity of an organization or regime to centralize sufficient authority so that implementation may be effectively decentralized. In the McClintock study of agrarian reform in Peru, for example, this was not the case. It is clear, then, that decisions made about how to go about implementing a program must take both political realities and program objectives and criteria into consideration.

Part Three: Deciding Who Gets What

The three chapters in Part Three also explore strategies for program implementation but they are more centrally concerned with the analysis of who benefits from the implementation of public policies in the Third World. More specifically, the case studies address the question of why programs intended to benefit certain groups in the society often do not do so. Thus, the authors are concerned with how choices made during implementation affect the outputs of particular policies or programs. The studies integrate considerations of both the influence of regime type and the impact of politics on the local level in the determination of who will have influence over resource allocation processes. This is a particularly important question to address in the context of the Third World. An overwhelming characteristic of Third World countries is that large proportions of their populations live at, below, or only slightly above, subsistence level, and thus the need for the goods and services promised by various government programs is great. At the same time, an increasing number of governments in Latin America, Asia, and Africa have chosen authoritarian solutions to the problems of managing political participation and conflict. This suggests that the capacity of low-income groups to acquire benefits from their governments may be strictly limited in an environment that minimizes the influence of numbers on political decision making through the elimination of open elections and rotation of political leadership.

Such a statement is in fact borne out by the case studies on Mexico, Kenya, and Brazil in this section. They explore interactions at the local level between administrators, politicians, recipients, and elite groups, and examine how choices made in response to the demand making of these groups were influenced by the

30

general nature of the political regime.[31] Thus, while dealing with political inputs into administrative decisions on the local level, the studies also explore more explicitly why government allocation decisions are not generally responsive to low-income groups in authoritarian regimes. They suggest that there is an enduring structure of relationships between the bureaucracy and the political system in which it is embedded and to which it is responsive. They also indicate that the conflict engendered by the content of redistributive policies may have a decided impact on allocation decisions. The relationship of regime type and local politics to implementation highlights the problems of compliance and responsiveness that were introduced by Quick, McClintock, and Hadden. While in some specific cases low-income groups such as peasants or urban squatters are able to affect the policies of the government, in general it seems that authoritarian political systems necessitate bureaucracies that are responsive primarily to the regime itself rather than to low-status clienteles.

This is a concern addressed in the chapter on Mexico, where government officials were given responsibility for implementing a rural development program. This study, described in Chapter Eight, suggests that resources allocated for the achievement of specific program goals may be reallocated at the site of implementation in order to achieve more pressing and general regime goals, such as maintaining the political peace. Implementing officials, the focus of a variety of often conflicting demands, may frequently

---

[31] A number of books and articles have been written that describe and analyze subnational political systems in Third World countries. These studies demonstrate how local concerns become translated into political demands and how these are articulated by individuals and groups. See, for examples, N. Abedin, *Local Administration and Politics in Modernizing Societies: Bangladesh and Pakistan* (Dacca: National Institute of Public Administration, 1973); R. Bates, "Ethnic Competition and Modernization in Contemporary Africa," *Comparative Political Studies*, 6, No. 4 (January 1974); W. Cornelius, *Politics and the Migrant Poor in Mexico City* (Stanford, Calif.: Stanford University Press, 1975); S. Kothari and R. Roy, *Relations Between Politicians and Adminstrators at the District Level* (New Delhi: Indian Institute of Public Administration, 1969); A. Kuper, *Kalahari Village Politics* (Cambridge, England: Cambridge University Press, 1970); H. Tinker, "Local Government and Politics, and Political and Social Theory in India," in M. Swartz, ed., *Local Level Politics* (Chicago: Aldine, 1968); E. Valsan, *Community Development Programs and Rural Local Government: Comparative Case Studies of India and the Philippines* (New York: Praeger, 1970).

31

find that the daily exigencies of performing their duties with a minimum amount of conflict require them to ignore the demands of low-status actors in favor of elites or subelites at the local level. Clearly, the behavior of these officials is affected by national regimes that place a high priority on stability and the maintenance of political support from important sectors of the population. It must be recognized, however, that because of the tentative nature of many of the political regimes in the Third World and their basis in coalitions of support groups, this is a concern of a large number of such governments. Although individual officials may have the best of intentions, political realities may dictate that redistributive policies are implemented effectively only when they do not threaten interests whose support is essential to the regime. It is, moreover, unlikely that many redistributive policies would meet this criterion.

In a study carried out in Kenya, Frederick and Nelle Temple analyze why public housing was built, not in response to the needs of low-income urbanites in Nairobi, but to serve middle- and high-income groups. After independence, the national government of Kenya committed itself to building a large number of housing units to be let or sold at prices that could be afforded by the poorest sector of the population. However, during the implementation of this policy, benefits again eluded low-income target groups, to be allocated instead to the political and economic elites most closely tied to the government. The reluctance of government officials to become involved in schemes that might prove economically unsound, the desire of the national politicians to establish a level and quality of benefits clearly superior to those provided by the colonial government, and the attitudes and elite relationships of political officials and bureaucratic implementors acted together to skew the allocation of resources. At the same time, the closed nature of the political process effectively prohibited access of low-income sectors to demand making channels or, when the poor were able to make their needs known, government officials saw little personal or political benefit to be gained from responding to them. The example of what occurred with public housing in Kenya is suggestive because of the large number of political regimes in the Third World in which political participation by low-status actors is similarly discouraged.

In Brazil, for example, a military regime, in agreement on policy goals and willing to use force to implement them, was able to pursue a policy of squatter settlement eradication in spite of the intense opposition of those affected by it. While in Peru low-income beneficiaries of agrarian reform were able to achieve their own goals because of the failure of political and administrative actors to agree on program goals, in Brazil the military government was firmly committed to slum eradication. The demise of electoral politics in the early 1960s made a significant difference to squatter settlement residents because they were no longer taken into consideration by policymakers and implementors, a change documented by Janice Perlman in Chapter Ten. Not only were settlement inhabitants unable to affect government policy, but they also became increasingly less willing to oppose the government's plans at all, a response to a real perception of the limited possibilities for success and the ability and willingness of the military regime to use its repressive capacity. Once again it is evident that the distribution of political power within a regime has a fundamental impact on the manner in which programs are implemented. In Brazil, low-status groups lacking power and the resources to acquire power became victims of a regime whose goals dictated that squatter settlements be eliminated. At the same time, however, the regime's lack of responsiveness to squatter settlement inhabitants and their conditions of life led to the failure of the resettlement schemes. The new housing complexes to which the squatters were moved did not provide for the economic and social life of the inhabitants; many began to abandon the housing units or to fail to make payments on their apartments. While the military regime was successful in forcing evacuation of choice urban land, it was unable to provide for low-cost and secure housing for those who were displaced. It succeeded in eliciting compliance, but its failure to be responsive at the same time was costly not only in terms of the physical, emotional, and economic strains imposed on "beneficiaries," but also because policies were pursued that ultimately were not effective solutions to the problem.

These three case studies underscore the variable nature of the implementation process in a setting of political conflict due to the scarcity of available resources, the wide range of actors involved, and the willingness or capacity of various regimes to be responsive to demands. Importantly, the studies indicate that the content of public programs can be considerably affected during their execution due to the nature of political participation, demand making, and bureaucratic response. They deal significantly with the broad political context of policy implementation. The authors would agree that the study of public policy in general, but especially in the Third World, must include a study of the political system itself and the distribution of effective power within it if the implementability of public programs is to be assessed. This is a task taken up in the last chapter of this volume.

In his conclusion, Peter Cleaves does not report findings from a field investigation but rather attempts to provide a means for anticipating and manipulating the potential implementability of various types of public policies in various political contexts. Drawing on the case study material, he discusses how political and bureaucratic leaders can attempt to introduce change oriented policies in their societies by manipulating the content of the policy or its political context. He refers to the *problématique* of policies—the range of characteristics that make a policy more or less easily implemented—and the resources that are available for mobilization to achieve the objectives of any given policy. Interestingly, he finds that the resources available vary by regime type, and he discusses the potential for mobilizing low-status sectors of the population in support of reform policies.

Cleaves' contribution is a fitting conclusion to this volume. In it, he suggests how policy planners and strategists might go about making the kinds of choices that would ensure greater implementability. Because of the large number of instances in which program outcomes fail to resemble the ends specified in original policy declarations and the even larger number of instances in which no results at all are achieved, it is important to attempt to understand as fully as possible the reasons for failure and what conditions might lead to more successful performance in the future. The potential to misuse such knowledge for illiberal ends is considerable and ever-present, but so, too, is the possibility that it may be used to change and better the conditions of those who live in poverty, ill-health, and insecurity. It is greatly hoped that the case studies and commentaries collected in this volume will provide some insights and guidance for those who are concerned with improving the economic, social, and political futures of peoples in the Third World.

34

Part One · FROM FORMULATION
TO
IMPLEMENTATION

THE first point at which choices influencing implementation are made is when policies or programs are being initially defined. Both political and administrative actors are involved in the task of goal setting. In the Third World, the guidance provided by political leadership may be particularly important because there may be little agreement among members of the political community about the fundamental beliefs, values, and goals of the society itself. In the absence of such cues from political actors, the normal condition may be a considerable amount of conflict and confusion over the ends pursued in public activities. Political leaders, in their public statements, private conversations, official directives, and formal emphases indicate the general direction that government actions should take. They may give cues, for instance, about the degree of social or economic change they consider to be appropriate for the political regime to encourage. This information allows policymakers to judge the extent to which their programs should seek to affect the distribution of economic and political power in the society.

Political leaders also provide general guidelines about priorities among policies and policy emphases, and by doing this, indicate to the planners the most politically acceptable ideological framework for the programs they develop. Resources are scarce in the Third World and because all desired policies cannot be pursued optimally, it may fall to the political leadership to indicate which among a variety of public programs and activities should be given special attention. Leaders also have a significant input into deciding the extent of material and human resources to assign to the achievement of particular programs. These actions, in addition to public statements of support, provide a degree of legitimacy to the goals enunciated in policy statements. It must also be recognized that the failure of political leaders to agree on policy goals, or misperceptions about each other's intent, also have a great impact on how goals are defined. The most common outcome of a lack of agreement among leaders is vague and unclear objectives that generally lead to implementation failures, as a number of studies in this volume indicate.

There are also administrative decisions made at the definition stage that may have great impact on the future implementability of the policy. Examples of such decisions are the degree of specificity embodied in policy goals and the practical soundness of the goals themselves. For example, the extent to which recipients of government programs are defined categorically may be crucial in ensuring that they do in fact benefit from the policy. Political leaders may be agreed that low-income agriculturists should be the beneficiaries of a particular range of public programs. The manner in which these individuals are identified more specifically may be a decision that bureaucratic officials are expected to make, with a view to political support-building activities perhaps, but also in consideration of more technical kinds of information, such as size of landholdings, type of crop produced, relationship to the market economy, and degree of need of various sectors of the agricultural population. A decision to specify that peasants who own less than one hectare of land, who grow crops for domestic consumption, and who live in a specific arid region are to be the recipient group is a fairly concrete definition that allows those individuals to be identified easily. The consequences of this definition are likely to be far different from those of a decision to specify only that peasants earning less than $100 a year are to be the target population. For one thing, demands for a share of program resources may be limited legitimately under the first condition; saying "no" under the second definition may be far more onerous. Of course, it may be that greater specificity will jeopardize policy flexibility, but it also indicates a more fundamental agreement among elite actors on the ends to be pursued by the policy.

In addition, discussions of policy failures are replete with evidence that the goals defined for policies are frequently unrealistic in terms of the amount of change, the type of change, or the time allowed for change that is specified. Economic planning efforts in the 1950s and 1960s, for example, were often characterized by unrealistic expectations about normal growth rates in the economy or by failure to consider the impact of population expansion. This kind of definitional problem may result from inaccurate information, lack of information, or failure to appreciate the complexities involved in achieving the goals. The result, however, is often the expenditure of resources in the pursuit of objectives which, by their very nature, may never be realized.

The two chapters in Part One demonstrate that choices made— consciously or unconsciously—at the outset of the policy process condition subsequent implementation efforts. The content of programs pursued in Zambia and Peru is seen to have been affected by the goals of the national political leadership and by the choices made by bureaucratic officials in response to such policy leadership. The authors are then able to show how the content of the programs affected the activities of officials as they set about carrying them out.

TWO · *The Paradox of Popularity:*
"Ideological" Program
Implementation in Zambia

STEPHEN A. QUICK

PROGRAM TYPES AND THE POLITICS OF IMPLEMENTATION

Students of policy implementation and development administration in the Third World are centrally concerned with analyzing and explaining failure. Public policies often do not get implemented at all, and those which do manage to get through the tortuous process of implementation often look very different from what their framers originally intended. The clear implication of existing studies is that policy implementation in the Third World bears little resemblance to the classical understanding of implementation as a process of rationally linking broad goals to specific programmatic decisions.[1]

In seeking explanations for this phenomenon, scholars started off by assembling information on the general obstacles to effective implementation in Third World countries. This orientation quickly produced a massive catalog of constraints on administrative rationality, ranging from organizational weaknesses, to cultural obstacles, to the dysfunctional nature of political conflict.[2] This list was indeed impressive, but it tended to give the impression that *all* policies suffered under the *same* implementation problems. As more fieldwork was done, however, it became clear that different

[1] See D. Waldo, ed., *Temporal Dimensions in Development Administration* (Durham, N.C.: Duke University Press, 1970); F. Riggs, ed., *Frontiers of Development Administration* (Durham, N.C.: Duke University Press, 1970); C. Thurber and L. Graham, eds., *Development Administration in Latin America* (Durham, N.C.: Duke University Press, 1973); E. Morgan, ed., *The Administration of Change in Africa* (New York: Dunellen, 1974); F. Weidner, ed., *Development Administration in Asia* (Durham, N.C.: Duke University Press, 1970).

[2] For a description of this literature, see Chap. 1 of this volume.

40

policies had different problems in implementation, and it was therefore much more interesting to examine the problems unique to a specific program rather than those which were general to a whole range of programs. This orientation was useful in that it produced a variety of interesting case studies, but so much attention on the specific made the development of general theory rather difficult. The next task, and the one faced by the authors in this volume, is to discover ways of generalizing about the implementation problems of specific programs.

The first step in this process is the construction of typologies— grouping specific policies into categories that have some relevance to the question of implementation. This sort of exercise has already been carried out in the realm of legislation, where it has long been observed that different types of policies face different legislative obstacles.[3] Presumably the same holds true in the area of implementation, and the problem becomes one of finding the best ways of grouping and typing policies in terms of their "implementability."

Because this theory-building process is still in its infancy, a wide variety of possible typologies can and should be proposed. In this chapter, we will examine a specific program—the creation of rural cooperatives in Zambia—as an example of one general *type* of program, a type which, for want of a better word, we will call the "ideological" program type. We will begin by exploring the general nature of this type of program, then move to a consideration of the Zambian example, and finally conclude with some general hypotheses about the implementation problems associated with ideological programs. Throughout the chapter, we will be attempting to show how certain general characteristics of ideological programs, in particular goal ambiguity and political popularity, create serious obstacles to effective program implementation.

THE "IDEOLOGICAL" PROGRAM TYPE

Most national leaders in the Third World possess a generalized view of how things should be in their countries. They acknowledge their present underdevelopment, and believe that some day things will be different. Their view of the good society usually includes a

[3] The most important early statement of this perspective is T. Lowi, "American Business and Public Policy: Case Study and Political Theory," *World Politics*, 16 (July 1964), 677-715.

large number of variables; economics, politics, social relations, and international relations are usually included, and spiritual values and subjective attitudes are frequently present in the vision. This vision of how things should be acts as a guide for transforming the existing situation, but in most cases government programs are directed at the solution of immediate problems and therefore bear but a tenuous relationship to the grand vision. There are some policies, however, that are linked much more closely to this grand transforming vision, and they engender programs that are expected to realize elements of the good society in the near future. These programs confirm the wisdom and accuracy of the transforming vision and serve to inspire both the masses and the elite by convincing them that a major transformation of the society is indeed possible. Such programs can be labeled "ideological" because of their importance as confirmers of the transforming ideology, and these ideological programs have specific characteristics that are relevant to the process by which they are implemented.

A first characteristic of ideological programs is that they are expected to realize a multitude of goals at the same time. They represent the first working models of the new society, and are therefore expected to introduce changes in many aspects of existing social relationships. In addition to being numerous, the goals set for ideological programs are also ambiguous in that national elites rarely have a clearly worked out view of what is required to move from the existing state of affairs to the new one. There is no hierarchy of goals, no clear statement that goal A is more important than goal B, or at least that goal A should be achieved before embarking on goal B. The ambiguity of goals presents the implementing organization with the clear message that everything must be done at once and that there are no priorities that can be used to orient implementation. A third characteristic of the goal structure of ideological programs is the immeasurability of many of their objectives. The target population is expected to live differently, to act and think differently, and to progress toward many of these goals, but such objectives cannot be measured with any precision. Agencies charged with implementing ideological programs thus have a goal structure which consists of a few measurable goals and many nonmeasurable ones.

Ideological programs are also affected by the high expectations of the national political elite. Such programs are endowed with a sense of urgency and vital importance, placing the implementing agency under extreme political pressure to produce results. So important is success in these programs that political appointees are selected to head the implementing agency, and resources are made available to this agency that are unavailable to other programs. The organizations charged with implementing ideological programs are also relatively immune from criticism, shielded as they are by the political popularity of their program. These, then, are the basic characteristics which define an "ideological program": multiple, ambiguous, and nonmeasurable goals; high expectations; political popularity; resource availability; politicized leadership of the implementing organization; and immunity from public criticism. In the remainder of this chapter, we will explore the hypothesis that these characteristics will influence the dynamics of the implementation process in significant and important ways. In fact, we shall attempt to argue that ideological programs suffer from problems in the course of implementation that are different from those of other programs.

An adequate exploration of this hypothesis would, of course, require a comparative analysis of several different ideological programs in different countries. The village resettlement program in Tanzania, the *animation rurale* effort in Senegal, and the self-help programs of Kenya and Tanzania might possibly fall into this category, but unfortunately the available literature on these policies does not throw sufficient light on the question of implementation to be of use to us. Lacking comparative data, we are forced to fall back upon the simpler expedient of a single case study. Generalizing from one example is always problematic, since it is never possible to separate the general from the idiosyncratic with any degree of confidence. The value of case studies is that they suggest possibilities for future comparative research, not that they constitute proof of a general hypothesis. Elsewhere I have argued that the Zambian experience can produce intriguing hypotheses about the relationship between bureaucratic organizations and socialist development goals, and in this chapter I hope to pose some hypotheses about the dynamics of implementation that emerge from this same case study.[4] These hypotheses are meant to be suggestive, not definitive, and are intended as a stimulant to future comparative research. It is too early at this point to establish with any degree of certainty the generalizability of the Zambian experience,

[4] S. Quick, *Bureaucracy and Rural Socialism: The Zambian Experience,* Ph.D. diss. Stanford University, 1975.

but the attempt to put this case into a broader framework will hopefully begin the process of generalization and theory building.

COOPERATIVES IN ZAMBIA: HUMANISM AND RURAL DEVELOPMENT

Zambia achieved her independence in October of 1964 under the leadership of the United National Independence Party (UNIP). Kenneth Kaunda was the president of UNIP and like many other African leaders he felt the need for a national ideology to guide his country after independence. A deeply religious man, Kaunda sought an ideology that would emphasize brotherhood, mutual support, equality, cooperation, and participation.[5] He eventually collected all of these elements into a partially coherent whole which he called "Humanism," and during the first few years of independence he sought to make it a guide to state policy. In many areas, however, it proved impossible to link Humanism to state policy because the freedom of action of the state was constrained by technological, economic, or political factors that mandated actions bearing little resemblance to the ideology.[6] Since there were fewer of these constraints in the area of rural development, however, it was here that Kaunda first sought to put his ideology into practice.

Like many other African ideologies, Humanism praised and respected the "traditional communal solidarity" of the rural village. In the realm of political structure and social relations, the village was something of a model for the future of Zambian society, and the only significant problem with village life was its economic structure. It was thought that if modern forms of production could be grafted onto the village social and political structure, the rural population could soon be living the good life as defined by Kaunda's Humanism. Kaunda believed that this transformation could be brought about by encouraging the development of new institutions in the rural areas—agricultural producers' cooperatives.

[5] For a discussion of Zambian Humanism, see H. S. Meebelo, *Main Currents in Zambian Humanist Thought* (Lusaka: Oxford University Press, 1973).

[6] C. Elliott, ed., *Constraints on the Economic Development of Zambia* (Nairobi: Oxford University Press, 1971); W. Tordoff and R. Molteno, "Introduction," in W. Tordoff, ed., *Politics in Zambia* (Berkeley: University of California Press, 1974), pp. 15-30.

These institutions could increase production, encourage producers to work together, strengthen democratic and participatory forms of decision making and create a sense of mutual trust and support —all at the same time. Kaunda obviously had high expectations for the cooperative movement as a vehicle for realizing Humanism in the rural areas.

When the president took his plan for cooperative development to the party, he encountered substantial rhetorical support but a basic unwillingness to assume responsibility for the program.[7] Frustrated by the resistance of the party, Kaunda took his case to the people, and in January 1965 he issued his famous Chifubu Declaration calling on the people of Zambia to form cooperatives of all kinds.[8] In this declaration, he promised the people that the government would provide support and assistance to the new co-operatives. This meant that an administrative apparatus to devise and carry out this program of support and assistance was needed. By default, responsibility fell to the Department of Cooperative Societies, a small, poorly staffed, low-status department in the colonial administrative structure. Although this organization had a number of unique problems that made it largely unsuitable for the task of supervising and supporting a network of rural farming cooperatives, this was the institution Kaunda chose to implement his ideological vision because no other agency of the government would assume responsibility.[9]

It may seem odd that the choice of an implementing agency was made in so haphazard a fashion. Given the importance of cooperatives to Kaunda's vision, one might have expected the creation of a new and powerful agency to implement the policy, or at least the selection of a competent and prestigious agency from the colonial administration. This did not happen, however, and the reason probably lies in the inexperience of the UNIP

[7] The nature and extent of this resistance is discussed in Quick, *Bureaucracy and Rural Socialism*, pp. 152-153.

[8] K. Kaunda, "Speech at Chifubu Rally, 17 January 1965," Zambia Information Services, "Press Background no. 3/65."

[9] The most serious organizational problems were a high vacancy rate in senior staff positions, rapid turnover in field staff, and a chaotic system of information-processing within the agency. These problems are analysed in: P. Wiffin, "The Staffing and Organization of the Department of Cooperative Societies," Zambia, Ministry of Finance, Establishments Division, Staff Inspection Unit, mimeographed report, 1970; Quick, *Bureaucracy and Rural Socialism*, pp. 182-211.

regime. The party had never been a "government" before, and the colonial practice of keeping civil servants out of politics made the party leadership relatively unaware of bureaucratic subtleties. UNIP elites apparently gave little attention to the mechanics of implementation of this or any other program, and it was only at a much later date that energy was devoted to administrative reorganization to facilitate implementation. At this point in the new nation's history, the leadership apparently felt that if they had a Department of Cooperatives, it would be natural and reasonable for that entity to supervise the new cooperative program. The pitfalls in this "natural" assumption soon became apparent.

The department was immediately confronted with the peculiar goal structure of an ideological program. No clear statement was ever provided by Kaunda as to precisely what the immediate goals of cooperative policy were to be, and yet it was made abundantly clear in a variety of public speeches made by the president that cooperatives were supposed to do a great deal and do it very quickly. During the early months of 1965, the president spoke frequently about the cooperative movement, and in these speeches he articulated no fewer than ten specific goals that he expected the movement to achieve in the next few years. The cooperatives were expected to provide employment and stem the flow of population to the towns, increase the income of members, promote equality in the distribution of income, create collective goods for the rural population, preserve the traditional values of the village community, increase political participation, strengthen procedures for the democratic control of elites, promote a sense of national identity, increase and diversify agricultural output, and develop a spirit of self-reliance in the rural population.[10]

This is a multiple goal structure, but it is also an ambiguous one. It was unclear precisely how these goals could be realized, and there was a substantial measure of contradiction among them. An emphasis on creating collective goods such as grinding mills and local shops might conflict with the goal of increasing and diversifying output because these collective goods might divert capital from investment to consumption. Or, to take another example, preserving traditional values and practices might conflict with the goal of developing procedures for the democratic control of elites. The problems of ambiguity were compounded by the problem of

[10] Quick, *Bureaucracy and Rural Socialism*, pp. 155-161.

immeasurability. How could the department measure progress toward the goal of creating a "spirit of self-reliance," and what were the reliable statistical indicators of a "sense of national identity?" Even some of the more concrete goals which could have been measured in a society with a more developed communications network were largely immeasurable in the Zambian context, and it was thus impossible for the department to prove in any reasonable fashion that progress was being made by the local societies toward the achievement of most of Kaunda's goals.

This problem in no way diminished the enthusiasm of the president for the cooperative ideal, and in speech after speech he made it clear that he expected immediate results from the new program. Other politicians, both national and local, soon joined Kaunda in urging the rapid development of cooperatives, and it became clear that the entire Zambian elite had high expectations of the department and its program. Along with these high expectations, however, went a substantial amount of suspicion. The UNIP politicians saw the civil service as a conservative force which was ideologically opposed to the new government's programs for rapid political and social change.[11] This suspicion was especially directed at agencies, such as the Department of Cooperatives, that were responsible for ideologically important programs. To prevent sabotage of the cooperative program by a conservative civil service, Kaunda appointed a UNIP activist to the post of director of cooperative societies.[12] This was further indication of the importance the president attached to cooperatives, for while political appointments were commonplace at the ministerial level at this time in Zambia, they rarely extended to the level of departments.

Once the administrative leadership of the department had been adequately politicized, the political elite felt safe in granting that organization a high priority in the allocation of government funds. The department was guaranteed access to loan funds to use in developing cooperatives, and it was further promised that the government would make cash grants available to local societies to give them the necessary amount of working capital. In addition

[11] R. Hall, *The High Price of Principles: Kaunda and the White South* (New York: Africana Publishers, 1969), p. 39.

[12] The new director had formerly been the accountant general of UNIP, chairman of the Lusaka Township council, and an active militant in the anti-color-bar campaigns of the early 1960s. See K. Mlenga, ed., *Who's Who in Zambia* (Ndola, Zambia: Falcon Press, 1967), p. 71.

47

to making resources available, the national elite virtually guaranteed the department immunity from public criticism by its constant and enthusiastic support for the movement. This set of factors defined the environment within which the department was to make a host of administrative decisions designed to implement the cooperative policy proposed by Kaunda. The incentives and constraints built into this environment unfortunately encouraged the department to make implementation decisions in a way that was disastrous for the development of the country's cooperative movement.

PROGRAM IMPLEMENTATION IN THE DEPARTMENT OF COOPERATIVES

In devising routines for implementing cooperative policy, the department was faced with the multiple, ambiguous, and immeasurable nature of the goals articulated by the president. It was clearly impossible to focus on all of these at once, and yet the total set of goals was so diverse that almost any action could be justified in terms of some goal. This reality paralyzed the planning and program development capacity of the department, for it was difficult, if not impossible, to define a course of action that would optimize all of these values at once. The agency could not remain inactive, however, for the high expectations of the political elite demanded immediate action of some sort. Neither could the agency follow the usual bureaucratic strategy of getting clarification from above concerning priorities for action. The Zambian political elite was trying to come to grips with all of the nation's problems at once and did not have the time to devote to a close analysis of each program. In addition, Kaunda had made it clear when he put a political appointee at the head of the department that he distrusted the conservatism of the agency, and any request for further clarification would have been interpreted as vindication of his suspicions.

This situation put the decision makers in the agency in a dilemma: the task before them was so enormous and complicated that it was impossible to develop a rational set of policies to implement the entire range of goals. Given the impossiblity of rational criteria for decision making, the agency was forced to turn to political criteria. The operational question became "What can we do quickly that will demonstrate to the political elite that we are doing our job?" The criterion for decision making became satisfying the short-run expectations of politicians, even if these were in the end counterproductive, rather than promoting a successful and viable cooperative movement over the long run.

One of the clear and unambiguous expectations of the political elite was that new cooperatives be established in large numbers as quickly as possible, and the department swiftly adopted this goal as its immediate task. The number of new cooperatives registered provided a good statistic to use in justifying the existence of the agency, and so the first program guideline established was the speedy registration of as many new societies as possible. The substantive rationality of such a move was immediately questioned by the more experienced field staff, who pointed out that many of the groups that were clamoring for registration as cooperatives knew nothing about farming and were interested in joining the movement only as a way of getting a handout from the government. This was a reasonable objection, for a policy of unrestrained registration would produce a network of ill-prepared societies scattered throughout the rural areas in a pattern that would make regular supervision difficult. In spite of the logic of these arguments, the logic of political necessity was stronger, and in a circular letter to all provincial cooperative officers, the registrar defined the attitude of the agency:

> We are only equipped to give advice on the purely business side of a society's activities and that of marketing. We are not qualified to pass on technical advice. . . . If a group of people, for example, wish to set up a cooperative poultry enterprise, the intending members may have no knowledge of keeping poultry but it is not for officers of this department to decide whether or not the society is likely to be a success. Members of a proposed cooperative may have no knowledge of the business they intend forming, but if they wish to form the society then it is their business, and we cannot refuse to register them for that reason.[13]

This letter clearly endorsed a program which would undermine the ultimate success of the cooperative movement, for it abdicated any responsibility for promoting rational decision making by the

[13] "Circular Letter to all Provincial Cooperative Officers from the Registrar of Cooperatives, 3 February 1965," in File 24/12/1, Department of Cooperatives, Eastern Province Files.

local societies ("we are not qualified to pass on technical advice") and it tacitly acknowledged the incompetence of cooperative members who "may have no knowledge of the business they intend forming." In terms of any of Kaunda's formal goals for the movement, this registration policy was a mistake, but it did have the immense political advantage of registering an impressive number of new societies. Everyone interested in the cooperative movement could read and praise the statistics on registration, and few would have the time, interest, or energy to enquire into the precise nature of these myriad new "cooperatives." The combination of ambitious substantive goals and intense pressure for results produced a shift in agency orientation from the achievement of substantive results to the purely formalistic goal of creating more paper cooperatives.

The policy of unrestrained registration was politically necessary for the agency but not politically sufficient. Everyone in Zambia knew that the president had promised governmental assistance to the new cooperatives, and so the department had to develop a set of routines for handing out money. Ideally, the loans procedure should have been tied in some way to the broad goals of the cooperative movement, for loans and subsidies are powerful incentives and these incentives should have been designed to encourage "cooperative" kinds of behavior on the part of the societies. Unfortunately, the definition of "cooperative behavior" was just as complex and ambiguous as the definition of "cooperative," and the task of devising incentives for such behavior was beyond the capacity of the organization. Once again, the logic of politics was substituted for reasoned analysis, and the criterion for granting loans became "give away as much as possible, as fast as possible."

Because of the popularity of the cooperative movement, funds were readily available to the department, and they were handed out with abandon. Large subsidies were granted to societies for each acre of land they cleared, and both seasonal and long-term loans were granted in huge amounts.[14] There was no supervision on the use to which these loans were put, and since it was easier to distribute cash than seed or fertilizer, most societies received their loans and subsidies in the form of cash deposits in their bank accounts. Under these circumstances, it was logical for members to

[14] National figures on total indebtedness of cooperatives are not available, but in the eastern province this author estimated that the average society received £1,500 in subsidies and over £3,000 in short- and medium-term loans.

50

assume that the funds were theirs to do with as they pleased, and most societies either wasted or consumed the bulk of their government support. The availability of substantial amounts of cash encouraged conflicts about distribution, and many cooperatives broke up over the tensions this engendered. An additional problem was that land-clearing subsidies encouraged the clearing of acreage instead of the cultivating of it. Many societies ended up with huge cleared areas, which often remained uncultivated because the land itself was poor and had been cleared only because the tree cover was less dense there than on more fertile land.

As with the registrations policy, the loans and subsidies program was injurious to the long-run development of the cooperative movement. But once again, this approach possessed substantial political advantages. The statistics on loans distributed were readily produced and clearly indicated that the department was doing something, and few were able to look beyond the statistics to examine the kinds of behavior which the loans were encouraging. Registration and loans were the two main routines developed by the department in its first few years of implementing Kaunda's cooperative policy, but there was an additional minor decision which provides an interesting insight into the problems of organizations with multiple and ambiguous goals.

André Gunder Frank has pointed out that agencies that are expected to achieve a long list of goals but which actually have the capacity to achieve only a few are extraordinarily vulnerable to external pressure. There are so many things for which they can be faulted that these agencies are extremely anxious to discover ways in which they can please their political superiors.[15] Frank was primarily interested in the manipulative power that this gave to the superiors, but this anxiety can affect agency decision making even when there is no conscious attempt at manipulation. Agencies in such vulnerable positions will seek clues about the desires of the political leadership and strive to fulfill these wishes as a way of protecting themselves from criticism.

In the Department of Cooperatives, the speeches of Kaunda were eagerly examined for hints about his special expectations for the movement. In a number of speeches he seemed to imply that members of farming cooperatives should all work together in

---

[15] A. Frank, "Goal Ambiguity and Conflicting Standards: An Approach to the Study of Organization," *Human Organization*, 17, No. 4 (1958-1959), 8-13.

cultivating a single plot of land instead of cultivating individual fields and sharing common services. Although this was a misinterpretation of Kaunda's views—he had always held that Zambia should have different types of cooperatives—it quickly became departmental policy because it seemed to be the immediate interest of the president. The same agency that refused to screen applicants for competence in farming and economic management began to screen them for compliance with this model, and in several cases societies that wished to farm individually and pool services were denied registration.

This decision further undermined the nation's cooperative movement, for it was usually the more efficient farmers who were reluctant to give up their individual fields to farm communally. Their exclusion from the movement jeopardized the economic success of farming cooperatives, and in later years both the department and the movement were to suffer greatly from the poor economic performance of cooperatives.

The Failure of Feedback

Zambia's cooperative movement had obviously gotten off to a bad start, but this is a familiar phenomenon with new and innovative public programs, and these initial troubles need not have meant the ultimate collapse of the movement. Under normal circumstances, the implementing agency could change its behavior in response to feedback from the environment, modifying its policies so that problems were eliminated and productive behavior encouraged. In the Zambian case, however, the peculiar nature of cooperative policy inhibited the operation of normal feedback mechanisms, so that while information about the poor performance of cooperatives was available to the department, it was not used to modify the behavior of the agency.

When the agency launched the movement there was no recognition of the need for feedback and evaluation. The agency was so little concerned with the effects of its actions that field staff were given no instructions about what they should observe, and were provided with no standardized reporting forms for the systematic presentation of information on the state of their societies.[16] It was suggested that officers visit their societies at least once a month, but this suggestion was rarely enforced. The principal method for

[16] Wiffin, "Staffing and Organization," p. 47.

communicating back to the capital city, Lusaka, on the performance of cooperatives was the yearly report by the senior cooperative officer in each province, and no effort was made to standardize these reports so that a comprehensive picture of the nation's cooperative movement could be assembled.[17]

In spite of these obstacles, the field staff did try to tell the department that things were not going well in the rural areas. In their annual reports and special letters to headquarters, provincial and district officials constantly emphasized that their societies were small, inefficient, and poorly located, that they were wasting the loans and subsidies that they had been given, and that closer supervision of them was necessary if the movement was to operate successfully. Provincial cooperative officers were unanimous in their call for a moratorium on new registrations until they could adequately supervise the existing societies, but throughout 1965 and 1966 their pleas received no support from the agency director.[18] Eventually, the threat of a staff revolt persuaded him to declare a halt to new registrations in the spring of 1967, but this concession came long after the field staff had demonstrated the necessity of this move, and it was the *only* staff suggestion that was followed. The department seemed peculiarly incapable of responding positively to feedback generated within the organization.

There are several reasons for this failure of the feedback process. First, the politicization of the department's leadership created an atmosphere that discouraged the rational examination of the task performance of the agency. Kaunda had appointed a politician as director because he distrusted the civil service, and in subsequent public speeches the president chastised the bureaucracy for excessive caution in the implementation of development programs.[19] This attitude could not help but affect the director, who naturally regarded gloomy reports from the field as an inevitable bureaucratic response to innovation. The political importance of the cooperative program provided an automatic excuse for discounting or belittling negative reports from the field, thus isolating the process of decision making from the rest of the activities of the agency.

[17] International Labor Office, "Report to the Government of Zambia on Cooperative Finance, Banking and Credit" (Geneva: I.L.O., 1968), p. 31.

[18] See the *Annual Reports* from the various provinces, 1965 and 1966, File 12/1, Department of Cooperatives, Lusaka Files.

[19] See the report on Kaunda's address to a seminar of civil servants in the *Times of Zambia*, June 27, 1966.

53

A second reason for the failure of feedback to produce change in the agency's behavior was that the feedback of the field staff was directed at goals that the department had not yet defined to be of central importance. The field staff was conerned about the inefficiency of the economic performance of local societies, and although this was part of the formal goal structure of the agency, it was not a part of its operational goal structure. As we have noted, political necessity forced the department to define its short-run operational goals as: 1) registering more societies; and 2) granting them loans. Achieving these goals had immediate payoffs, while the longer range goals of producing an efficient and productive cooperative movement were pushed into the background. In a sense, the information supplied by the field officers was not defined as relevant to the immediate tasks of the agency and so could be conveniently ignored.

A third difficulty lay in the isolation of the department from the critial expertise of other agencies. Three other institutions, the Department of Agriculture, the Land and Agricultural Bank, and the Credit Organization of Zambia, had participated in granting loans to cooperatives, and yet none of these provided the department with any informed criticism of its policies. The political popularity of cooperatives discouraged criticism, so rather than precipitate a conflict, the other agencies merely gave pro forma approval to the decisions of the department. In the case of the Department of Agriculture, a direct rival of the Department of Cooperatives for funds and prestige, bureaucratic jealousy resulted in a conscious withholding of critical information on cooperatives. The agriculture field staff was discouraged from reporting problems with cooperatives to the Department of Cooperatives so that the Department of Agriculture could slowly build up a case for the abolition of the whole cooperative movement.[20] Information that might have encouraged the department to improve its policies was therefore deliberately withheld, because improvement would not have been in

[20] In one case, an eager agricultural assistant had written directly to the Department of Cooperatives to describe the problems with one society. He was firmly told by his superior in the Department of Agriculture that: "Your job is to advise farmers on how to grow more and better crops. It is not, repeat not, writing letters to other departments." See: "Letter from the Provincial Agricultural Officer, Eastern Province to the Agricultural Assistant, Sinde Misale, 23 September 1966," File 2/70, Department of Cooperatives, Eastern Province Files.

the best interests of the Department of Agriculture. This bureaucratic hostility would not have been as intense if the political elite had not been so favorably disposed toward cooperatives that the Department of Agriculture felt seriously threatened in the rural development sphere.

This kind of isolation from bureaucratic feedback is probably inevitable in resource-poor countries, but the Department of Cooperatives also experienced the additional problem of being isolated from its own target population. Cooperative members were never consulted about policy, and their criticisms of the program (which were substantial) were never brought to the attention of agency decision makers. This insensitivity to feedback from the client population was produced by a variety of factors: the colonial heritage of bureaucratic authoritarianism; the status insecurity of low-level field staff who could not bear to listen attentively to the criticisms of illiterate "bush" natives; the communications problems within the department; communication and transportation difficulties in the rural areas; and a structure of information-processing in the department which proceeded from the top down instead of the bottom up. Whatever the precise cause, agency decision makers were effectively cut off from the feedback of cooperative members, a factor that further increased the informational isolation of the department.

This brings us to the fourth factor that inhibited the operation of the feedback process—the political popularity of cooperative policy. Kaunda and his supporters were prepared, for ideological reasons, to defend the cooperative movement even if it was in serious trouble. So important was this program that problems could be rationalized as initial and minor difficulties that would soon clear themselves up. This attitude meant that the department had little to fear from its political superiors; its budget was secure and its activities guaranteed of support. In the Zambian administrative system, this kind of popularity meant power, and the power of the agency reduced the salience of feedback. This is the problem of *hubris* identified by Karl Deutsch: the more powerful an organism, the less need it has to learn from its environment and the less responsive it is to critical messages.[21] In Herbert Kaufman's terms, popularity raises the threshold at which negative feedback must

[21] K. Deutsch, *The Nerves of Government* (Glencoe, Ill.: Free Press, 1963), pp. 200-242.

TWO · *Quick*

be listened to: the more popular an agency, the less it needs to pay attention to critical information.[22]

A final barrier to the rational processing of feedback was the availability of financial resources to the department. In a resource-rich situation, the department did not have to take a hard look at its policies and reevaluate them in light of the performance of cooperatives. Instead, it could take the easier route of pumping more resources into the movement on the grounds that whatever the problems were, more resources would surely solve them. Armed with this logic, the department proceeded to give tractors to the ailing farming societies as a device for increasing their productivity.[23] Needless to say, this innovation proved no solution, and in fact, the tractors merely added another burden to the already troubled movement. An agency with less access to financial resources would not have been able to "buy its way out of trouble" in this fashion, and perhaps would have been obliged to take a closer look at its existing policies.

The inability of the Department of Cooperatives to respond rationally to the negative feedback that it received from its own staff was thus largely a product of the peculiar nature of cooperative policy in Zambia at this time. Eventually, the situation changed; cooperatives lost their privileged position, and the department was forced to initiate sweeping changes in order to safeguard its own existence. We will discuss these changes briefly at the end of the chapter, but they really belong to another story. Once they occurred, cooperative policy ceased to have the characteristics we have defined as "ideological" and the policy took on quite a different form with very different problems of implementation. At this point, therefore, we should step back from the narrative and examine the general hypotheses that emerge from this analysis of ideological program implementation.

THE PARADOX OF POPULARITY

The argument we have developed in this chapter can be quickly

22 H. Kaufman, *Administrative Feedback* (Washington, D.C.: The Brookings Institution, 1973), p. 53.

23 See Zambia, Department of Cooperatives, *Annual Report for 1966* (Lusaka: Government Printer, 1967). For an analysis of the problems with tractors, see R. Roberts and C. Elliott, "Constraints in Agriculture," in Elliott, ed., *Constraints on the Economic Development of Zambia*, p. 285.

summarized in the form of seven general propositions about decision making in organizations that are attempting to implement vaguely defined but politically important policies.

1. Agencies with multiple, ambiguous, and immeasurable goals find it difficult to develop technically rational solutions to the problems of implementation. They have no logical way of setting priorities or organizing routines, since *any* activity can be justified in terms of *some* goal. This paralysis of rational planning inhibits the agency from taking decisive or effective action on its own.

2. If political pressure makes inaction impossible, agencies will use political criteria for setting priorities and organizing action. Such criteria demand a simplification of the agency's operational goal structure, eliminating many of the nonmeasurable or long-run goals and focusing attention exclusively on activity that will yield short-run, measurable results. Immediate results have a political utility for the organization regardless of the contribution that such activity makes to the long-run success of its program.

3. Agencies implementing multigoaled programs are made vulnerable by their inability to achieve all of their goals, and this vulnerability increases their sensitivity to the desires and expectations of their political superiors. They rush to respond to clues from their superiors, and are so anxious to demonstrate at least a small measure of success that they may entirely misinterpret the desires of the national leadership. This hypersensitivity is a further obstacle to effective program implementation.

4. The politicization of leadership in an agency inhibits the operation of normal processes of feedback and learning. A political appointee is encouraged, by the very nature of his position, to discount or belittle any negative information on agency performance that comes from the staff.

5. Political popularity isolates an agency from feedback from other bureaucratic actors who are either afraid to criticize a popular department or anxious not to tip their hand until their criticism can destroy the popular rival. In either case, the implementing agency receives little assistance from others in improving its task performance.

6. Resource availability inhibits the feedback process by allow-

57

ing an agency to postpone critical examination of its actions. Spending more money is a convenient and painless alternative to critical self-inspection.

7. Popularity increases the power of an agency and decreases its sensitivity to messages from its environment. Critical information need not be listened to because it is largely irrelevant in determining the status or budget of the agency. Popular organizations can afford not to learn from their mistakes.

The overall import of these propositions can be summed up in a single paradox. Vague but ambitious programs that are favored by a nation's leaders owe their popularity to the importance that they have in the elite's overall scheme for national development. The success of such programs matters greatly, and to succeed in such complex undertakings the implementing agency must be adaptable, flexible, and responsive to problems that arise in the course of implementation. While it is important that popular programs succeed, their very popularity reduces the likelihood of success. Popularity inhibits the feedback process and reduces the capacity of the implementing agency to respond creatively to problems.

The reverse of this "paradox of popularity" is the hypothesis that ambitious programs would stand a better chance of success if they were slightly *un*popular with the political elite. Agencies with unpopular programs are likely to demand a clear formulation of goals before launching an operation, to monitor their own performance quite closely, and to solve problems quickly before they become ammunition for political opponents. Agencies with unpopular policies to implement are less likely to be given political directors, and will be less able to hide their problems by random and irrational increases in spending.

Some support for this hypothesis can be found in the experience of the Department of Cooperatives after 1967, for in that year Zambia's cooperative movement lost a large measure of its political popularity and became just one more rural development program among many. The events that precipitated this change in status were an extremely critical report on cooperatives by the French agronomist, René Dumont, and a budget crisis which forced Zambia's political elite to take a closer look at the economic productivity of all the nation's development programs.[24] Once coop-

[24] On the Dumont Report see "Dr. Dumont's Diagnosis," *Business and*

erative policy lost its unique popularity, the behavior of the implementing organization became much more rational and effective, confirming our hypothesis about the inverse relationship between popularity and implementation rationality. This connection is made even more convincing by the fact that the leadership of the department, including the director and the registrar, remained the same throughout this transition phase. The same organization behaved in a very different way, and this change in behavior can only be explained by the changed external environment of the department, an environment that ceased to regard cooperatives as a particularly popular program.

The changes after 1967 were remarkable. To begin with, the department was not troubled by problems of multiple and ambiguous goals. The Dumont Report had focused its major criticism on the economic performance of farming cooperatives, and the post-1967 productivity drive made it absolutely clear that economic criteria were to be the sole goals of departmental policy. When cooperative policy became less popular, elite expectations became much more specific, allowing the department to focus its activities on one particular and unambiguous goal.

Goal clarification was swiftly followed by a determined effort to improve the feedback mechanisms within the department. The regime's productivity drive had drawn critical attention to the performance of farming cooperatives, and the agency quickly learned that if it did not detect problems with the movement, someone else would.[25] Fear of external criticism brought about a number of changes, the most significant of which was the development of a standardized reporting form so that Lusaka headquarters could have detailed information on the performance of each cooperative society available on short notice.[26] Procedures for supervising the work of field officers were tightened up considerably,

Economy of East and Central Africa (May 1967), pp. 26-29. On the government's productivity drive see Zambia Information Services, "Press Background no. 6/68, 13 January 1968."

[25] For a discussion of the public criticism of cooperatives in the news media and the National Assembly, see Quick, *Bureaucracy and Rural Socialism*, pp. 279-285.

[26] Zambia, National Institute for Public Administration, "Report on the Cooperative Movement in Zambia," mimeographed report, December 11, 1967, p. 1. For information on other pressure on field staff, see the report in the *Zambia Mail*, December 12, 1967.

and the post of internal auditor was created to monitor the behavior of lower level field staff.[27] Finally, the normal system of feedback and monitoring was supplemented by several teams of foreign "experts" who were recruited by the department to evaluate both the cooperative movement and the performance of the agency.[28] It was obvious that the post-1967 department was not going to have the same problems receiving and acting on negative information that had plagued its efforts at cooperative development in the 1965-1967 period.

On the operational level, steps were soon taken to correct the more obvious problems that departmental policy had encouraged. Cooperative officers were given much greater supervisory authority over local societies, acquiring the power to veto society expenditures and to control the books and the bank accounts of each society in their district.[29] These measures reduced the misuse of government funds, and offered some assurance that the economic affairs of the farming cooperatives were managed in a reasonably effective fashion. With the cooperative officer in control of the loan funds, there was much less waste and many fewer conflicts between members over the distribution and use of money. In another move to increase the rationality of cooperatives' economic behavior, the department launched a campaign to take tractors away from societies that were not making productive use of them and to locate these tractors at a central mechanization station.[30] These stations were called Cooperative Mechanization Unions, and in theory the tractors still belonged to the individual societies that were coerced

[27] Quick, *Bureaucracy and Rural Socialism*, p. 306.

[28] The first group of expatriates were volunteers from the Netherlands who arrived in early 1967. They were soon joined by volunteers from Sweden, Denmark, and Israel. Most of the volunteers were posted to rural areas to assist the local farming cooperatives, but the leader of the Swedish team was made planning officer in the Lusaka headquarters of the department. He was soon joined by a Swedish agricultural economist who became the main research officer in the department, and in 1972 the department recruited an entire cooperative research team from Sweden. In addition to these expatriates, the cooperative movement was studied by an I.L.O. mission, and the department itself was the focus of a study by the Ministry of Finance.

[29] "Review of Department Policy by the Director of Cooperative Societies for the Cooperative Conference, May 1967," File 12/1, Department of Cooperatives, Lusaka Files.

[30] "Circular Letter from the Registrar to all Provincial Cooperative Officers, 2 October 1968," File 2/392, Department of Cooperatives, Lusaka Files.

into joining the union. In practice, the supervision of the tractors was the responsibility of the farm manager, an employee of the Department of Cooperatives. The position of farm manager was created late in 1967 as a device for overcoming the obvious ignorance of cooperative officers about agricultural production. The farm managers were recruited as agricultural experts, and were hired as contract and not civil service employees, because the department believed that contract employees could be controlled by the agency more effectively than civil servants with guaranteed security of tenure.[31] The farm managers were given extensive authority to regulate the day-to-day performance of the mechanization unions, and in practice their authority extended down to the level of the member societies. Farm managers decided on planting schedules, crop rotation, the allocation of labor, and virtually every other area of agricultural performance. After 1967, the department's laissez faire policies were replaced with strict management and close supervision of farming societies.

From this brief discussion, it is obvious that the process of implementing cooperative policy changed rather dramatically after 1967. Criticism of the cooperative movement forced the department to define its operational goals clearly, to develop systems of monitoring and feedback, and to organize its field staff in such a way as to implement its operational goals effectively. The implementation process in the post-1967 period was considerably more rational and coherent than in the earlier years, lending some support to our view that criticism may be more successful in producing effective policy implementation than unqualified support. However, while it is clear that departmental behavior after 1967 was more rational, it is not the case that this period saw a dramatic improvement in the state of the cooperative movement. A more rational implementation process does not guarantee the success of a program, especially one which got off to so poor a start. In the post-1967 period, the department was unable to solve the acute problem of demoralization within the cooperative movement and to attract back to the movement those skilled and energetic farmers who had left it in disgust during its first phase. Similarly, the agency could not secure a minimum level of elite support, for by 1967 too

[31] This rationale for hiring farm managers as contract employees was spelled out in: "Letter from the Director of Cooperative Societies to the Permanent Secretary, Ministry of Rural Development, 3 December 1969," File 2/392/2/2, Department of Cooperatives, Lusaka Files.

many Zambian politicians had written the cooperative movement off as a failure.

The failure of the department to respond effectively to the problems of the movement, combined with the elite's early support for it, created a reservoir of resentment that was finally released when the Dumont Report broke the dam. After two years of negative experience, many felt that the cooperative movement was clearly an unsalvageable failure, and so they were reluctant to grant the department additional resources to solve the problems that it had created. The agency was repeatedly denied requests for increases in field staff, and was also cut off from access to government loan funds that were needed to get the mechanization unions off the ground and to serve as incentives for more productive economic behavior.[32] Perhaps the most significant problem, however, was the encouragement that the political elite gave to alternative, noncooperative modes of production in agriculture. After 1967, elite attention turned to mechanisms for increasing the productivity of individual farmers, and the profitability of participation in these schemes drew members away from the cooperative movement. Thus, although the behavior of the Department of Cooperatives was more rational in the post-1967 period, it was unable to solve the problems that it had created in the 1965-1967 years, and the movement was essentially moribund after 1970. Had the agency behaved in 1965 as it did after 1967, however, the story of Zambia's cooperatives might have been very different. Had cooperative policy been defined in less ideological terms, and had the department been less popular in its initial phase of operations, the movement might have stood a considerably better chance of success.

CONCLUSION

This chapter has tried to demonstrate how certain characteristics of ideological programs act to undermine the effectiveness of the implementation process. Political popularity appears to encourage goal ambiguity and to inhibit the normal processes of feedback and evaluation within the implementing agency. Thus while it has long been observed that a lack of political popularity

[32] "Record of the Ad-Hoc Meeting Held in the Credit Organization of Zambia Conference Room, 5 September 1969," File 2/392, Department of Cooperatives, Lusaka Files.

may doom a development program, this chapter suggests that the alternative of excessive and uncritical support may be equally injurious to successful program implementation.

The present study should be viewed largely as a corrective to the simplistic assumption that political popularity is a sufficient condition for program success. It should *not* be seen as an assertion that *un*popularity is necessarily a useful device for ensuring program success. Given the resource limitations of Third World countries, programs which do not enjoy a large measure of political popularity are likely to be abandoned, as David Pyle demonstrates in Chapter Five of this volume. Alternatively, programs that lack strong elite support may founder under the problems of goal conflict within the political elite, as Cynthia McClintock describes in the next chapter. It would appear that unpopular programs have their own set of implementation problems, and these problems may be as severe as those facing popular ones. The major import of this chapter, therefore, is not that unpopular programs are likely to succeed, but that popular ones also face a formidable set of obstacles to rational implementation.

THREE · *Reform Governments and Policy Implementation: Lessons from Peru*

CYNTHIA McCLINTOCK

THE successful implementation of public policy is difficult in First World countries; it is more difficult in the Third World; and it may be most difficult for reform-oriented governments in the Third World, as this chapter will suggest. Reform-oriented governments share many major impediments to policy implementation such as resource scarcity and faulty communication among state agencies and citizens with other Third World countries. In addition, however, these governments are by definition embarking on more ambitious, problematic programs that are harder to implement.[1] Further, these governments generally claim to be concerned not only with national economic redistribution but also with popular political participation, and, in the new political arenas, conflict over program goals is likely to emerge, further impeding policy implementation.[2] If the political leadership abides by its commitment to respond to popular concerns, conflict over correct policy implementation reverberates back to the leadership as conflict over correct policy formulation. Indeed, when the ideology of the reform government is uncertain and many voices are heard in the

Note: I would like to thank the Social Science Research Council, which supported not only a year's fieldwork in Peru but also a return trip and write-up time. In Peru, I was fortunate to be helped by many kind people, especially Luis Deustua, Pedro Ortiz, and Rodolfo Osores Ocampo. This chapter has been greatly improved by the helpful comments of Suzanne Berger, Wayne Cornelius, Merilee Grindle, and Henry Deitz.

[1] General discussions of this issue are provided by Merilee Grindle and Peter Cleaves in this volume, and by D. Van Meter and C. Van Horn, "The Policy Implementation Process: A Conceptual Framework," *Administration and Society*, 6, No. 4 (February 1975), 460-461.

[2] This point is also emphasized by Van Meter and Van Horn, "Policy Implementation Process."

major political arenas, incoherent and indecisive policy formulation is likely, thus hindering effective policy implementation.

In this study, the obstacles to successful policy implementation by reform-oriented Third World governments are examined through the experience of the Velasco regime in Peru (1968-1975) and its efforts to carry out a meaningful agrarian reform. Velasco's agrarian reform program certainly warrants classification among the most problematic government programs on the basis of the criteria established by Merilee Grindle and Peter Cleaves in their introductory and concluding chapters to this volume. The program was redistributive rather than distributive, expropriating haciendas from the previous owners and transferring them to the peasants. The agrarian cooperatives were sudden innovations in the Peruvian countryside, similar in many respects to the self-managed enterprises in Yugoslavia, in Chile under Allende, and in Mexico under Cárdenas, but a dramatic change from the typical Peruvian hacienda. The reform involved many goals and multiple actors; the goals were long-range and complex in nature, including both specific, quantifiable aims such as increased agricultural productivity, and abstract goals such as greater peasant self-confidence and respect. Moreover, as Grindle points out, agrarian reform is necessarily a decentralized program, with dispersed sites and decisional units, and thus is more difficult to implement.

Nor was the political context of the Peruvian agrarian reform propitious for coherent policy formulation and implementation. Like many reform governments, the Velasco junta came to power unexpectedly and embarked suddenly on programs that called for major changes in the society. The extent and character of the reform policies were uncertain. As in Bolivia under the MNR (Revolutionary Nationalist Movement), Chile under Frei and Allende, Mexico under Cárdenas, and Venezuela under Betancourt, some analysts thought Velasco was masking socialist programs with moderate rhetoric to calm national elites and the United States, and other observers thought he was cloaking moderate programs with socialist rhetoric to win popular support.[3] This

[3] Consider, for example, the distinct evaluations of the Peruvian reforms by various scholars. A. Lowenthal, "Peru's Ambiguous Revolution," in A. Lowenthal, ed., *The Peruvian Experiment* (Princeton: Princeton University Press, 1975), and P. Knight, "New Forms of Economic Organization in Peru: Toward Workers' Self-Management," ibid., perceive Velasco's efforts as dramatic reforms. Less positive evaluations are found in J. Cotler, "The

was particularly the case with respect to the Velasco reform government because it was a military regime, and the military had an inglorious past in Peru, frequently acting to block reform efforts.

In the midst of the confusion and uncertainty, many factions emerged and made policy demands on the government. Elites who stood to lose from the implementation of the reform policies tried to block them. Technicians asserted the importance of their knowledge and experience. Marxist intellectuals and disadvantaged citizens emphasized the need for greater redistribution to attain the goal of social justice. Since the Velasco government claimed to seek not only greater economic equality in Peru but also increased political participation, it was committed to respond to these various voices rather than to repress them. Intense conflict over the direction of the agrarian reform program ensued at various political levels. Although, in the abstract, the agrarian reform program was probably the most popular effort of the Velasco government, both civilian bureaucrats and military leaders did not hesitate to advance their own ideas about specific points in the program, even if their actions might threaten the progress of the reform; the Peruvian officials thus stand in sharp contrast to the compliant Zambian officials described by Stephen Quick in the preceding chapter.

To win compliance from administrators, the Peruvian government might have used the tried-and-true strategy of high salaries and massive benefits. As a reform government, however, the Velasco government was trying to move toward more equal income distribution, and thus hoped to decrease rather than increase officials' salaries. Strict maximum salary levels for top officials in all government ministries were set in Decree Law 21058, and the salaries of lower level officials and cooperative managers were generally not commensurate with their potential earning power in the private sector or in other Latin American countries.[4]

The relatively low salaries of administrators in the agrarian

New Mode of Political Domination in Peru," ibid.; K. Middlebrook and D. Palmer, *Military Government and Political Development: Lessons From Peru* (Beverly Hills, Calif.: Sage Professional Papers in Comparative Politics, 1975); and R. Webb, "Government Policy and the Distribution of Income in Peru, 1963-1973," in Lowenthal, *The Peruvian Experiment.*

[4] See C. McClintock, "Self-Management and the Peasant: Agrarian Cooperatives and Changing Political Culture in Peru, 1969-1975," revision of Ph.D. diss. Massachusetts Institute of Technology, 1977, pp. 377-378.

sector did not reflect reluctance on the part of the Velasco government to provide resources for the agrarian reform program. Evaluation of the resources of agrarian reform actors is critical to an analysis of the reasons for the success or failure of the program, as Cleaves emphasizes, but this is difficult because various kinds of resources must be considered. Relatively, the agrarian reform program was well financed. The budget of the Ministry of Agriculture multiplied about eight times in current *soles* (the Peruvian currency) between 1967 and 1975, and agriculture rose from ninth to fourth in terms of total ministry allocations over the same time period.[5] Agricultural investment increased sharply and loans to agricultural enterprises jumped.[6] Yet, salaries to officials were low. Moreover, and perhaps most importantly, despite the *relatively* great allocation of resources to the agrarian reform in comparison to previous allocations, in *absolute* terms, resources were still limited vis-à-vis the task at hand. Resources were sufficient for the actual expropriation of Peruvian haciendas, but not for the full support of the new cooperatives. Because such problems as the inadequate communications network could not be ameliorated overnight, support for the new cooperatives required not only very large sums immediately but also for a considerable period of time.

Given the immensity of the task, the charged political context in which many civilians were skeptical of the military government, and the limited resources available, it is not surprising that the formulation and implementation of the agrarian reform were difficult. This chapter analyzes these difficulties, emphasizing in particular the problems created by disagreement among virtually all political groups over the correct direction of the reform program. First, the conflict within the military leadership during the prolonged "formulation" of the reform is examined. The next section of the chapter indicates that this conflict at the top was transferred into conflict among reform implementors and beneficiaries: SINAMOS (National System for the Support of Social Mobilization), the Ministry of Agriculture, and the agrarian cooperative members. The following section explores the actual confrontation among these actors in the countryside. The agrarian cooperative members emerged as the victors of this struggle, but it may have been a Pyrrhic victory, contributing to the demise of Velasco and the rise of his relatively conservative successor, Morales Bermúdez.

[5] Ibid., p. 397.   [6] Ibid., pp. 397-398.

Although this study emphasizes the shortcomings of policy formulation and implementation during the Velasco government, the Peruvian agrarian reform should not be construed as a total failure. It "failed" according to many of the goals of its formulators because: 1) it apparently did not increase agricultural production; 2) it neither enhanced the capacity of the government to guide peasant political activity, nor even built popular support for the Velasco government; and 3) it did not help the poorest peasants, the *comuneros*, residents of highlands peasant communities who constituted approximately 40 percent of the agrarian population, and who frequently had to migrate to the coast for temporary seasonal work. However, these were lofty goals. By the standards of many Latin American agrarian reforms, the Peruvian program did not do so badly on redistributive criteria. Considerable hacienda expropriation actually occurred. As of September 1976, almost 8,500,000 hectares, accounting for 35 percent of Peru's agricultural land, had been expropriated and about 285,000 families had benefited from the reform, approximately 24 percent of all rural farm families.[7] Although all figures must be treated with caution, the impact of the Peruvian reform was generally similar to or greater than that of the agrarian reforms in Chile, Bolivia, and Mexico.[8] In contrast to these previous reform programs, in Peru virtually all of the large, lucrative tracts in the countryside were expropriated intact; subdivision of haciendas was minimal. It must be noted, too, that although during 1976-1978 Morales Bermúdez was reversing many of Velasco's reform programs, to date the agrarian cooperatives have endured, standing as the major legacy of the Velasco government.

This study is based on research conducted in Peru from March 1973 to April 1974, during May and June of 1975, and in July of 1977. Three agrarian cooperatives were studied. The largest of them, Huanca, was a major livestock enterprise in the central highlands near the provincial city of Huancayo. The Huanco coopera-

[7] Figures on the number of hectares expropriated and families benefited are from *Reforma Agraria en Cifras*, a serial publication of the Ministry of Agriculture in Lima. Percentage figures are derived from various sources; see McClintock, "Structural Change and Political Culture in Rural Peru: The Impact of Self-Managed Cooperatives on Peasant Clientelism, 1969-1975," Ph.D. diss. Massachusetts Institute of Technology, 1976, Appendix 2.

[8] For comparative figures for these reforms see McClintock, "Structural Change and Political Culture in Rural Peru," pp. 150-154.

tive included both ex-haciendas and peasant communities as members. There, I did research in one ex-hacienda, Monte, and three peasant communities, Patca, Varya, and Rachuis. I also studied two smaller crop enterprises, Estrella and Marla, on the coast near the provincial city of Trujillo. A sample survey was conducted in each of these three cooperatives.[9] I visited other cooperatives in the southern highlands (Puno), the south coast (Cañete), and the north coast (Chancay). The analysis of official attitudes and actions is based on interviews in Trujillo, Lima, Huancayo, Cañete, and Puno. Twenty SINAMOS officials were interviewed informally, in addition to twenty-five Ministry of Agriculture officials, and a sprinkling of employees in other agencies.

POLICY FORMULATION BY THE MILITARY LEADERSHIP

As of 1968, when General Velasco overthrew the constitutionally elected civilian president, Fernando Belaúnde Terry, Peru was behind most Latin American nations with respect to economic and political reforms. In contrast to many Latin American countries, Peru's most significant reformist party, APRA (American Popular Revolutionary Alliance), had never won executive power and had never been able to advance its core programs. Political, economic, and social inequities were severe in Peru. Its political and economic systems were generally considered to be dominated by "forty families."[10] These families controlled the great bulk of Peru's exports, productive land, and industry, and were closely tied to international interests. Peru's income distribution was one of the most skewed in the continent.[11] Inequality was especially severe in the agrarian sector. In 1961, Peru's Gini index of land distribution ranked lowest among 54 nations profiled by Taylor

[9] Details on survey methodology are provided, ibid., pp. 667-672.

[10] On the pre-1968 system, see C. Astiz, *Pressure Groups and Power Elites in Peruvian Politics* (Ithaca, N.Y.: Cornell University Press, 1969); and F. Bourricaud, *Power and Society in Contemporary Peru* (New York: Praeger, 1970). Specific discussion of the "oligarchy" is given by C. Malpica, *Los dueños del Peru* (Lima: Ediciones Ensayos Sociales, 1968).

[11] In 1961, Peru's per capita GDP was $237; the top 5 percent of the income recipients received 48 percent of the income, a considerably larger percentage than in Brazil, Bolivia, Colombia, Chile, Mexico, or Ecuador. See J. Howe, *The U.S. and World Development: Agenda for Action 1975* (New York: Praeger, 1975), pp. 214-215.

69

and Hudson.[12] Major land invasions shook the Peruvian highlands during the early 1960s; they were stopped only through violent repression.

When the military came to power in 1968, there was considerable agreement that it was time for a change. Most top military
officers believed that Peru's dependence on the United States and
on the "forty families" should be reduced. More specifically, high-
level officers agreed upon the need to expropriate the International Petroleum Company, a subsidiary of Standard Oil that was
widely perceived to have violated Peru's national sovereignty. The
military leadership also concurred on the need for some kind of
agrarian reform.[13]

However, with respect to the ultimate goals of the reforms and
with respect to their extent, agreement among top military officers
was scant.[14] The political conflict resulted in a kaleidoscope of
shifting leadership groups and tenuous, incoherent policies. This
will be illuminated here with respect to the agrarian reform, but it
was evident in other policy spheres as well. The overall designs of
the government were never clear; the most common label for the
regime was a description of what it was not: "neither capitalist nor
Communist." The government's ideology was really an ideological
collage. In the international arena, Peru seemed to seek greater
economic autonomy, and to this end expropriated first the International Petroleum Company, and then various other large foreign
enterprises. Yet, the state did not carry its ambitions for independence into the arena of financing; the foreign debt rose sharply
between 1968 and 1975. The military's designs for reform in the
industrial sector changed markedly over time. In 1970, a program
of workers' participation was established, called the Industrial
Community, under which workers were eventually to own and
control 50 percent of the enterprise. However, alongside the industrial communities, many state-run enterprises were developed.

[12] C. Taylor and M. Hudson, *World Handbook of Political and Social
Indicators* (New Haven: Yale University Press, 1972), p. 267.

[13] Agreement among military officers on the need for both the expropriation of the International Petroleum Company and a measure of agrarian
reform is emphasized by A. Stepan, *The State and Society: Peru in Comparative Perspective* (Princeton: Princeton University Press, 1978), pp. 136-
144.

[14] The most detailed analysis and description of the controversies is H.
Pease García, *El Ocaso del Poder Oligárquico: Lucha Política en la Escena
Oficial, 1968-1975* (Lima: DESCO, 1977).

In 1974 the Social Property scheme was announced, for the advancement of new enterprises that creatively mixed worker and state control.

With respect to the military's agrarian reform program, several distinct groups of officers with distinct policy goals have been delineated.[15] One group, dubbed the "bourgeois liberals," seemed most interested in checking the monopoly powers of traditional foreign and domestic elites to enable the development of a more truly capitalist system in the Peruvian countryside. These officers saw the aim of the agrarian reform as primarily the encouragement of agricultural productivity. In their view, only the largest and least efficient estates should be expropriated, in part as a threat to stimulate other enterprises to become more efficient. Another set of officers hoped that the agrarian reform would be a means to social justice. Various key allies of Velasco—known as "the progressives" and "the four colonels"—were by and large convinced that the agrarian reform should redistribute as much land as possible "to those who worked it" and that it should encourage vigorous political participation by the peasants as well as social solidarity among them. Redistribution was not seen as contradictory to growth; nor was political participation seen as contradictory to regime stability. These officials desired the development of worker-managed cooperatives as the key institutions in the countryside.

A third set of officers promoted reform with less concern for social justice and more concern for national security. These military leaders apparently feared that, without an agrarian reform, peasant revolts would inevitably recur—entailing massive civil disruption and conceivably Communist revolution, or else repressive action by the military (action that was increasingly distasteful to many officers). These officers would presumably want the reform to help in particular the poorest peasants, the *comuneros*, who had been the most politically disruptive in the past. These officers would also be most eager to enhance the political capacity of the state in order to channel and guide peasant political activity more effectively in the future. In the view of some scholars, the concern for national security colored the political thought of even the most committed radicals in the Velasco regime.

[15] This delineation draws heavily from Pease García, ibid.; and H. Pease García, "La Reforma Agraria Peruana en la Crisis del Estado Oligárquico," in DESCO, ed., *Estado y Política Agraria* (Lima: DESCO, 1977).

71

The conflicts within the military leadership about the desirable degree of redistribution and the desirable degree of state and/or technocratic influence upon the peasantry were evident in the many alterations and gaps in the agrarian reform law. Indeed, it is difficult to speak of "formulation" of agrarian reform "policy" at any one time because so many key points of the original 1969 law were changed, and so many other critical issues were not discussed in the law. Overall, as Velasco was able to place more of his radical allies in important posts, the agrarian reform program gradually moved toward the left between 1969 and 1975.[16]

During the first nine months of the military government, there was considerable doubt that any agrarian reform law of any significance would be implemented. The major reason was the opposition of General José Benavides, the minister of agriculture and a "bourgeois liberal." Although drafts of the agrarian reform law were being prepared without the support of Benavides, the general's opposition seemed a serious obstacle; Benavides was the son of a past Peruvian president and a respected officer (not to mention a wealthy landowner with close ties to other wealthy landowners). However, in June 1969 Velasco charged that Benavides' public opposition to the law was tantamount to flagrant insubordination and forced him to resign. Only twelve days later the principal agrarian reform law was proclaimed and, the following day, the largest agrarian enterprises, the agroindustrial sugar complexes on the north coast, were occupied by military officials.

Even after the proclamation of the agrarian reform law and the expropriation of the agroindustrial sugar complexes, however, it was widely believed that the reform would not affect most haci-

---

[16] The account in the next few pages on the gradual formulation of agrarian reform policy draws upon the author's own interviews and observations, and also upon J. Agut, "The 'Peruvian Revolution' and Catholic Corporatism: Armed Forces Rule Since 1968," Ph.D. diss. University of Miami, 1975; C. Harding, "Land Reform and Social Conflict in Peru," in Lowenthal, *The Peruvian Experiment*; K. Middlebrook, "Land for the Tiller: Political Participation and the Peruvian Military's Agrarian Reform," B.A. thesis Harvard College, 1972; P. Ortiz Vergara, "El Proceso de la Reforma Agraria Peruana," unpublished manuscript, University of Venezuela at Alto Barinas, 1978; D. Palmer and K. Middlebrook, "Corporatist Participation under Military Rule in Peru," in D. Chaplin, ed., *Peruvian Nationalism: A Corporatist Revolution* (New Brunswick, N.J.: Transaction Books, 1976); Pease García, *El Ocaso del Poder Oligárquico*; and Stepan, *The State and Society.*

endas. Through mid-1971, subdivision of haciendas among family members was permitted, allowing the estates to remain much as they had been, except in name. Many government officials (including the new minister of agriculture, General Barandiarán) emphasized that the key goal of the reform was not to nationalize or collectivize land but to increase agricultural productivity, stimulate private industry, and achieve social peace. It was only in 1971 that it became clear that most large coastal estates would in fact be expropriated. During this year, decrees were issued prohibiting subdivision, and doing so retroactively as well, and the legal landholding limits (approximately 150 hectares on the coast and 50 hectares in the highlands and jungle) began to be enforced.

Moreover, to the consternation of the landowners as well as some military officers, soon haciendas under the legal landholding size were also being expropriated. "Secondary" clauses in the agrarian reform law, such as requirements that the landowner comply with social security regulations, were invoked to expropriate these haciendas. It was not until 1975, when a firm leftist ally of Velasco, General Enrique Gallegos Venero, took over as minister of agriculture, that the former de facto limits (approximately 50 hectares on the coast and 30 in the highlands and jungle) were officially decreed.

There were also many changes and omissions in the 1969 law with respect to political participation in the new cooperatives. The original law devolved considerable power over important decisions in the cooperatives to the members. Each and every member was to have one vote in the General Assembly, which was the maximum formal authority in the enterprise and which elected members to the executive organ, the Administrative Council; this council was responsible for formulating, with the help of a technical manager, the policy for the cooperative.

After the enactment of the reform law, however, many officers apparently had second thoughts. Official fears were kindled by the threats of administrative and technical employees to resign en masse if the law were implemented. Thus, six months later, a new decree was passed that severely restricted workers' participation in the cooperatives. Under the original law, only workers were allowed to be members of the cooperative, and each would have one vote. The new decree stipulated that technicians and white-collar employees would be represented in the cooperative's leadership organs in equal numbers to the field and mill workers; it also prohibited union activists from assuming leadership posts in the new enterprises.

Opposition to the new decree was vehement in the agroindustrial sugar cooperatives, which were the most important rural enterprises in the country and the primary ones to have been expropriated in 1970. Military coordinators in the enterprises enraged workers by repeatedly trying to block salary raises. Between December 1971 and February 1972, strikes erupted in several sugar enterprises, and the military intervened to arrest labor leaders. Velasco was apparently sympathetic to the workers: when the then minister of agriculture, General Barandiarán, wanted the military to intervene at the cooperative Tumán, Velasco vetoed the minister's recommendation, spurring Barandiarán to resign.

Velasco's preference for participatory democracy finally triumphed in March of 1972. By this date, the general could persuade skeptical officials of the desirability of greater worker participation with a barrage of practical arguments.[17] Repression did not seem to be a feasible long-term strategy; as a result of its use, sabotage of technical equipment was a constant threat in the sugar cooperatives. By satisfying workers' demands for participation, the regime could expect to win vitally necessary political support. Further, SINAMOS could be hurried into action, and some officials may have hoped that SINAMOS would control the mobilization of workers. The weight of these arguments apparently persuaded officials to rescind all the restrictive norms of the previous decree. Free, one member/one vote elections were held in the cooperatives.

Yet, the law still remained silent on many key issues of political participation. The main law, Supreme Decree 240-69-AP, said very little about the role of the technical manager in the cooperative, and nothing about how he was to be chosen. It evolved that the Administrative Council would select three candidates for the position, and the ministry would choose one of these three for the post. The law was also silent on the question of the right of members to decide their own salaries, a right some officers wished to reserve for the Ministry of Agriculture.

Nor did the law resolve the question of private versus coopera-

[17] See Stepan, *The State and Society*, p. 205; and Agut, "The 'Peruvian Revolution' and Catholic Corporatism," pp. 513-516.

tive enterprise as the modal form in the new agrarian structure. The law outlined various potential enterprise modes, some entailing limited cooperativization (the Service Cooperative and the Peasant Group) and some entailing a considerable measure (the Agrarian Production Cooperative, or CAP, and the Agrarian Social Interest Society, or SAIS). Only gradually did it become clear that the CAP and the SAIS would be the predominant modes in the more prosperous agricultural areas. According to the Ministry of Agriculture, as of November 1976, 480 cooperatives, primarily CAPs, and 57 SAIS, had been established. There are various important differences between the CAP and the SAIS. Most CAPs, such as the two I studied, Estrella and Marla, incorporate only one ex-hacienda and are geographically integral units. In contrast, the SAIS, like the research site Huanca, comprise not only one or more ex-haciendas but also contiguous peasant communities. The SAIS aimed to help the disadvantaged peasant communities, most of which had seen some of their land seized by the haciendas in the past.

Goal Conflict Among Implementors and Beneficiaries

The intense conflict over goal priorities within the military leadership almost inevitably resulted in a subsequent struggle over the actual implementation of agrarian reform. The division among military leaders became institutionalized in the conflict between the two major agencies operating in the rural sector from 1973 to 1975,[18] SINAMOS and the Ministry of Agriculture. Although there

[18] P. Cleaves and M. Scurrah, *Agriculture, Bureaucracy, and Military Government in Peru* (Ithaca, N.Y.: Cornell University Press, forthcoming), describes all the agencies operating in the rural sector under the Velasco government. The most important ones that functioned throughout the 1972-1976 period that I have omitted are the Agrarian Bank and CENCIRA (National Center for Training and Investigation for the Agrarian Reform). Agrarian Bank officials were charged with responsibility for granting loans to the peasants. However, the bank did not employ many field extension agents, and had to rely on the Ministry of Agriculture's information in many cases. Agrarian Bank officials had the highest professional qualifications and the largest salaries of all agrarian sector bureaucrats. They also tended to be the most hostile to agrarian reform and peasant participation. CENCIRA was a much smaller agency that offered adult education in administration, agricultural economics, Peruvian law, politics, and the like. Politically, it was relatively passive; its officials often had a "wait-and-see" attitude toward the agrarian reform. Cleaves calls the political orientation of CENCIRA

75

was a great variety of ideological preferences within both organizations, and also some purely opportunistic, nonideological attitudes, on balance SINAMOS officials were more committed to massive immediate redistribution and political participation for the most disadvantaged peasants, namely the peasants excluded from the cooperatives, whereas Ministry of Agriculture officials were concerned that the cooperatives themselves be strengthened and their productivity maintained. Gradually, SINAMOS and the ministry became not so much organs of state policy as rival pressure groups. The conflict was intensified further by the opposition of the peasants to the policy goals of both agencies. Cooperative members wanted social and political independence from all government agencies, but they also wanted economic aid from the state.

SINAMOS

What was SINAMOS? Just as the mission of the Velasco government was never entirely clear, neither was the mission of SINAMOS. Characteristically, SINAMOS was usually described by what it was *not*—it was not a political party, it was not Peru's FBI, and it was not a corporatist trick. But, what was it, then? Apparently, Velasco wanted SINAMOS to be the organizational centerpiece of his government, a kind of superministry that could overrule the decisions of other ministries. Velasco also apparently hoped that SINAMOS would push other ministries toward the left; two leftists, both close allies of Velasco, were catapulted to national prominence in 1972 as the leaders of the new organization: Leonídas Rodríguez Figueroa as its military head, and Carlos Delgado as its civilian chief.

---

officials "collaborative"—the reform model would work in time. Other agencies, specifically the Ministry of Food (an offshoot of Agriculture) and the Support Agency for Peasant Enterprises (an offshoot of SINAMOS), were not active in the countryside until at least 1975, after the major period of my research. An idea of the relative importance of the agencies can be gained from a comparison of their 1975-1976 biennial budget allocations:

Agency	Soles
Ministry of Agriculture	16,696,056,000
SINAMOS	3,369,304,000
Ministry of Food	2,216,125,000
CENCIRA	65,010,000

Fifty or sixty soles to the dollar was a practical exchange rate during 1975-1976.

76

The law creating SINAMOS emphasized that the priority functions of SINAMOS were to extend and amplify the participatory rights of citizens. In fact, these functions were the primary ones of most base-level SINAMOS officials. However, a considerable number of military leaders hoped—and in all probability had been led to believe—that SINAMOS would at the very least enhance popular support for the regime and perhaps even guide and channel popular participation in directions favored by the government.[19] When it became clear that SINAMOS was not performing these supportive roles, Rodríguez was replaced in 1974 by a general who did pay them heed.

The pattern of recruitment into SINAMOS made the effort to build popular support for the Velasco government virtually impossible for the agency. SINAMOS hired both conservative officials (especially at the middle ranks) and many young Marxists (especially at the lower ranks, as "promoters").[20] Officials with conservative or Marxist perspectives were rarely interested in building support for Velasco. Indeed, the low scores of new SINAMOS recruits on examinations after a "Basic Course on the Peruvian Revolution" led the national SINAMOS office to judge that the degree of commitment to the government was disturbingly low.[21] Most of these new recruits were young and idealistic, recent graduates of university programs in the social sciences, with limited practical experience in the Peruvian countryside. High-level officials may have thought that they could coopt radical students through SINAMOS, but in fact they could not. The young radicals accepted salaries from SINAMOS but preached their own politics in the field. Weak supervisory practices and the vast distance between zonal offices and field sites afforded the promoters substantial political independence.

As perceived by its radical leaders and base-level promoters,

[19] Agut, "The 'Peruvian Revolution' and Catholic Corporatism," pp. 513-516, is especially instructive on this point. Many scholars have also emphasized a hidden agenda for SINAMOS of cooptation and control of political activity. See, for example, Palmer and Middlebrook, "Corporatist Participation under Military Rule in Peru" and Cotler, "The New Mode of Political Domination."

[20] A detailed description of the ideologies of SINAMOS officials at various ranks may be found in S. Woy, "SINAMOS: Infrastructure of Participation," paper presented to the seminar on the "Faces of Participation in Latin America," University of Texas, San Antonio, Texas, 1976.

[21] Ibid., p. 24.

the major goals of SINAMOS were to encourage both "authentic participation" and "equal participation."[22] Authentic participation" meant the free and accurate expression of the citizens' will, by means of formal organizations based on one member/one vote principles. "Equal participation" meant the inclusion of all peasants, especially previously marginal ones, in these organizations. At times, these two goals were contradictory—as, for example, when prosperous cooperative members would "authentically" vote to restrict the access of disadvantaged temporary workers to membership in the cooperatives, thereby impeding equal participation. Generally, at these times SINAMOS promoters opted to encourage equal participation, and thereby proved intrusive in the view of many peasants.

During 1973 and 1974, the most specific policy target of SINAMOS in the countryside was the development of the major new peasant organization, the National Agrarian Confederation (CNA). The CNA was to provide the institutional channel for peasant participation—at the local level in Agrarian Leagues, at the regional level in Agrarian Federations, and at the national level in the General Assembly of Delegates and Leadership Board of the CNA. It was hoped that the CNA would express the concerns of the peasants to the military leadership and would in turn build understanding and support for the Peruvian government. The CNA was also to unite peasants of different socioeconomic strata and geographic regions. SINAMOS worked hard to incorporate disadvantaged peasants into the CNA.

The Ministry of Agriculture

The background and goals of Ministry of Agriculture officials were distinct from those of their SINAMOS counterparts, although as in SINAMOS there was considerable variation among hierarchical levels and regions. Whereas most SINAMOS officials were young graduates of the social sciences, most Ministry of Agriculture personnel were experts in agriculture and livestock production or business administration. Especially at higher ranks, ministry employees had often worked previously on haciendas. With these professional backgrounds, ministry officials tended to

[22] See the numerous SINAMOS pamphlets, including "63 Preguntas y Respuestas"; "Movilización Social: ¿ De Quién y Para Qué?"; and "8 Preguntas a la Revolución Peruana." See also C. Delgado, *Testimonio de Lucha* (Lima: Biblioteca Peruana, 1973), pp. 221-267.

be more knowledgeable about the Peruvian countryside than SINAMOS administrators, but also at times ambivalent about the agrarian reform. They had seen the hacienda owner's arrogance and exploitation of his workforce, and they also recognized the deficiencies of production in the hacienda system. They were generally sympathetic to the plight of the peasants, but also felt that the burdens of the past could not be obliterated overnight. Said Estrella's manager, for example: "The people here are not prepared for these reforms. They're not even thankful for them. They're not educated. They know very little. It's too much, too fast."

Ministry officials feared that the lack of preparation of the peasants jeopardized agricultural production and that in the long run, a decline in production hurt the peasants themselves and threatened the entire reform program. They favored some peasant political participation, but argued that it should be carefully guided by technicians and the government so that peasants would gain what they really wanted: greater production and higher standards of living. The new cooperative members, they argued, should not be suddenly torn from an old system and placed in a completely new one without direction.

The ministry's concern with guiding the cooperative members and improving production led it to consider the employment of managers in the cooperatives to be a critical priority. The agrarian reform law required that each cooperative hire a manager, but it also allowed the cooperative to fire him. Managers were fired from the Peruvian enterprises in enormous numbers and with considerable dispatch, often within twenty-four hours of hiring. During 1973-1975, the ministry promoted a number of revisions in the law to stabilize the employment of managers in the enterprises. It was hoped that managers, who lived every day in the enterprise, could advise and persuade members to adopt favorable attitudes toward hard work, economic collaboration, and saving. Some ministry officials also promoted the employment of managers by the cooperatives with an eye to their own professional futures, hoping that they would win these relatively lucrative positions.

Placement of managers in the cooperatives was considered so critical by ministry officials that other means to enhance economic development were not advanced in much detail between 1973 and 1975. Gradually, however, as the limitations of the manager's influence in the cooperative became clear, new laws were promot-

79

ed more vigorously. The ministry feared that members were consuming enterprise profits in higher salaries, thus reducing investment and threatening future production. Although the Ministry of Agriculture was supposed to authorize all wage increases, the specifics of the authorization process were vague,[23] and many officials wanted tougher measures for government control over salary increases. Finally, by Decree Law 21583 under Morales Bermúdez, a special commission was created to evaluate, review, and authorize all wage increases. Moreover, to assure that members would work hard for the enterprise, some top ministry officials further recommended that production levels be stipulated for geographical regions, and that enterprises in the area be required to meet this quota. No action had been taken on this recommendation as of mid-1977, however.

This picture of the perspectives of Ministry of Agriculture officials on the agrarian reform is painted with a broad brush. Like the aims of SINAMOS officials, the goals of agriculture functionaries tended to vary by region, hierarchical level, and individual background. Although most officials who opposed any kind of agrarian reform and denigrated peasant participation in the enterprises found their bureaucratic home in the Agrarian Bank, and later in the Ministry of Food, some men of this ideological persuasion were also employed by the Ministry of Agriculture. On the other hand, especially in regions where SINAMOS was weak, the ministry also employed radical young men with social backgrounds that resembled those of the SINAMOS promoters.

Moreover, after 1974, the ministry moved to the left. After General Valdez, minister of agriculture from 1972 to 1974, was implicated in a marketing scandal and imprisoned, the top post was won by General Gallegos, a committed leftist. At approximately the same time, SINAMOS was sidelined, officially under "reorganization," and some progressive SINAMOS officials transferred to the Ministry of Agriculture. Meanwhile, various technocratically oriented ministry officials were attracted into the better-paying positions of the newly created Ministry of Food.

Agrarian Cooperative Members

In comparison with government officials, agrarian cooperative

[23] As mentioned above, no reference to ministry power over wage increases is made in the basic cooperative law (Supreme Decree 240-69-AP).

members were united and certain of their goals for the agrarian reform programs. The members wanted complete political autonomy from their former hacienda patrons and potential governmental patrons. On the other hand, members were eager to improve their standard of living, and they desired economic support from the government.

In most cooperatives, members were delighted by the demise of the traditional patron. The idea that a few people—patrons—were born to command and others born to obey was firmly rejected by them.[24] Among them, to say that a man "wants to be the new patron" was to denigrate him. Moreover, the great majority of peasants wanted to participate in important decisions, even if their participation would mean delays.[25] Members made comments such as the following:

> Before, the patron exploited us and took everything away with him, and the only thing that assured our defense was the union; before, we really didn't have ways to talk about problems. Now it's different—in the cooperative, everybody participates.

> At times, there's no unity, and I don't like the meetings. But in general you can learn what's going on and agree about investments, planting. You vote about what you want. Sometimes too we kick out the manager.

Members such as these feared that the managers would become "new patrons," asserting their right to traditional prerogatives and status. They were especially fearful of functionaries whom they could not oust by any legitimate means, as was the case with SINAMOS officials. Said one cooperative member vehemently, "SINAMOS can't tell us what to do. This is our place."

Although the cooperative members rejected political interference from the state, they nevertheless needed government loans

---

[24] An item in my sample survey, applied in coastal sites only, asked respondents whether the statement that "a few have been born to command and others to obey" was true or false. Seventy-three percent of the coastal cooperative respondents said it was false (N = 118).

[25] One item in my sample survey asked respondents to choose between an authority that encouraged people to participate in important decisions, entailing delays, and a second authority that did not allow people to participate in decisions, entailing no delays. Averaging the three ex-haciendas, 68 percent of respondents (including women) opted for the authority that encouraged participation (N = 230).

81

and other kinds of economic aid. When asked about positive actions of the government, the members' most frequently cited responses were, "more loans, technical help, or economic development," and "agrarian reform" (see Table 3-1). Although members worried that loan money would be exploited by cooperative leaders for private purposes, they recognized the need for the investments that the loans would allow; further, they felt that all cooperative workers, not just the leaders, would have the capacity to dip into the public till for private ends.

TABLE 3-1
POSITIVELY PERCEIVED ACTIONS OF GOVERNMENT
(percentages)

	Agrarian Reform	More Equality, Social Justice	More Loans, Technical Help, or Economic Development	Better Education	Other Specific Types of Help	Other
Responses to the item, "You think that the government is doing some good things. What?" N = 58	33%	22%	33%	24%	10%	9%

Note: Percentages do not add to 100 as some respondents gave more than one answer. Only respondents who said they thought the government "was doing good things" were asked this item.

Members were, of course, eager to improve their standard of living. However, this desire did not necessarily entail commitment to the cooperative enterprise. To achieve a higher living standard, they turned to working harder on their private plots and livestock rather than on the cooperative enterprise. The peasants' behavior was rational from their standpoint, for there were few incentives to work hard for the cooperative; it was unlikely either that working hard for the cooperative would bring a better job with higher pay, or that working little would lead to being fired. Moreover, to gain a higher living standard, members preferred higher salaries to greater enterprise profits that could be invested in the cooperative. Members feared, often correctly, that enterprise profits would slip into the pockets of enterprise leaders. Further, a portion of the gross enterprise profits was allocated neither to the consumption of the peasants nor to enterprise investment, but to payment of the so-called "agrarian debt," owed to the ex-owners of the hacienda and paid through the Ministry of Agriculture. Finally, members were reluctant to invest in the enterprise because they were uncertain about the direction of Peruvian politics. They worried, on the one hand, that Velasco might fall and the previous hacienda owners would regain their land, and, on the other, that Velasco's turn to the left would accelerate and culminate in the transformation of "their" cooperative into a state-run enterprise. Although this limited commitment to hard work and investment in the enterprise was rational from the perspective of the cooperative members, it was rarely seen in this light by ministry officials, who often regarded the peasants as lazy and ignorant.

Cooperative members also worked to prevent new members from joining the enterprise and claiming shares of its economic and political benefits. The cooperative was perceived as a pie, and members did not want their portions to become smaller.[26] Hence, they did not want to admit temporary workers to permanent positions, even if the "temporary" workers had in fact been regularly employed for years. Given the severe land scarcity in Peru and the relative wealth of the cooperative enterprises, this hostility to the admission of temporary workers to the cooperatives was a serious obstacle to further redistribution of wealth and power.

THE STRUGGLE OVER AGRARIAN POLICY PRIORITIES

By and large, government agencies active in the Peruvian agrarian reform failed to implement their policy priorities. The major reason for this failure appeared to be the intense ideological conflict among and within the agencies charged with implementation. One agency often promoted one policy in the cooperatives and the second, a virtually contradictory policy. For example, SINAMOS officials frequently denigrated the work of the managers while the ministry applauded it. The rapid promulgation and then retraction of policy directives alienated and confused both officials and peasants and contributed to a tremendous waste of resources. Perhaps most importantly, the ideological conflict impeded the clarification and elaboration of policies. As officials tried

[26] Such a perception may reflect the peasant's "image of limited good," a perception first emphasized as characteristic of the peasantry by George Foster. See G. M. Foster, "Peasant Society and the Image of Limited Good," *American Anthropologist*, 67, No. 2 (April 1965).

to implement policies, they often encountered peasant resistance. To overcome this resistance, administrators needed to support each other and work together to develop an appropriate government response. Especially critical was the establishment of guidelines for the legitimate use of sanctions against recalcitrant cooperatives. The disagreement among officials over the validity of the policy target inevitably signified even more vehement disagreement over the legitimacy of various carrots to encourage cooperation and sticks to enforce policy.

The difficulties in implementing the agrarian reform program were exacerbated by the limited resources available to the government. Despite the considerable attention and funding given to the agrarian reform program relative to many other programs of the Velasco government, the absolute amount of resources available was still inadequate to the very large task at hand. Because of the dearth of agency vehicles and the absence of telephones, officials could not keep in touch with the enterprises, nor ask that members prepare critical information for the official visits. Because field personnel were meagerly reimbursed, they could often be bribed and manipulated by the peasants.[27] Problems of scarce resources and inadequate communication facilities were yet further exacerbated by the functional division between state agencies. This division meant that an official with political responsibilities might visit the enterprise once every two months and a different official with economic responsibilities might also appear once every two months. Greater frequency of visits by a single official charged with both political and economic responsibilities would have facilitated supervision. Further, cooperative members were often able to play officials off against each other. For example, the peasants would claim that they had given certain information to SINAMOS, compelling the ministry to check with SINAMOS before it could take further action; if SINAMOS said it had not received the information, cooperative members would claim that it had been lost en route.

[27] Full information is provided in McClintock, "Self-Management and the Peasant," p. 397. A typical SINAMOS or Ministry of Agriculture official in Huancayo or Trujillo earned under $4,000 per year. The lowest level officials, like Ministry of Agriculture field agents, made less than $1,000 per year. See D. Palmer, "Social Mobilization in Peru," in L. Bradfield, ed., *Chile and Peru: Two Paths to Social Justice* (Kalamazoo, Michigan: Western Michigan University, Institute of International and Area Studies, 1974), p. 67. (All figures are calculations from Peruvian currency.)

84

SINAMOS and Peasant Political Participation

Broadly, the goals of SINAMOS were the achievement of equal participation, authentic participation, and support for the Velasco government. These goals were difficult to attain—indeed, it soon appeared that they were contradictory. In the midst of the national ideological debate, SINAMOS promoters were not advised about how they should resolve the contradiction. Most promoters chose to stress the policy target of equal participation. This emphasis was supported neither by many top-level SINAMOS officials, nor by the Ministry of Agriculture, nor by cooperative members. SINA-MOS promoters were not given the resources that might have allowed them to implement their policy priority—for example, they could not threaten enterprises with loss of their bank loans or promise the liquidation of the agrarian debt. More than anything else, perhaps, SINAMOS needed time—time to talk with the peasants, to persuade, to negotiate—but this resource was not granted either.

The tension between authentic participation and equal participation that confronted SINAMOS was evident in conflicts among distinct peasant strata in the cooperatives.[28] Perhaps the most important instance in the highlands peasant communities I studied involved the implementation of the "peasant community statute."[29] This law disqualified commercial middlemen from membership in the community and called for the equalization of landholdings in the community. The statute was vague, however, and during

[28] For the sake of brevity, I am only discussing two instances of the tension between "authentic participation" and "equal participation." SINAMOS officials confronted this problem in other important areas, including the rise of relatively privileged workers in many SAIS cooperatives and the conflict between workers and ex-sharecroppers in coastal cooperatives. See McClintock, "Structural Change and Political Culture in Rural Peru," pp. 560-569.

[29] These points were evident from my own research as well as that of other scholars. See N. Long and D. Winder, "From Peasant Community to Production Cooperative: An Analysis of Recent Government Policy in Peru," *The Journal of Development Studies*, 12, No. 1 (October 1975); B. Roberts, "Center and Periphery in the Development Process: The Case of Peru," in W. Cornelius and F. Trueblood, eds., *Urbanization and Inequality: Latin American Urban Research*, 5 (Beverly Hills, Calif.: Sage Publications, 1975); and G. Alderson-Smith, "Peasant Response to Cooperativization under Agrarian Reform in the Communities of the Peruvian Sierra," Paper presented at the nineteenth International Congress of Anthropological and Ethnological Sciences, Chicago, Ill., August 28-31, 1973.

85

1973 SINAMOS was encouraging peasant communities in SAIS Huanca to adopt a stricter program of disqualification of village commercial elites and land equalization, called the Community Enterprise system. The program could have increased the participation and wealth of peasants from the low- and middle-income ranks of the community. But, threatened middlemen opposed the program and campaigned against it, calling it an example of government control of the communities. Many peasants who were economically dependent upon the middlemen for trade or employment feared to act against their wishes. Thus, the great majority of peasant communities in SAIS Huanca voted against the Community Enterprise system in their general assemblies. As a consequence, SINAMOS was frustrated to see that it could not bring about greater participatory equality in the peasant communities except by violating this "authentic" expression of will. SINAMOS retreated, but many peasants continued to believe that the agency had tried to gain control of their villages through the Community Enterprise system.

The most significant instance of tension between equal participation and authentic participation for the entire Peruvian agrarian reform occurred in the coastal cooperatives, involving cooperative members and temporary workers, who in their highlands residences were generally *comuneros*. The agrarian reform law entitled only permanent workers to be cooperative members. However, as was noted earlier, these members were a relatively prosperous minority, whereas the temporary workers were socioeconomically disadvantaged and politically disenfranchised. Between 1972 and 1974, most cooperative members vehemently opposed the incorporation of temporary workers into the enterprises as full members. Thus, SINAMOS could not simultaneously promote authentic participation and equal participation. Under the mandates of authentic participation, SINAMOS had to accept the will of the cooperative members, impeding the equal participation of temporary workers.

In this dilemma, SINAMOS chose to encourage equal participation. It helped temporary workers to organize unions in many sites, including my research cooperative, Estrella. In some regions of the country, SINAMOS agents collaborated with temporary workers in the organization of land invasions, not only on hacienda land but also on cooperative land.[30] These strategies ultimately

---

[30] *Latin America*, 7, No. 28 (July 13, 1973), 223; 7, No. 16 (April 26,

failed, however. Estrella and other threatened cooperatives reacted by firing some temporary workers who were active in unions.
SINAMOS was powerless to stop this backlash, in part because the
Ministry of Agriculture failed to support the agency's efforts. Petitions of complaint against the cooperatives sent by temporary
workers were ignored by top ministry officials. SINAMOS thus held
neither carrots nor sticks with which to modify cooperative members' policy toward nonmembers. Gradually, the number of members in most cooperatives declined as they became more and
more exclusionary.

The conflict between cooperative members, on the one hand,
and *comuneros*, on the other, signified difficulties for SINAMOS
not only with respect to political participation locally within the
cooperatives but also nationally within the new peasant federation,
the CNA. In its organizational work for the CNA, SINAMOS
promoters once again emphasized the goal of equal participation.
Throughout 1973 and 1974, SINAMOS worked hard to incorporate
disadvantaged highlands *comuneros* into the CNA, and its effort
succeeded. As of late 1974, 73 percent of all CNA local organizations were peasant communities and eight of eleven members of
its leadership board were from peasant communities, making
comunero representation in the CNA greater than their proportion
of the rural population.[31] Not surprisingly, the CNA expressed
primarily the concerns of disadvantaged *comuneros* and other
low-status rural inhabitants.[32] The number one priority of the CNA
was the acceleration and intensification of the agrarian reform,
especially the reduction of the landholding limit, a goal that was
irrelevant to cooperative members. It also advanced demands
that actually threatened the position of cooperative members. The

1934), 127; and 8, No. 40 (October 11, 1974), 319. See also Agut, "The
'Peruvian Revolution' and Catholic Corporatism," pp. 522-527.

[31] Comprehensive data on the backgrounds of CNA organizations are pro-
vided in SINAMOS, *La Confederación Nacional Agraria: Información Básica*
(Lima: Dirección General de Organizaciones Rurales, January 1975), p. 4.
Information on the Leadership Board is from interviews and *El Comercio*
(Lima), October 5, 1974.

[32] Information on the CNA's demands derives from interviews with the
vice-president of the CNA, on June 2, 1975, and with Ingeniero Luis Deustua,
who worked closely with the CNA; from the commission reports in the Confederación Nacional Agraria, *Congreso de Instalación de la Confederación
Nacional Agraria* (Lima, October 1974); and from *Latin America*, 8 No.
40 (October 11, 1974), 319.

peasant organization wanted sharper price increases in basic foods, especially the potato, whereas CAP members, because they were generally consumers of potatoes and producers of export foods, wanted to see prices for basic commodities remain low. The federation also requested new programs to prevent exploitation by wealthier peasants acting as middlemen. Most threatening to cooperative members was the CNA's proposal that more temporary workers be admitted to the cooperatives.

Cooperative members rejected the CNA. In 1975, most members of the Agrarian Production Cooperatives of Estrella and Marla, including three of four delegates selected to attend a CNA league conference, evaluated the CNA's league system negatively. They resented the efforts of SINAMOS to organize previously marginal peasants into the CNA, and argued that SINAMOS would control the CNA because the *comuneros* were poorly educated and, therefore, easy to manipulate.

The failure of cooperative members to participate enthusiastically in the CNA leagues signified failure for SINAMOS on various counts. First, the CNA was not an integrative institution that could aggregate the demands of distinct peasant strata. The military leadership and the Ministry of Agriculture wanted an organization incorporating well-to-do cooperative members and independent coastal farmers so that the government could work closely with these economically significant groups, but the CNA was primarily an organization of disadvantaged peasants. Second, the limited participation of cooperative members indicated their lack of support for the Velasco government. SINAMOS had thus failed in one of its most important missions. Moreover, not only did cooperative members show little enthusiasm for the military regime, but the CNA itself often seemed hostile to the government,[33] indicating SINAMOS' inability to stimulate popular support for Velasco even among organizations that were indebted to the regime for their creation.

In short, SINAMOS failed to achieve its policy goals. Its priorities were complex, contradictory, and disputed by other agencies. Among the original policy goals assigned to SINAMOS, promoters chose to emphasize "equal participation." When this goal conflicted with cooperative members' "authentic participation" or

[33] The CNA sharply criticized officials in most agencies and made strong demands for greater peasant participation. See Confederación Nacional Agraria, *Congreso de Instalación*.

jeopardized their support for the government, the military leadership and the Ministry of Agriculture withdrew their backing of SINAMOS. SINAMOS thus often intervened in peasant communities and cooperatives to no avail, threatening cooperative members without the capacity to implement the threat.

The Ministry of Agriculture and Rural Development

The primary concern of Ministry of Agriculture officials was that agrarian reform contribute not only to social justice but also to agricultural productivity. To this end, the ministry advanced three policy priorities for the cooperatives: the employment of administrators in the enterprises; increased investment rather than greater consumption; and collective production rather than individual landholdings. As of 1975, the ministry had largely failed to implement these priorities with the exception of the employment of managers in the cooperatives, and even in this case, the managers were generally not as effective as the ministry had hoped.

The employment of an administrator in the cooperatives was a very critical issue from 1973 to 1975, pitting the ministry against both SINAMOS and cooperative members. In this battle, the ministry had the agrarian reform law and the Agrarian Bank on its side, and gradually emerged victorious. As indicated previously, the ministry joined the bank to threaten the enterprises with the loss of loans if they did not hire a manager. Both research CAPs, Marla and Estrella, were so threatened and both finally hired managers in 1974 and 1975, respectively. The ministry also developed new measures so that the managers would not be fired within a few months. For example, by 1974, many regional offices were trying to require that a dismissed administrator not leave the cooperative until his replacement arrived. The ministry was also persuading enterprises to give the manager a one-year contract at the minimum. The proportion of cooperatives with managers rose from about 30 percent in 1973 to between 50 and 60 percent in 1975.[34]

By and large, however, the adminstrators were not able to change the economic dynamics of the cooperatives. Although the typical manager promoted the ministry's policy preferences, he still

[34] Data of 1973 are from the Dirección de Producción, Ministry of Agriculture, Lima, December 1973; 1975 data are from Dr. Rodolfo Masuda Matsuura, Dirección de Apoyo Técnico Contable a Las Empresas Campesinas, Ministry of Agriculture, June 4, 1975.

failed to persuade members of their validity. If the administrator tried to enforce these preferences too vigorously by enlisting the support of the Agrarian Bank to withhold loans or by other means, the cooperative generally reacted by firing him. Marla's manager in 1974-1975, for example, adamantly pushed members to work harder for the cooperative and was fired at the end of his one-year contract. Further, the incomes of many administrators were small in comparison not only to pre-1968 days but also to those of the most prosperous peasants in richer cooperatives.[35] Thus, managers were frequently found to be involved in economic misdoings in cooperatives, as was SAIS Huanca's manager in mid-1976. In other cases, the manager lacked the institutional authority to provide forceful leadership. CAP Estrella's manager, for instance, was a humble man who had few qualifications for the job. He owed his position to the cooperative's truck driver, a prosperous individual who was president of the Administrative Council from 1975 to 1977. The manager was therefore often unable to offer effective advice to the peasant leader.

Wage increases were another point of contention between cooperative members and the ministry. As noted above, the ministry wanted to limit wage increases so that enterprise profits would be available for investment, the agrarian debt, and the like. However, by and large the ministry failed to limit salary jumps, in part because it lacked the necessary sanctions and in part because it lacked the resources and personnel to monitor the enterprises adequately. In prosperous export-oriented enterprises, the production of the cooperative was important to the national economy. A strike thus posed a significant threat. In various enterprises, such as SAIS Huanca, workers demanded salary increases that were opposed by the enterprise manager and the ministry. However, the workers had forged a strong union and threatened to strike. The ministry regularly allowed salary increases. Even in cooperatives where members were not as vehement as in Huanca, the ministry often capitulated to peasant demands. Between 1970 and 1975, wages at least doubled in most cooperatives, an increase well above the rate of inflation.[36]

In smaller enterprises that did not contribute greatly to the

[35] Salaries of enterprise managers dipped from about $8,000 in my sites to approximately $6,000.
[36] Data are provided in McClintock, "Self-Management and the Peasant," pp. 288-289.

national economy, the ministry was not as afraid to veto a salary increase, but it was not able to supervise the enterprise to prevent subversion of the wage moratorium. For example, the ministry refused to approve a salary increase in Marla in 1974, threatening the enterprise with the loss of its bank loan. Officially, Marla accepted the ministry's veto. However, unofficially, the cooperative devised schemes to raise wages. Elaborate modifications were hidden in a special set of books (if written down at all) so that the ministry official would not discover them on his monthly visit. Exorbitant overtime payments were made because members would claim more overtime than they worked and would charge overtime at several times the regular wage. Routine jobs were elevated to the status of specialized skills. For example, guarding machinery, an undemanding task, earned double pay. Another device was to alter the daily work quota so members could perform two or three "daily" work quotas and thus receive two or three "daily" wage allocations.

Another issue of contention between cooperative members and the ministry was private as opposed to cooperative production. Members sought increased private production, but most officials believed that private production was not as efficient as cooperative production because economies of scale were lost. Ministry technicians thus tried to persuade members to limit their private parcels and to pool their livestock into mini-cooperatives. Most cooperatives simply refused to do so, however. Both Estrella and Marla voted down managers' initiatives for a livestock cooperative; especially in Estrella, the number of members with private parcels continued to increase through 1974 and 1975. The number of hours worked for the enterprise continued at approximately 75 percent of the hours worked for the hacienda. In some SAIS, such as Huanca, *comuneros* rather than workers dominated the enterprise politically, and the *comuneros* did legislate requirements for the cooperativization of private livestock. However, even though SAIS Huanca employed more technicians than the average cooperative, it could not implement these requirements; workers hid their sheep in craggy nooks in the mountains, and they lied to inquisitive technicians.

The Victors in 1973-1975: The Agrarian Cooperative Members

Lacking resources and official support for the application of sanctions against cooperative members, SINAMOS and the Ministry of Agriculture lost the policy battles to the peasants. In most cases, members ran their cooperatives independently of government officials. In most cooperatives, members were politically very active, resolving many key concerns within the community and also formulating new demands that they pressed on regional government agencies. Members rejected manipulation by SINA-MOS officials and by managers.

The standard of living of most cooperative members improved. In Estrella, Marla, and the two SAIS Huanca communities, Patca and Varya, over 50 percent of respondents felt that they were better-off in 1974 than in 1969; they generally cited higher incomes and easier loans as the reason (see Tables 3-2 and 3-3). The improved standard of living reflected both the increased salaries of members and their work on private plots. Production did not decline between 1970 and 1975, as some ministry officials had feared, but neither did it increase, as other officials had hoped.[37] Members' preference for consumption over investment signified that new investment to maintain production in the future would

TABLE 3-2
PERCEIVED QUALITY OF LIFE, 1969-1974[a]
(percentages)

	N^b	Better-off Now Than 5 Years Ago	The Same	Worse-off Now Than 5 Years Ago
Cooperatives/Ex-haciendas				
Estrella & Marla, 1974	123	51	20	29
Estrella & Marla, 1969	118	42	33	25
Monte, 1974	71	11	56	32
Monte, 1969	44	18	61	20
SAIS Communities,				
Patca & Varya, 1974	90	56	37	7

[a] Answers to the item, "Five years ago, the people of this place were better-off, about the same, or worse-off than now?"

[b] Not applicables, don't knows, etc., have been omitted.

[37] The Peruvian government reported agricultural growth rates of 7.8 percent in 1970, 3.0 percent in 1971, 0.0 percent in 1972, 2.4 percent in 1973, 1.8 percent in 1974, and 1.0 percent in 1975 (*Latin America Economic Report*, April 11, 1975), p. 54; 1975 figure from DESCO, *Informativo Político*, No. 40 (January, 1976), p. 23. Data on the economic performance of the agrarian cooperatives, which of course constituted only part of the agricultural sector, are provided in McClintock, "Self-Management and the Peasant," pp. 309-325.

TABLE 3-3
POSITIVELY EVALUATED FEATURES OF COOPERATIVES[a]
(percentages)

	N^b	More Money (Profit Shares, Better Salaries, Easier Loans, etc.)	Better Work Conditions (Easier Tasks, No Firings, etc.)	Better Facilities, (New Houses, Easier Transportation, etc.)	More Individually Owned Animals	More Union and Equality	More Technical Help	Other
Cooperatives, 1974								
Estrella and Marla	84	90	35	44	18	24	8	18
SAIS Communities, 1974								
Patca and Varya	90	70	0	57	0	8	52	4

[a] Responses to the item, "You think the SAIS/CAP helps in some ways? Why?"
[b] Only applicable respondents. As some respondents gave more than one answer, percentages do not always add to 100.

have to come from the government. For most cooperatives, the government obliged; the amount of loan money more than quadrupled between 1968 and 1975, an increase well beyond the inflation rate.[38] With the exception of the issue of employment of a manager, the government did not use loan money as a sanction to gain its policy priorities, although some officials wanted to do so.[39] Cooperative members thus maintained their political independence but still won economic aid from the government.

CONCLUSION

In implementing policy for the agrarian cooperatives, the Velasco government confronted an array of difficulties. It faced one set of problems that is endemic to Third World countries: resource scarcity and inadequate communication networks. Moreover, these difficulties were greatly exacerbated by the fact that Velasco's regime was a reform government, steering Peru on a dramatically different course that was very ambitious and relatively uncharted.

Perhaps the most important obstacle, however, was that con-

[38] See DESCO, *Informativo político* (Lima, July 1976).
[39] See Cleaves and Scurrah, *Agriculture, Bureaucracy, and Social Class.*

93

tradictory ambitions were held, even among the top military leaders. Political disagreements at the top were never resolved, and they were translated into similar controversies among implementing agencies. During the period of this study, leftists who favored greater redistribution and participation tended to align with SINAMOS and more technically oriented officials who favored production priorities tended to join the Ministry of Agriculture, although officials of all types could be found in both agencies. Various policies of the two agencies were contradictory.

Especially with respect to an agrarian reform policy carried out in isolated areas where communication networks were rudimentary, disagreement at the center almost inevitably entailed decentralization. Policy was only really "made" in each region, enterprise, or community when it became clear which officials—those with a technocratic, a statist, a radically redistributive, or even an opportunistic bent—would emerge on top of the bureaucratic heap in that area. But policies devised in this way were very vulnerable to change. They were, of course, prey to the vagaries of bureaucratic politics.

Moreover, policies became more vulnerable to the demands of citizens. The clout of the implementing apparatus was necessarily reduced in the decentralization process. The sticks available to implementors were decreased because the various officials did not support each other; peasants could play one official off against another. Divided over policy priorities, officials could not agree on the yet more difficult question of sanctions against their peers who resisted "advice." Nor did implementors have juicy carrots readily available as incentives to change peasant attitudes and behavior. The most important carrots, the land expropriation and loans, were awarded to cooperatives generally regardless of their political and economic performance, and were handled largely by the Agrarian Bank rather than by either of the two agencies more active among the cooperatives, SINAMOS and the ministry. SINAMOS and the ministry were often unable even to offer such minor rewards as transportation assistance, office help, and aid for small local projects.

The vulnerability of policy to peasant demands can also be seen more positively, however, as the greater power of the peasants over decisions of significance to them. Agrarian cooperative members were able to block such key initiatives as SINAMOS' effort to incorporate more temporary workers into the enterprises and the ministry's attempt to impose more rigorous control over cooperative policy through technical managers. This intense suspicion of SINAMOS was one reason behind the military's decision to downplay the agency after 1974. The peasants' tendency to favor private landownership over cooperatives was in all likelihood one factor in the move away from CAPs and SAIS to the looser "Peasant Group" mode in 1975 and 1976. The power won by the peasants because of leadership factionalization and decentralization is especially interesting because their power probably surpassed the intentions of even the leftist officers who most favored peasant participation in policymaking; it certainly did not jibe with the widespread image of hermetic decision making by the Velasco government.

Were alternatives available to Velasco that might have kept his reform government in power? This study suggests various recommendations. Generally, leaders of reform governments should not assume that to legislate is to implement; they must recognize that implementation entails complex organizational tasks and requires incentives for eliciting compliance and support from administrators and citizens.

More specifically, a reform government should realize the problems of monitoring and controlling new political agencies like SINAMOS. Many scholars of political development exaggerate the ease with which national leadership can subordinate and coopt low-level officials and politically aware individuals. Perhaps this is because inappropriate generalizations are drawn from the experience of the Mexican government, which has been very successful in this respect.[40] In reform governments where political conflict is intense, high-level officials may want to delay the establishment of large political bureaucracies until they are more united in their ranks and can agree on the ideological contours of new institutions. The Cuban revolutionary leadership exercised tremendous caution in the development of political institutions,

[40] For example, the Mexican political system is explicitly a key model in S. Huntington, *Political Order in Changing Societies* (New Haven: Yale University Press, 1970). In *The State and Society*, Stepan compares the Peruvian case to the Mexican frequently, but not to the Bolivian, with which perhaps it has more in common. In early works emphasizing the Velasco government as a corporatist system, the Mexican model seemed the reference point also, at least implicitly. See Cotler, "The New Mode of Political Domination," and Middlebrook and Palmer, "Military Government and Political Development."

perhaps for these very reasons.[41] When a reform government does establish political bureaucracies, the leadership must watch that the administrators share commitment to key policy goals. Recruitment must be handled carefully. If economic rewards cannot be offered administrators due to redistributive concerns, great attention must be given to the provision of other rewards, such as prestige or the personal attention of political leaders.

Further, a reform government should be careful not to announce policies that cannot be implemented. Of course, it may be difficult to know in advance whether or not a policy can be implemented; one guidepost, however, would be the establishment of sufficient consensus about the policy within the top leadership so that sanctions can be applied to enforce the policy if necessary. The announcement of redistributive policies that cannot be implemented is especially dangerous because it frightens groups who stand to lose, but still does not satisfy groups who stand to gain. Fears are fanned and expectations raised, but as years go by and nothing happens, the government is criticized as muddled and ineffectual.

Exercising caution in the announcement of unimplementable policies is one component in an overall strategy for maintaining political support. The cultivation of political support must, of course, be of major concern to a reform government that rejects coercion. A reform government knows it will create many enemies, so it must be careful to keep its friends. Too often, political leaders and scholars perceive reform, especially agrarian reform, as a program that wins the everlasting support of beneficiaries.[42] In many cases, however, reform may build beneficiaries' political confidence and involvement, and increase their demands on the government.[43] Velasco, as well as Allende in Chile, may have taken the support of agrarian cooperative members too much for granted. In their proposals for redistribution from cooperative members to more disadvantaged peasants, neither the Peruvian nor the Chilean leadership was sufficiently sensitive to the prob-

[41] The cautious development of Cuban political institutions is pointed out by E. Gonzalez, *Cuba Under Castro: The Limits of Charisma* (Boston: Houghton Mifflin Co., 1974); and J. Dominguez and C. Mitchell, "The Roads Not Taken: Institutionalization and Political Parties in Cuba and Bolivia," *Comparative Politics*, 9, No. 2 (January 1977), 173-197.

[42] See especially Huntington, *Political Order in Changing Societies.*

[43] See McClintock, "Structural Change and Political Culture in Rural Peru," pp. 261-391.

lems these initiatives raised for political support. Without a doubt, agrarian cooperative members were the biggest winners from the Velasco government and should have been enthusiastic supporters; yet, threatened by programs of social property and admission of temporary workers into the cooperatives, they actually resented the government.[44] Velasco should have paid greater heed to the way in which available resources and benefits were allocated, doing so in a more regular and organized way, in order that peasants would perceive all government officials, not just the Agrarian Bank, as both helping them and, in return, requesting their support and trust in the new endeavors.

In short, Velasco's Achilles' heel was not necessarily that he tried to do "too much, too fast," as is often said of reform governments. More specifically the problem was that so much of what was done was contradictory. Political confusion was massive. The contradictions and confusion were in part inherent in the process of rapid reform, but they were also the result of efforts to shortcut the problems of reform by the impetuous formation of policies and bureaucracies at cross-purposes to each other. A thorough consideration of the problems of policy implementation in the Velasco government should be instructive to future leaders in search of a "Third Way."

[44] In the two cooperatives surveyed, support for the government declined between 1969 and 1974. In 1969, 58 percent of respondents in Estrella said that the government "helps to improve conditions in the country," at least "more or less," compared to 45 percent in 1974; the corresponding figures for Marla are 61 percent and 47 percent.

Part Two · CHOICE AND CONSEQUENCE
OF IMPLEMENTING
STRATEGIES

AFTER the broad parameters of a policy are chosen, political and administrative choices crucial to its outcome are made concerning the strategy by which it will be pursued. In the Third World, such strategic choices are centrally important because of organizational, managerial, and political problems arising from bureaucracies that may be unfamiliar with or resistant to programs requiring new forms of behavior, greater coordination and planning, and more flexible and responsive styles of management. As is indicated in the following chapters, the choices that are made are difficult to predict, categorize, or control, so extensive are the factors that influence the decisions and the success or failure of the strategy chosen. Some of these choices, however, can be pointed out briefly to indicate both their sources and possible consequences.

In terms of politically inspired choices, the decision to select one agency rather than another to carry out a program may result from criteria based on patronage, or the personal loyalty, ethnic identity, or party affiliation of the bureaucratic leadership of specific organizations. At the same time, a lack of political intervention at this point may indicate disinterest in the policy by political leaders and may easily be the reason why a program is poorly implemented. Similarly, a decision that several agencies should collaborate in the pursuit of a given policy is also a crucial one, for the organizational problems involved in bureaucratic cooperation are different from those involved if a single agency is given responsibility. In a related aspect, political leaders may decide to favor bureaucratic officials and agencies with public support and access to resources and problem solving mechanisms. Conversely, failure to make such a commitment may seriously damage the chances for implementation. Political leaders may also have influence over assuring the steady and regular flow of resources to the program components of various policies.

There are other decisions made concerning the implementing strategy which, while less overtly political, are no less important in determining the capacity to implement a given program. These include a variety of administrative and management decisions. Some are deliberate choices: the degree of staff hierarchy involved in program management; organizational flexibility to deal with unforeseen circumstances; the amount of staff assigned to a given program; the level of their training; scales of remuneration and

101

incentives; the mechanisms employed for checking and controlling administrative behavior; the procedures for channeling the supply of resources where and when they are required. While there are constraints on the alternatives available—the number of staff is limited by funding, for example—there are many possible choices and combinations of structures that can be experimented with in the search for means to encourage successful delivery of goods and services.

Other factors, however, may be more resistant to tinkering. Perhaps most obvious in this category are organizational variables, such as administrative culture and traditions, which tend to influence the behavior of both individuals and institutions. Thus, those who have studied bureaucratic organizations and delivery systems in India have frequently commented on the ubiquity of rigid hierarchies and lack of initiative, the result of colonial civil service practices, which plague almost every effort at implementing development programs. While cultural, traditional, and institutional patterns may be difficult to alter, it is nevertheless possible to become aware of these variables and to try to establish practices and methods for avoiding or minimizing them. The design of the organizational context for implementation thus presents a focus for thinking strategically about how best to pursue program goals.

The chapters in Part Two address the questions involved in these strategic choices. They suggest the range of political and administrative variables that may determine the success or failure of a particular design for achieving program goals. Once again, the political context in which a particular range of decisions is made affects the type of strategy chosen and this in turn affects the future of the development program. The authors of these four chapters dealing with experiences in India and Colombia are able to explore why particular strategies are chosen and what factors seem to be important in affecting the utility of the strategy.

FOUR · *The Pilot Project and the*
Choice of an Implementing
Strategy: Community Development
in India

GERALD E. SUSSMAN

LACK of resources limits severely the options available to a developing country for pursuing policies whose goals stress social and economic change. Each choice of a national program must be carefully weighed; any new program that deviates substantially from established practices may involve considerable risk of failure and loss of resources. The pilot project has frequently been considered a useful mechanism because program investment can be hedged until the prototype of the new design is pretested on a small scale. Community development programs in India in the post-independence period, for example, were preceded by pilot experiences that were to offer lessons about the design and operation of subsequent programs.

The generic question faced by the leadership of India in 1947 was how to go about implementing policies of social and economic change at the grass roots level, notably in rural areas. The number of proposed changes listed in various five-year plans was impressive, but the machinery to deliver services and mobilize community support was lacking. As one USAID (Agency for International Development) expert noted, "there was nothing at the end of the trolley line" that would aid the government in achieving its developmental goals. The creation of an infrastructure of administration at regional and local levels, with strong links to national planning institutions, would therefore be critical to the success of the development plans. Traditionally, the way of responding to this problem of reaching the grass roots was through the utilization of the existing bureaucratic machinery. But this structure tended to consist of "centralized, vertical, sectoral institutions, each with its

103

FOUR · *Sussman*

own narrowly defined area of activity," and each with an autonomous organization extending from the capital city to the field.[1]
New alternatives were needed that would break with traditional
and undynamic implementing strategies, but on a scale that would
allow experimentation without an irreversible commitment of resources. In a situation such as this, in which new organizational
and delivery system prototypes are sought by government planners,
the pilot project seems to present itself as a useful means to test
ideas, to develop technical, organizational, and behavioral knowledge, and to save on scarce resources. If successful, it could provide a model for the further design of broader implementation
efforts.

This chapter presents a case study of a pilot project in community development in India as well as an analysis of the use and
abuse of lessons learned during the pilot experience in the later
national program of community development. Several questions
address the interaction of program content and the environmental
context in which it was pursued and evaluated for expansion.
What were the characteristics of the political and bureaucratic
contexts in which the pilot project developed? What lessons did
the pilot project suggest about implementing strategies for community development? Why did the criteria for judging the success
of the program change as the development effort moved to the
national scale? How did changes in both the time frame for achieving goals and in the criteria for evaluating the program affect implementation? The study indicates that the strategy chosen to
implement a program nationally is subjected to different bureaucratic and political considerations that can negate the lessons of a
pilot project for implementation design. But before addressing
the central questions, it is useful to explore briefly the context in
which the movement toward community development emerged in
India.

THE HISTORICAL CONTEXT OF COMMUNITY
DEVELOPMENT IN INDIA

Early efforts at helping improve village conditions in India took
two forms: government service under the British Raj, and various

[1] D. Korten, "Management for Social Development: Experience from the
Field of Population," paper delivered at the Conference on Public Management Education and Training, Bellagio, Italy, August 11-15, 1976, p. 5.

experiments in rural development. The first placed its emphasis on revenue collection and maintaining the peace, with some limited interest in development functions such as public works, agriculture, health, and education. But it was not until the 1930s that these efforts received real impetus. Unfortunately, attention to development needs was shortlived due to the eruption of World War II. However, even at its height, the administrative and resource base for establishing any large-scale development effort was insubstantial. Programs in the field depended heavily on the district officer, whose main functions included tax collection and the maintenance of law and order. The area of his responsibility was extensive, covering approximately 1,500 to 2,000 villages and including from one to three million people. Although there was some attempt to decentralize power under the colonial administration, the pattern of program development, decision making, and authority still moved from the top down. Ultimately, the district officer remained the most influential person in the district.

Below the district, the bureaucratic machinery was ineffective. Generally there was only one qualified government representative of individual ministries for each aggregate of 60,000-100,000 villagers. The efforts that were made concentrated on physical rather than on human development.[2] There was no real attempt to involve local participation in the planning and decision-making process and, in fact, the relationship of the government to the people fostered the latter's dependency.[3] In addition, the government's efforts in the rural areas, carried out by the separate departments concerned, made no attempt at coordination.

Besides the limited development efforts of the government under the British Raj, there were a number of interesting voluntary

[2] For example, in West Bengal before independence, there was one agricultural graduate for each district assisted by two workers (2,000 square miles). Under community development there were 3 to 6 agricultural graduates and 10 to 20 village level workers in each "block" of 100 villages. See West Bengal Department of Agriculture, *The Innovators*, Research Bulletin No. 1 (Calcutta: West Bengal Department of Agriculture, 1963).

[3] "The Government started new departments such as Public Works, Agriculture, Public Health. . . . The villagers who had hitherto been neglected, now started demanding for more and more help from the Government. Villagers came to look up to the Government and in fact to depend on the Government's assistance for most of the problems of the villages. Villagers' self-reliance declined rapidly." B. Rudramoorthy, *Extension in Planned Social Change* (Bombay: Allied Publishers, 1964), p. 21.

efforts to manage rural reconstruction.[4] These projects emphasized factors such as the use of local village resources, the necessity for an integrated approach to rural problems, and experimentation with workers at the village level. They were also strongly influenced by the religious, philosophical, and social convictions of their founders. However, these projects generally suffered from a lack of government support. One area of experimentation under the Raj that was influential in forming official perspectives about approaches to rural development was the Grow More Food Campaign, launched in 1943 to increase food production. Ultimately, the project failed, affecting only two to four percent of the cultivated area of the country, probably due to poor organization and lack of experience as well as to the deficiencies of program backup. The framers of the community development approach to rural development saw in this experience the need to emphasize a more integrated approach. As stated by the chairman of the Grow More Food Enquiry Committee, "All aspects of rural life are interrelated and no lasting results can be achieved if individual aspects are dealt with in isolation."[5]

The scope of the development problems following independence was enormous. India, in 1951, was populated by nearly 360 million people, 80 percent of whom lived in the rural areas. Of this number, it was estimated that over 20 million were permanently unemployed while another 3 million were being added to the labor force each year. Per capita income was estimated at about $50-60 a year. Of this, not less than 80 percent of the farm labor family's consumption budget went for food. Illiteracy was around 84 percent nationally and 90 percent in the rural areas. Agricultural yields were among the lowest in the world—670 kilograms per hectare in wheat, 690 in maize, and 1,103 in rice. Table 4-1 indicates

[4] There were Sriniketan in Bengal founded by Rabindranath Tagore, India's greatest modern poet and writer; Spencer Hatch's Marthandam project in Kerala to carry out YMCA activities; the village agent approach, developed in part by the Englishman F. L. Brayne; the Gandhian constructive movement at Saburmati Ashram and Sevagram; the Sarvodaya Scheme of Bombay and the Firka development scheme of Madras also based on Gandhian philosophy; the Nani Institute, sponsored by the Allahabad Agricultural Institute; and the Friends projects at Barpali in Orissa and Rasulia in Madhya Pradesh.

[5] V. T. Krishnamachari quoted from the "Report of the Grow More Food Enquiry Committee," in Rudramoorthy, *Extension in Planned Social Change*, p. 28.

106

India's rank among a number of developing countries in the yields of these crops per hectare. Moreover, village industry was moribund and village institutions were dominated by a rigidly stratified social structure. Fifty-five million people carried the stigma of a socially undesirable group—the untouchables—and another 30 million were tribals living in even more depressed conditions. National unity remained tenuous as the 17 states making up the new Indian Republic spoke 15 major languages and over 800 dialects. The transportation system, while fairly good by standards of other developing countries—it ranked fourth in the world in 1951 with one mile of rail per 2,559 square miles—was still inadequate for India's needs. The use of mass communication such as the radio and newspaper had little prominence outside the urban areas. The rural-urban gap was great.

TABLE 4-1
INDIAN AGRICULTURAL PRODUCTIVITY AMONG 26 DEVELOPING NATIONS, 1951

Crop Yield per Hectare	Number of Countries Reporting	India's Rank
Wheat	24	21
Maize	24	23
Rice	20	20

Source: U.S. Department of Agriculture, Economic Research Service, *Changes in Agriculture in 26 Development Nations, 1948 to 1963*. Foreign Agricultural Economic Report No. 27, November 1965, p. 46.

In an intensely ideological period the community development approach to the problems of rural life was launched with considerable high-level support, as the political leadership responded to the problems of rural isolation and stagnation. First and foremost there was the burning social idealism of Gandhi and his disciples with their intense concern for the village. Political leadership was provided by Nehru who had pledged to improve conditions in the villages during the fight for independence and who seemed determined to honor that pledge.[6] His efforts were supplemented at the bureaucratic level by social visionaries such as V. T. Krishnamachari, deputy chairman of the Planning Commission, and its workhorse, Tarlok Singh, both well experienced in rural construction efforts. Also important was S. K. Dey, an engineer by training but a strong devotee of social change. Nehru selected him to head

[6] D. Ensminger, *Rural India in Transition* (New Delhi: All India Panchayat Parishad, 1972), p. 16.

107

the newly established Community Projects Administration. Within the states there existed political support for community development not only among the committed, but also among other state officials, because community development promised to provide additional resources from the central government.

The efforts of the proponents of community development, based on both pragmatism and idealism, were further favored by their timing. The colonial power had withdrawn from the subcontinent and because of the widely held Indian view that the British had been exploiters, it was easy to arrive at the conclusion that having removed them, Indians had also removed the major obstacle to their country's progress. Equally optimistic were the Americans who came to assist the Indians. Especially prominent during the early period was Albert Mayer, an engineer-architect who provided one prototype for community development with the Etawah Project. There was also Horace Holmes, an agricultural extension specialist who worked at Etawah and in other community development projects. Most importantly, there was Chester Bowles, who advocated the need for the Congress party of India to build strong grass-roots support. While he was ambassador, the first Indo-American Agreement provided $55 million to help the government of India initiate the community development program. In summary, the political leadership was supportive of community development; there was assistance from abroad, and although part of the bureaucracy was skeptical, there was strong backing in the powerful Planning Commission and Ministry of Finance. The cumulative result was that on October 2, 1952, the national program of community development was launched with tremendous enthusiasm and interest in 55 community projects throughout India.

But policy must be implemented to be effective and this requires organization based on a series of strategic choices about implementing machinery. Are staff in position? How are they recruited and screened? What is the staffing pattern? What skills are represented? If training is needed, do the facilities exist? What is the budget for the program, its source, and duration? Within the bureaucratic framework, what is the jurisdictional responsibility of the new organization? And closely related to this, where is the program located and what is the base of its political support? These were some of the internal questions of the new national program of community development that had to be answered before it could even begin its work. On the output side there were other questions. What functions would the program perform? Which geographical areas and populations would be covered? What services would be provided? What would be the government's role toward the people serviced? Finally, how would the organization know it was succeeding in meeting its objectives?

Of course, these questions are difficult to answer for any public sector operation. They presume, according to management theory, clarity of objectives, a solid information base from which to make decisions, which in turn requires both control and surveillance systems to gather information, some model against which to measure performance, and ideally, an external mechanism to provide objective and constructive evaluation.[7] The British left a bureaucratic structure that provided a nucleus of unusually well qualified administrative officers. However, its contour was essentially non-developmental and unconducive to developmental activities. It was also one that placed a premium on the rule of an administrative elite, emphasized an impersonal, rigidly stratified bureaucratic hierarchy, and further entrenched the status concept among these strata and between the administrative and technical cadres. The existing administrative structure in 1952, at the time when the community development program was launched, was therefore one which had some serious built-in defects for the effective implementation of a development program requiring more than a routinized pattern of operation. As a result of these and other constraints, the political leadership looked to the experiences of a pilot project to discover how to pursue the goals of community development.

THE PILOT PROJECT

India was particularly fortunate in having an excellent model to use as its point of reference for the community development program—the Etawah Project. This pilot project began operations in October 1948 in 64 villages of the Etawah District of Uttar Pradesh. Albert Mayer, with his own handpicked team, designed

[7] P. F. Drucker, *Management Tasks, Responses, Practices* (New York: Harper and Row, 1974); H. Koontz and C. O'Donnell, *Principles of Management: An Analysis of Management Functions,* 5th ed. (New York: McGraw-Hill, 1972). J. G. March and H. Simon, *Organizations* (New York: John Wiley and Sons, 1958); *Science Quarterly,* 9, No. 1 (June 1964) are insightful on this subject.

and headed the project. Mayer brought to it skills, enthusiasm, and personal involvement. Further, he enjoyed the confidence and backing of the prime minister and of the chief minister of the state of Uttar Pradesh. In keeping with the philosophy of community development, he built the project on self-help and community participation.[8] As stated, the general aim of the pilot project was:

> [To] see what degree of productive and social improvement as well as of initiative, self-confidence, and cooperation can be achieved in a village or district not the beneficiary of any set of special circumstances [and] to see how quickly the results may be attainable, consistent with their remaining permanently part of the people's mental, spiritual, and technical equipment and outlook after the special pressure is lifted.[9]

Mayer laid down the fundamentals of operational technique and key inputs for working at the grass-roots or community level. In summary, he outlined the following guidelines.

1. Assess the local situation by beginning with "felt needs" and gradually move to induced needs, based on a carefully planned and graduated approach.
2. Go only as fast as the people's development can absorb it. To do this requires a careful study of the local situation, systematic planning, and realistic setting of priorities.
3. Be thorough—assemble resources and move systematically step by step, taking time to evaluate the results and correct deficiencies; work intensively, saturate the target area; emphasize team work, open communication between staff and line functionaries, and provide support for the latter.
4. In the government's work with the villagers, involve them, develop their initiative, and use local resources as much as possible.

Mayer indicated that the critical tests for determining the success

[8] This subject is covered by an extensive literature. In addition to Mayer's book there is T. R. Batten, *Communities and their Development* (London: Oxford University Press, 1957); L. J. Cary, ed., *Community Development as a Process* (Columbia, Mo.: University of Missouri Press, 1970); S. C. Dube, *India's Changing Villages: Human Factors in Community Development* (Ithaca: Cornell University Press, 1958); W. H. Goodenough, *Cooperation in Change* (New York: Russell Sage Foundation, 1973).

[9] A. Mayer, M. Marriott, and R. Park, *Pilot Project, India: The Story of Rural Development at Etawah, Uttar Pradesh* (Berkeley: University of California Press, 1958), p. 37.

or failure of the Etawah Project were whether the community would continue the program if outside support were withdrawn and whether the program, if successful, could be replicated elsewhere.

Possibly the two factors most stressed in effective implementation of this government program were competently trained personnel and a reliable supply line. The project stressed recruitment and careful screening and built a prestigious program that attracted well qualified and highly motivated personnel at each operating level. But while extension staff could educate the villagers about options for their own development, the government still had to deliver on the implied promise that the inputs to sustain the development would be made available. This required reliable supply lines and proper scheduling. More than once Mayer and his staff had to do battle with the government to secure these principles of operation.

The project left an operational design that was sound and thoroughly tested during the period of Mayer's direct involvement. In addition to the principle of replicability, which was the overriding criterion used for evaluating the success of the project, Mayer and his staff strove to meet the following objectives:

1. Personnel were to be meticulously selected and given adequate training.
2. Once the staff was in position, the meaningless tradition of personnel transfer was to be avoided.
3. Project workers would accept their task as being in the service of the people, and avoid traditional domineering behavior.
4. Relations between field workers would be "open," allowing for feedback of problems from the field on the effectiveness of suggested remedies.
5. Targets would be based on a proper understanding of the conditions in the field, rather than imposed from above, and then time-tabled to serve as guides for action.
6. Projects would build on local self-reliance and local sources of supply when possible.
7. The staff would strive to obtain the fullest cooperation from other government departments at the district and local levels.
8. An essential element was the involvement of the village leadership in initiating and organizing the work to insure continuity and viability in the program.[10]

[10] Paraphrased from S. Dasgupta and B. N. Singh, *History of Rural Development in Modern India*, I (New Delhi: Impex, 1967), p. 119.

111

The project staff consisted of four deputy development officers, one each in agriculture, village participation, agricultural engineering, and training. There was a senior economics intelligence inspector to do the survey work, record progress, and maintain data. Supporting them were a number of assistant development officers in agriculture, mechanical engineering, civil engineering, public health, social education, and training. In the field were the village level workers (VLWs), multipurpose agents with some training in agriculture and with experience in rural life. Once selected, each was given an additional six months of training. Although the duties were broad, the service area included only four or five villages. As an incentive for rural work, a higher pay scale was in effect than for the field agent of the agriculture ministry.

Although there had been other community development experiments which employed the multipurpose worker concept, Etawah systematized it for the first time. Organizationally, the whole project was a support system that used the VLW in a flexible way to help ascertain local problems and organize villagers for demonstrations and education. More specialized expertise was provided to the villages from the project headquarters. Finally, at the district level, a development officer worked to coordinate the project's activities, secure the supply lines, and maintain a high level of cooperation with other departments.

Measured both in terms of service inputs and production outputs, the gains at Etawah were impressive. The projects completed included the construction of drains, storage tanks, roads, and canals; the delivery of improved health measures, sanitation, and adult and primary education; the introduction of better implements, technology, and improved seed in agriculture; the use of better feed and breeding in animal husbandry; and even the publication of a village newspaper. Although the project had social and cultural benefits, its underpinning was economic development. One of its accomplishments was in the field of small industry—the development of brick kilns. This local industry was encouraged because the brick-making process was simple and easy to learn, materials were readily available, the kilns were not difficult to construct, the cost was low, and the industry was labor intensive. In addition, the brick-molding season didn't conflict with agricultural operations and the market was potentially great.[11] The

[11] Mayer, *Pilot Project, India*, pp. 272-279.

Etawah Project had shown that by considering local conditions and resources, needed and economically profitable efforts could be designed to benefit the local people.

The major emphasis of Etawah as a production experiment was in agriculture. It was the introduction of a new variety of potato, the Patna Phulwa, which provided the early breakthrough for the project. Project workers facilitated the sale of seed at cost to the farmers and provided technical information. Because the price of the new seed was less than the local variety, the size of the potato larger, and the yield greater, it was quickly adopted by local farmers. The average potato crop yields more than doubled.[12] The history of the introduction of wheat as the major crop in the area was similar. This operation included an intensive education campaign, instruction on proper storage, planting, fertilizing, hoeing, and other improved practices, as well as facilitating the availability of seeds. The results were dramatic. Within three to four years, improved wheat strains completely replaced the traditional varieties.[13] Similarly, the production of improved varieties of peas almost tripled and spread over the entire state.[14] Moreover, these development efforts lasted long after Mayer's departure.[15]

Among the lessons extracted from the Etawah Project by program officials were the following important points.

1. Emphasis on economic programs is essential.
2. Targets for work should be fixed by local officials and farmers and not from above.
3. Every worker from bottom to top should know what has been planned and what his role is in the total plan.
4. The "multipurpose worker" is the most suitable pattern of staff at the field level.
5. Studying the difficulties of workers and solving them on the spot is important.
6. Establishing personal contacts with villagers to win their confidence is equally important.

[12] Dasgupta and Singh, *History of Rural Development in Modern India*, p. 217.

[13] Ibid., p. 218.

[14] Ibid., pp. 220-221.

[15] Horace Holmes returned to Etawah twenty years after its inception and enthusiastically commented on its continued progress. Letter from Horace Holmes, Agricultural Officer in the SEA Regional Office, U.S. Embassy, Bangkok, October 30, 1967.

7. The caliber of workers in the project can be improved by allowing them to assume responsibility and by free and frank discussion with them.
8. Rigorous planning and execution of the program, with concentrated effort, timely supply, follow-up, and demonstration are also crucial.
9. Fulfillment of promises, sympathetic treatment of farmers and other village workers, and successful demonstrations are other keys to success.[16]

Etawah was well managed, highly productive, and cost effective. It also enjoyed high visibility with the national and state leadership. But soon its carefully managed, highly intensive, "go slow" approach was abandoned by the supporters of community development—Nehru, V. T. Krishnamachari from the Planning Commission, and S. K. Dey, head of the Community Projects Administration—for a much more extended and rapid program of rural reconstruction.[17]

Formally, there were many organizational similarities between the pilot project and the national effort. But the formula approach and the rigid pattern that rapidly evolved in the national program ran directly counter to the Etawah philosophy of flexibility and responsiveness to local needs.[18] Moreover, the attempt to introduce community development widely made it impossible to achieve the kind of intensive, individualized development efforts that had been responsible for Etawah's success. An evaluation of later community development policy indicates that the lessons of Etawah were not applied. The reasons for this can be found in an analysis of the political pressures and bureaucratic relationships that formed around the broader implementation needs of the national program.

THE REPLICATION OF PILOT PROJECTS

A general criticism of pilot projects is that they approximate

[16] Dasgupta and Singh, *History of Rural Development in Modern India*, pp. 388-389.

[17] Mayer, *Pilot Project, India*; S. K. Dey, *Power to the People* (Calcutta: Orient Longmans, 1961); and interview with Douglas Ensminger, Champaign, Ill., January 13, 1974.

[18] H. C. Hart, "The Village and Development Administration," in J. Heaphey, ed., *Spatial Dimensions of Development Administration* (Durham, N.C.: Duke University Press, 1971).

the ideal more than the readily attainable even though they may, when properly managed, provide impressive results as had Etawah. But Mayer recognized this problem and the need to reproduce the organizational mechanism that gave these results. He therefore made replication his strongest criterion for judging success. Since Etawah's key organizational elements had been identified, its mode of operation made known, and its results field-tested, a "blueprint" existed for organizing the national effort. The experiment offered a coherent and persuasive answer to the question, What is the best way of doing community development? But even allowing that Etawah presented an operationally sound model, this is not enough. A critical factor in Etawah's success had been that it was *allowed* to be successful. The leadership—Nehru at the national level and G. B. Pant at the state level—had provided it with a protective environment and supported it against the inroads of the established bureaucracy. Given this political environment, a talented management could both develop and implement its programs to their maximum potential.

However, the change to the national scale raised problems different from those of a project of limited size and duration. Choices on national priorities involve heavy outlays of capital resources and expenditures. The question decision makers may therefore find themselves asking is not, What is the *best* way of doing community development? but, What is the most politically and bureaucratically *feasible* way to do community development? And, this may result in a trade-off between quantity and quality. Given the constraint of limited resources, a certain irreducible cost level in operations is quickly reached. Community development's resources, after all, were always quite modest—Rs. 90 crores ($180 million) in the First Five-Year Plan and Rs. 200 crores ($400 million) in the Second Five-Year Plan. The parameter is then not an "optimal funding level," it is the achievement of sufficient funding to make it feasible to try to attain the program's minimum objectives, assuming proper management. However, even at this suboptimal level of operation, another trade-off is required.

While proper management procedures are able to achieve a high degree of cost-effectiveness without sacrificing quality, they increase the time needed to gain coverage. If the area of program responsibility is limited and the population small, this may not be an important concern. In India, however, size, both in distance and

115

population, is a part of any national program formulation. The choice facing India's policymakers during the early days of community development was between general coverage with limited resources per unit of operation or limited coverage with a full complement of resources per unit of operation. As they weighed the impact of the 55 community projects launched in 1952 to cover 16,500 villages, they judged such coverage to be negligible in a country of over a half million villages. Even the planned 90 community projects would reach only five percent of the population and would exhaust all the resources that could be spared.[19] They therefore were willing to dilute effective program implementation to achieve the higher priority of general coverage.

The considerations were many. A concentrated effort of this type had political value, over the short run, for a national party anxious to build its grass-roots support. At the time of independence, most of rural India identified only vaguely with anything as nebulous as a national government, especially one as far away as Delhi. An often repeated story was that there were Indians who never knew the British had left; there were also Indians who never knew they had come. It is therefore not surprising that an important development theme for India in the 1950s and 1960s was national integration. India was faced with the problem of "integrating diverse ethnic, religious, communal, and regional elements into a national political community."[20] This priority pointed to quantity of effort rather than quality. The motto of community development could have been "make yourself visible to the people," for it was important to counter the centripetal pulls of the diverse groupings on the subcontinent with evidence that the government was attempting to meet the people's needs.[21]

A choice that would have favored operational quality was further complicated by a number of other factors. The Americans,

[19] Dey, *Power to the People*; and Chester Bowles to J. Nehru, "Memo to Prime Minister," May 1952 and November 9, 1953 (U.S. Embassy, New Delhi).

[20] J. D. Montgomery and W. J. Siffin, eds., *Approaches to Development: Politics, Administration and Change* (New York: McGraw-Hill Publishers, 1966), p. 61; K. Deutsch and W. Foltz, *Nation Building* (New York: Atherton Press, 1963); J. Palombara and M. Weiner, *Political Parties and Political Development* (Princeton: Princeton University Press, 1966).

[21] H. Wriggins, "National Integration," in M. Weiner, ed., *Modernization: The Dynamics of Growth* (New York: Basic Books, Inc., 1966).

concerned with the recent loss of China to the Communists, fearful that India might follow suit, argued for a broad national approach. There was an air of urgency in the American Mission about the need for the Congress party to build a strong base in the rural areas; the Americans were impressed by the fact that the Chinese Communists had won their revolution by isolating the Kuomintang in the cities.[22]

In addition, there were ideological pressures that militated against a choice for operational quality. Nehru and the other followers of Gandhi were intellectually committed to rural reconstruction for India. As Douglas Ensminger recalls, Nehru had promised India's millions that something would be done to alleviate their plight.[23] Correspondingly, since community development promised benefits to Nehru's constituents in the Congress party, there was political pressure from local areas to expand coverage. Since the Congress members of the legislative assembly did not want their areas excluded from community development's patronage, the national leadership and the Planning Commission were concerned with how long it would take to cover the rural areas and reach the population.

The consequence of this range of factors and their interaction was the decision to abandon to a "go slow" approach and to move as rapidly as possible to cover the country by means of a National Extension Service.[24] This meant a reduction in resources for community development's operating unit, the block, which consisted of administration and services for 100 villages. More importantly, it meant a reduction in organizational capacity because rapid expansion meant rapid recruitment of staff and field personnel. This could only result in the loss of management capability. It is primarily on the basis of the decision for rapid expansion that one can trace most of the deficiencies of the later community development effort. From this, it is easy to draw the conclusion that the national leadership made an "irrational" choice of implementing strategy. But did they? As argued below, a difference in perspective can change the criteria by which success is measured.

[22] Chester Bowles, *Ambassador's Report* (London: Y. V. Gollancz, Ltd., 1955).

[23] Interview with Douglas Ensminger, Champaign, Ill., January 13, 1974.

[24] V. T. Krishnamachari, *Community Development in India* (New Delhi: Government of India Press, 1958), p. 154.

THE CALCULUS OF DECISION MAKING

Interviews with many of those who were involved with or had access to decision making at the national level—Tarlok Singh, secretary to the Planning Commision, S. K. Dey, Chester Bowles, Douglas Ensminger, Clifford Willson, first head of the American Technical Cooperation Mission—indicate that there was a conscious decision by the government leadership, both political and bureaucratic, not to go the route of careful, slow, high performance, small unit operation. The reason for this decision, as previously noted, was the overriding concern to gain coverage. Although this became the highest priority, the reasons and motivation that brought the policymakers and their advisors to the same endpoint differed. Their evaluations of the form the community development program should take were based on political and bureaucratic criteria rather than on operational criteria.

Three sets of actors can be singled out to demonstrate the primacy of political and bureaucratic criteria over the program perspective in the choice between quality and quantity. The first set of actors consisted of Jawaharlal Nehru and the political leadership of the Indian government. For Nehru, the decision drew its antecedents from his socialization under Gandhi, Marxism, and socialist philosophy; from his role in the fight for independence; and from his commitment to do something for India's rural millions. There is some reason to believe he hoped community development would usher in a social revolution that would change the status quo of the conservative countryside. Because he had the political power, he was able to use his position and standing to initiate this "revolutionary" approach. Although his later speeches on community development suggest that he had reservations about the bureaucracy as the initiating force in what he hoped would be a "people's program," he agreed on the need for coverage.[25]

In more general terms, the Indian leadership was intellectually inclined toward community development, and due to a favorable set of circumstances, took the early decision to move on the program. It therefore created a supportive environment that was critical for the program's development. Although there was an early question as to whether the "rapid coverage" or the "intensive develop-

[25] Ministry of Community Development and Cooperation, *Jawaharlal Nehru on Community Development, Panchayati Raj, and Cooperation* (New Delhi: Government of India Press, 1965).

118

ment" approach would be adopted, the political leadership soon favored the former. This was due to the leadership's desire to strengthen the party's organization in the rural areas, to Nehru's advancing years, to his longing to see his vision of the new India take form, and to political pressures from states and politically articulate constituencies to acquire benefits like community projects from the government.

If Nehru represented the key political support for the national program of community development, V. T. Krishnamachari represented its strongest bureaucratic support. This individual was highly respected for his development work in the present-day state of Gujarat. He had headed the Grow More Food Enquiry Committee and later became the deputy chairman of the powerful Planning Commission. His desire for rapid coverage was not motivated by community development per se. Instead, he wanted an Administrative Services that was oriented to welfare and development. Since the services' prime functions were administering the law and revenue collection, this represented a major departure not only in function but in total perspective. It meant working with the village people and having them participate in the decision-making process. It also had a somewhat less understood meaning—that of management of limited resources in a public sector operation: setting objectives, planning, program development, and evaluation. On one thing V. T. Krishnamachari was quite clear; for his plan to work, the Administrative Services had to come under the aegis of the National Extension Service and this could only succeed if the expansion of the National Extension Service was pushed rapidly.

The community development program posed a number of threats to the bureaucracy's existing mode of operation. It was a generalist organization among specialists, with responsibility for integrating services. As such it was entrusted with some degree of control of resources and their allocation in the field. With its orientation towards implementing self-help programs, it viewed its role in a most unbureaucratic fashion as one of involving the community in the decision-making process. One may label the independence period as a time of flux, an open period for experimenting with new concepts. The established bureaucracy was on the defensive, and in a weak position to oppose the program. Following independence, the Administrative Services' previous association with the British brought it into disrepute, which weakened

119

its capacity to oppose the Extension Service. Moreover, V. T. Krishnamachari was in a formidable position on the Planning Commission to handle opposition to the program. The Planning Commission was then at the height of its power, was supported by the prime minister, and related well to the Ministry of Finance. This allowed Krishnamachari not only to espouse a policy of rapid expansion, but to see that the policy was, in fact, implemented.

Finally, there was the United States government and its representative in India, Chester Bowles. The U.S. for the first time entered into an aid giving agreement with a non-European, newly established developing nation in Asia. Bowles, a man of vision and energy, saw a model in the field, Etawah, and used it to foster a political interest in a national program of community development. As the American ambassador, he was in an influential position with the Indian leadership to do so. For him, the American national interest would best be served by supporting a strong, independent, and democratic India. In concrete terms, this was translated into a priority to encourage and support a strong political base in the rural areas for the Congress party. To this end, the American government was willing to make development funds available to the Indian government for the purpose of extending the community development effort. Bowles understood there would be a loss in performance per unit of operation since both funding and staffing levels would have to be reduced. But, he believed, such coverage would substantially increase total agricultural production over what could be expected from a limited number of projects.

These, then, are the most important reasons why a seemingly plausible operational approach to the implementation of development projects was not followed. Analyzing the results, it is difficult to envision a means for resolving problems created by the over-riding concern for coverage. But even so, the lessons of sound operation could have been sustained had the government supported the continuation of a limited number of regional models. Instead, Etawah, the Ford Foundation's 15 area development projects, and the early 55 community projects were all diluted and absorbed into the national program, and with that dilution went the exemplars for the national program. Another way of dealing with these problems would have been to acknowledge the primacy of the political factors in development. Then, once

120

coverage was obtained, efforts could have been made to strengthen the organizational structure. This happened, in part, with the Intensive Agricultural Development Program, and later with the World Bank's "Training and Visit System."[26]

Still, there are intriguing aspects to the community development experience in India. The early community projects were close approximations of the Etawah project, even by Albert Mayer's own admission.[27] Secondly, during this period of great enthusiasm and hope, several members of the old Indian Civil Service (ICS) and the new Indian Administrative Services (IAS) were drawn to the call for sacrifice and work on rural development. As members of the bureaucratic elite, they represented an enormous potential for affecting the implementation of community development. Bowles called the first group of development commissioners the finest group of civil servants he had ever seen.[28] U. L. Goswami, Dey's deputy in the Community Projects Administration and a member of the ICS, commented that had the bureaucracy maintained the priority and elitism surrounding entry into the early community projects and had the political leadership supported its efforts, community development could have succeeded.[29]

The lesson of Etawah and community development in India is that the calculus involved in the development of a national program is complex and depends even more on political and bureaucratic perspectives than it does on what is learned in the field trial, the pilot project, or the demonstration project. Thus, we might expect in other cases that the pilot project might well *not* be adopted as a model for the national program unless its political utility and feasibility can be demonstrated to be the most attractive alternative to decision makers. Viewed in this manner, seemingly irrational decisions—from the operational perspective —become understandable even though those implementing decisions may limit the program's ability to achieve its stated goals.

In the following chapter, David Pyle analyzes another pilot

[26] D. Benor and J. Harrison, *Agricultural Extension: The Training and Visit System* (Washington, D.C.: World Bank, May 1977).

[27] Albert Mayer's letter to Tarlok Singh cited in CPA/MIN. of Community Development and Cooperation, "Letter of May 14, 1954," *Important Letters*, II (New Delhi: Government of India Press, 1958), 219-225.

[28] Interview with former Ambassador Chester Bowles, Essex, Conn., September 25, 1973.

[29] Interview with U. L. Goswami, Vienna, Austria, October 31, 1974.

project pursued in India and explores the reasons for its failure to be replicated on a broader scale. In this second case, information of a technical, organizational, and behavioral nature generated by the pilot experience was again overlooked. This project was permitted to expire because there was little interest shown by the government in either the ultimate goals of the program or in the implementing strategy it suggested. As Pyle indicates, the case therefore lacks one vital component that encouraged community development in India—strong political commitment and support of its goals. Nevertheless, Pyle's evidence further substantiates the claim that the evaluation of pilot projects for replication on a broader scale proceeds on a plane distinct from the evaluation of the pilot project's capacity to achieve effectively its operational goals. Perhaps, then, pilot projects themselves ought to be designed to test political and bureaucratic variables as well as more technical and operational ones.

FIVE · *From Pilot Project to Operational Program in India: The Problems of Transition*

DAVID F. PYLE

CORPSES of pilot projects, particularly in the social sector, litter the development field. Although in many cases, such as the Etawah Project described by Sussman in the previous chapter, pilot schemes have proved eminently successful in achieving their objectives, very rarely have they been adopted on an expanded and/or permanent basis. Project Poshak, which will be discussed in this chapter, suffered the same igominious fate. The reasons the implementation strategy tested did not survive the traumatic transition phase from pilot study to operational program, however, are not what one would intuitively expect. The explanation of its demise does not rest on questions of the cost of the program or the effectiveness of the methodology as much as on a myriad of problems that are political and managerial in nature.

The wastage in terms of scarce personnel and financial resources, and more importantly, in terms of approaches that have proven effective, demands that those concerned with development programs devote more attention to the dynamics of pilot projects, especially to the transition stage that most never survive. Such a focus is a logical and necessary part of the recent emphasis on the analysis of policy output and implementation questions as mentioned in the first chapter of this book. Hopefully, this new direction and insights generated by case studies such as this on Project Poshak will help both planners and implementors understand the problems of institutionalization faced by pilot projects and, as a result, be better prepared to deal with them.

Note: I am extremely grateful to Dr. John O. Field for his interest in and thoughts on Project Poshak, which have been of considerable value to me. I also wish to thank Dr. Tara Gopaldas, research consultant and project director for Project Poshak, and CARE-India for their cooperation and assistance in this study.

123

Project Poshak, an integrated health and nutrition project, was conducted in the central Indian state of Madhya Pradesh between 1971 and 1975.[1] Poshak was originally conceived as a means of providing nutrition supplements to the "hut-bound" toddler (under three years of age) in isolated rural areas. In the early 1970s, the emphasis in childhood nutrition programs shifted from school lunch programs to schemes concentrating on the preschool age group. Although sensible from a nutritional standpoint, this shift gave rise to several operational problems. School feeding has two advantages—an existing infrastructure and "captive" beneficiaries. Neither apply to preschool schemes. Therefore, it was necessary to establish efficient delivery systems and capabilities to reach children between 6 and 36 months, those whose rapid development and whose exposure to the health hazards associated with weaning make them the "most vulnerable age group."[2]

It was the problem of reaching the neediest preschoolers that Project Poshak attempted to address.[3] Instead of requiring beneficiaries to come daily to a predetermined site to receive and consume the ration, Poshak tested the feasibility of a take-home implementation strategy. In this study the recipient would collect a week's ration or more at a time, enabling the child to consume the supplement in small amounts at home with his regular diet. In principle, it was thought that the take-home strategy would enable the children of economically active mothers and economically deprived families to participate in and benefit from the nutrition scheme.[4]

[1] Madhya Pradesh is India's largest state geographically; it is slightly larger than California. It has the largest tribal population in India; over 20 percent of its 41,650,000 (1971) population is classified as scheduled tribes. See B. Dube and F. Bahadme, *Study of the Tribal People and Tribal Areas of Madhya Pradesh* (Indore: Government Regional Press, 1969).

[2] Prior to Poshak, supplementary nutrition programs were restricted to supervised on-site feeding schemes that only attracted the older preschoolers (4-6 years old) and those with slightly better socioeconomic standing. The largest feeding scheme for preschoolers operating in India in the early 1970s was the Special Nutrition Program for children in the urban slums and in the tribal areas. Approximately three million preschool children were receiving daily rations under this program in 1973. See D. Gwatkin, "Health and Nutrition in India: Recommendations for Ford Foundation Support" (New Delhi, January 1974), p. 42.

[3] For a complete report of the study, see T. Gopaldas, et al., *Project Poshak*, Vols. I (Results) and II (Methodology) (New Delhi: CARE-India, 1975).

[4] The study points out that in most cases members of the lower castes and

The planners of the pilot project realized that it would take more than a food supplement to improve the nutritional status of the priority target group. To be effective, at least some of the "nutritional leaks" would have to be plugged so that the recipient could derive maximum benefit from the supplement.[5] For this reason the nutrition component was to be delivered through and linked with the existing health system. By drawing the needy to the health facilities, Poshak hoped to provide the target group with curative as well as preventive measures that, along with the nutrition supplement, would produce a positive synergistic effect upon the recipient. In order to reinforce the short-term effort while insuring long-term effect, Poshak included a third element—child-care education for pregnant and lactating mothers.

Poshak was, therefore, a pilot study designed to evaluate the operational feasibility, efficiency, impact, and economics of an integrated health-nutrition scheme. However, Poshak differed from most pilot projects in several ways. First, it was large. In the course of three years of fieldwork, the study involved some 15,000 beneficiaries in widely dispersed areas of the state.[6] Furthermore, the scheme was to operate through the existing health infrastructure instead of through an artificially expanded service that would have been impossible to duplicate because of economic and manpower limitations. The initiators of Project Poshak considered it of utmost importance that the integrated take-home feeding approach be continued and even expanded once the study had been completed. Therefore, they consciously avoided several of the principal pitfalls that, in their estimation, had prevented

those from the poorest class, the landless laborers, either did not, or could not, participate in schemes such as supplementary and public health programs because of economic or time constraints (e.g., more than 80 percent of the women in the tribal areas of Madhya Pradesh are in the labor force), or because they are discriminated against. Also, see D. Banerji, "Health Behavior and Rural Populations: Impact on Rural Health Services," *Economic and Political Weekly* (Bombay, December 22, 1973), 2261-2268.

[5] The term, "nutrition leaks," refers to all the environmental health problems, such as parasitic infestations, weanling diarrhea, and infections that reduce the child's ability to utilize fully the nutrients consumed. See A. Mitra, "Making Hard Choices Between Cost-Benefit Streams of Health and Nutrition," *PAG Bulletin*, 5, No. 1, 36-44.

[6] In general, the phases of the research can be described as follows: 1) Exploratory—to give insight, experience, and direction for the project; 2) Extensive—large geographical coverage with minimal supervision; and 3) Intensive—a series of substudies to investigate in-depth some important ecological and logistical problems that emerged from the Exploratory phase.

other pilot schemes from being adopted on a permanent basis. Poshak, as originally conceived, was to reflect the "real world" situation.

Moreover, interest in nutrition programs for the preschool age group was high in the early 1970s in India. The prime minister declared her "Garibi Hatao" (War on Poverty) and launched schemes such as the Special Nutrition Program to provide disadvantaged preschoolers as well as pregnant and lactating women in the urban slums and tribal areas with daily nutrition supplements. The Fourth Five-Year Plan (1968-1973) provided approximately $130 million to fund the scheme. In the fifth plan, the amount discussed for nutrition was increased to over $550 million, the majority of which was to be spent on supplementary feeding.[7] The government's interest in nutrition, supported by considerable funds (both internal and external), provided a supportive atmosphere for Project Poshak.

Despite the purposeful planning of Project Poshak and the encouragement given to the testing of nutrition interventions by the government, the Poshak concept ultimately was not adopted by the government of Madhya Pradesh as a permanent part of its nutrition programs. I found no evidence that the scheme was ever considered for implementation statewide. The most that was ever discussed was introducing the integrated concept in a portion of the feeding centers in the Special Nutrition Program and then extending it to all of the centers at some unspecified time in the future. However, when Poshak concluded its work in 1975, the state continued to employ the on-site supervised feeding approach as it had done before the Poshak concept was tested. Nothing changed, despite the four-year project that had involved five different organizations—the national government, the state government, USAID, UNICEF, and CARE—plus a considerable budget and countless person-hours. Ironically, interest generated by the Poshak experience led to the initiation of several integrated take-home feeding programs elsewhere in India.

Why was the Poshak approach not adopted, much less expanded, by the government of the state in which it was conducted and which had originally expressed an interest in the approach? The government's decision, one might assume, would be based on ques-

[7] The final version of this plan was adopted in 1976; it reduced the allocation for nutrition programs to little more than that of the Fourth Plan.

126

tions of effectiveness of the integrated take-home feeding approach and/or its cost. If the approach had been found to be ineffective or unworkable or had proven too costly to maintain, there would have been reason to discontinue it. This, however, was not the basis for Poshak's demise. Therefore, it is necessary to review the history of the project and to ask what the factors were that determined its fate. Such matters as personalities, bureaucratic practices, publicity, and political realities loom large when one examines the fate of Project Poshak in detail. However, it is these factors that are often overlooked when analyzing such projects. Instead, emphasis is usually placed on the academic aspects of pilot projects which, as in the case of Poshak, may not be the prime concern when the project's future is being decided.

The research for this paper was carried out in early 1976 in India. The agencies that had been involved in the study were contacted, and past and present officials of the Ministries of Social Welfare and Health in New Delhi and Bhopal, the capital of Madhya Pradesh, who were familiar with Poshak or had played a role in it, were interviewed. I took advantage of the opportunity to visit several rural health centers that had participated in the field study, thereby gaining an insight into the situation at the end of the bureaucratic chain. I also visited another integrated nutrition pilot study in a neighboring state, which provided some interesting comparisons. The field research enabled me not only to piece together the various parts of the puzzle as to why the strategy of Poshak was not accepted by the Madhya Pradesh government, but also to speculate about how other pilot schemes might avoid similar problems.

EFFECTIVENESS AND COST

In terms of success, defined as the "capacity actually to deliver programs as designed," Poshak can be considered successful. The project demonstrated that supplementary rations could be distributed on a take-home basis through the rural health facilities. The amount of food consumed by the different age cohorts was very close to what was observed in the supervised on-site approach.[8]

The scheme also showed that it could play a significant role in

[8] *Project Poshak*, I, 216. The definition of success is taken from the introduction to this volume.

improving the quality of life of the rural population. Some of the spin-off effects of Poshak were particularly encouraging. The utilization of the Primary Health Centers included in the study, for example, increased by approximately 40 percent. Considering the normal inability and/or unwillingness of the population in rural India to use the health services, this is a major achievement. Along with improved usage came a slight increase in the acceptance of family planning measures among the experimental group. Accessibility and a closer relationship between the health personnel and the community were identified as precipitating factors in this change. It is significant that the most peripheral health units had the highest participation rate.

There was also improvement in mothers' attitudes toward nutrition and health. While the lasting nature of this attitudinal change is not known, the multiinput interpersonal approach, in addition to involving the mother personally in the program, would seem to promise some behavioral change when extended over a longer period. There was also a slight, yet significant, decrease in the mortality rates among the experimental versus the control group. Considering that the controlled phases of Poshak lasted for only a year, it would not be farfetched to expect much greater results from an ongoing program using the same methodology.

Moreover, according to the official Poshak report, the cost of the integrated services delivered by means of the take-home approach provided considerable savings over the on-site system. Although there is some question about the accuracy of the figures, the cost data presented in the project report strongly favored the Poshak strategy over the on-site method.

Despite the general ability to deliver the services, there remain questions concerning the effectiveness or impact of the approach. First, the study showed the scheme was unable to reach a large portion of the priority target groups—the poorest sector and the early toddlers in the weaning period. The people taking part in the program were mostly from the small landowner class, already one step above the bottom economic stratum. Landless laborer families, who comprise over 30 percent of the population of Madhya Pradesh, did not participate as a rule, again because of time and social constraints. Moreover, the younger cohorts did not consume any more of the ration than they did in the supervised program. The overall impact of the integrated package on the development of the experimental group over the control group was not substantially different either. This was apparently due to the diversion of the food to other family members and infrequent or improper use of the health facilities and educational opportunities offered by the program.

In the final analysis, however, the effectiveness and cost findings mattered little. They were not the basis of the decision to discontinue the take-home approach. Indeed, it was apparent in interviews with those in positions to decide the future of Poshak that the results were either not known, not known in sufficient detail, or were not considered of great importance. The officials did not refer to the lower participation rates or the lack of significant nutritional impact. Nor were they aware of, or impressed with, the cost benefits reported in the project's findings. A similar reaction was apparent when discussing the increased utilization of the health facilities, a matter that should have appealed to those whose responsibility it was to improve the dismal performance of the rural health services. If the most important aspects of the Poshak record did not elicit a response, there must be other explanations for why the scheme was discontinued after the pilot phase.

REASONS FOR DISCONTINUATION

At various times during the course of the project the state government demonstrated interest in continuing the integrated take-home feeding method. A proposal for expansion of the Poshak concept, which reportedly would have brought some 54,000 beneficiaries in 18 districts under the Poshak system, was drafted in 1974. No action, however, was taken on this measure. Later, a smaller scheme involving 28 Primary Health Centers and 5,000 beneficiaries was to be started by mid-1975 by order of the Health Department of Bhopal. In January of 1976 no evidence existed to indicate that the scheme was in operation, or that anyone was even interested in its status. For all intents and purposes the Poshak concept was dead in Madhya Pradesh once the study had been concluded. A combination of factors provide some explanations for why Poshak failed to live beyond the pilot phase. They are grouped into four general categories: conceptualization, commitment, administration, and timing.

Conceptualization

Poshak was a complex project with a multitude of different

129

components. At the beginning it appeared to be a less complicated study, originally planned for 2 years, whose objective was to test the feasibility of a take-home feeding approach distributed through the health system. But as it developed, Poshak evolved into a 4-year project with considerably expanded scope. This was made possible by the flexibility that had been built into the project design to allow for follow-up on eventualities that had not been, or could not have been, foreseen in the planning stage.

While the value of and need for flexibility are recognized, the danger of overloading the project with purposes to meet the interests of different participants must also be appreciated. For example, the government of Madhya Pradesh was principally interested in the pilot study as embodied in the second (Extensive) phase. After this point, the government's participation, never as much as it might have been, was significantly reduced. CARE, on the other hand, became increasingly more involved and interested in the applied research aspects of the study.

Differences and disillusionment arose when the two aspects—pilot and research—were combined into one project. CARE's research produced 28 outstanding reports that were published in leading professional journals and some of which were presented and well received at international conferences, in addition to a 2-volume final report on the project. But the government neither understood nor was very interested in this aspect of the project, which did little to help it implement the scheme. It apparently wanted merely a demonstration that such a scheme was feasible and affordable.

There is also a difference between flexible planning and unspecific planning. In the former, the objectives remain fixed while the means to those ends are amenable to change. In unspecific cases, the objectives themselves are left somewhat vague. Poshak suffered from the latter—the original agreement did not specify how the take-home concept would be continued or expanded once the study had been completed. The five institutional participants in the initial stages of Project Poshak apparently agreed that this alternative delivery system would be continued, but the number of districts, centers, or beneficiaries was not specified. In fact, there is no evidence that any specific commitment to carry on this approach was mentioned in the original agreement among the participants. As the individuals in charge of the program changed, the outlines of the original implicit agreement became increasingly vague. A strong and irrefutable commitment by all the participating organizations would have served their purposes better. The agreement could have been amended at any time, but at least there would have been a basis for discussion when the time came to expand or continue the concept. The assumption, at least by CARE, was that the Poshak approach would be adopted to some extent in Madhya Pradesh, and this resulted in a complacent attitude on the part of CARE officials. The idea was not pursued with as much vigor as it might have been if CARE had realized earlier that the continuation of Poshak was not certain.

At the same time that there was a difference of opinion about what Project Poshak's principal objectives were and what its future would be, CARE and the state government apparently had different ideas of what the chances for duplication were. Even if the Madhya Pradesh government had wanted to continue the Poshak concept of delivering a package of services, it would not have been easy for it to do so. Despite the fact that the project was initiated with the explicit intention of operating within the existing infrastructure, this proved not to be possble. While no new personnel were hired for the project, all the participating health centers were brought up to full authorized strength by transferring personnel from nonparticipating health centers. As a rule at this time in India, several staff positions in all health centers were left unfilled. Thus, the health facilities of Project Poshak were exceptional to start with; this situation would make the system difficult or impossible to duplicate if fully staffed centers were thought to be essential for the success of the scheme. Moreover, the staff spent considerably more time than was originally allotted to carry out Poshak work. Most workers spent either a high percentage or all of their time on the integrated program, and as a result, had to neglect some of their other duties. This was possible on a short-term basis but would not have been feasible if the program had become a permanent fixture, unless the department ordered a change in work schedules or responsibilities, made the integrated scheme top priority, or provided additional personnel.

In a similar vein, there were problems with the continued availability of a precooked food like the ICSM (Instant Corn-Soya-Milk) that was used in Project Poshak.[9] Even though the

[9] Instant Corn-Soya-Milk is a fully processed, blended food that was presweetened and flavored. The recipient had only to mix with water before serving.

131

ICSM had experienced some problems (infestation, short shelf life), the government thought a fully processed commodity was necessary if the scheme were to succeed. CARE, as we shall see, was not in a position to supply ICSM on a continuing basis, and the government claimed that it did not have the expertise to develop such a food. While it was argued that the scheme could be carried out very well without such a sophisticated product as ICSM, the government could not be persuaded of this. Using a product that was not indigenous or readily replicable, or whose availability was uncertain, may have been an unwise decision if continuity were an important objective of the project designers.

Emphasizing a point made by Sussman in the preceeding chapter, it was unrealistic to expect significant results to be achieved in such a short time frame. Only part of the project extended for more than a year. This, it would appear, is not a sufficient period in which to test the full benefit of a complex scheme like Poshak with its many components. Yet, the problems that confront a multiyear project seem to increase directly with its time frame—it is difficult to maintain the interest, coordination, and cooperation of all participants over an extended period. Changes in personnel and circumstances may not favor the project. Nevertheless, a unified two- or three-year study may have given a better indication of what might be gained from the Poshak concept than the division of the program into various phases.

All of these problems—the flexible planning, unspecified future, unrealistic personnel and food inputs, brevity of the study phases—indicate an identity crisis. Was Poshak a demonstration, a pilot, or a research project? A distinction can be made among these three types of projects. A pilot project can be defined as the testing of a particular approach on a small scale to determine its chances for success if implemented on an expanded basis. A demonstration project, on the other hand, serves the purpose of showing the merits of a selected system; i.e., given certain inputs, something can be accomplished. A research project is a careful investigation aimed at identifying or testing new theories. The three types of projects serve different functions and must be distinguished one from another in order to avoid confusion in establishing a project's objectives.

The evidence clearly shows that elements of all these types were present in Project Poshak. The shift of personnel to fulfill the

132

project's requirements, as well as the use of exogenous foods, made Poshak a demonstration of what could be accomplished given certain conditions. At the same time, there was an explicit pilot aspect, the broadly based and less controlled Extensive phase, as well as the research aspect that seemed to increase in importance as Poshak progressed. The inability to define clearly the purpose of Poshak made it difficult for those involved to identify what the outcome of the project was to mean. Moreover, it complicated practical decisions since participants were often at odds with one another. Most importantly, the state government saw its primary interest in a pilot study being obscured by a research-cum-demonstration project that did not serve its purposes. As will be discussed, it had little or no control over Poshak's direction, and as a result, could not do anything to ensure that its interests were accorded proper attention.

Commitment

Commitment is a difficult thing to measure when a government's performance is concerned. The most obvious form in which an agency demonstrates its interest in a project is in the allocation of funds. In the case of Poshak, the two governmental bodies that were involved did not commit any resources over and above previously budgeted funds. The national government's contribution, for instance, paid for the project's administrative costs and the transportation of the food. However, this money had already been appropriated and allocated to Madhya Pradesh and would have been used in its regular Special Nutrition Program if Poshak had not been initiated. More significantly, the state government did not make any special appropriation for Project Poshak—its contribution was in the form of personnel who were already members of the staff.

Generally, proponents of new programs find that their most difficult task involves getting approval of funding. Neither the national nor the state government had to undergo this rigorous process, and, therefore, no political support for the scheme was required or received. In the end, neither the center nor the state had any financial stake in the outcome or continuation of Poshak. They had invested nothing but some person-hours, mostly of lower echelon personnel whose work tends to be undervalued in any case.

In addition to the lack of financial commitment, the Madhya Pradesh Department of Health, with the exception of a few individuals, had never demonstrated any dedication to nutrition or preventive health in general. Its first priority was family planning, followed by curative medicine. Moreover, at the time there was very little in the way of financial reward to gain from preventive medicine. Curative medicine was also politically more popular because of its use of impressive, visible facilities and services.[10] The local Madhya Pradesh paper in January 1976 carried statements by the state minister of health and family planning about supplying each of the 46 districts of the state with a "fully-fledged hospital complete with equipment including an intensive-care unit" and an air-conditioned operating room.[11] He went on to say that four centers for the treatment of cancer would be established in the four largest urban centers of the state!

Part of this curative bias may be explained as a reaction to feelings of technological inferiority. Since there is no glamour or status in preventive medicine, the government wanted to show its constituents, as well as outsiders, that it had the ability to do the more complicated and expensive "luxury" curative medicine. The principal incentive for investment in the more expensive curative side, however, was that this type of medicine was required and desired by the politically influential. Those who would most benefit from preventive medicine have little political voice and even less political power.

Such a deeply ingrained set of priorities increased the impact of, and dependence on, key personalities who supported the Poshak concept. The original secretary of health and the director of health understood the value of Poshak, yet these men were unable to change the department's orientation during their brief tenures in office. Once they left their respective positions, the department reverted to its traditional set of priorities. Poshak lost its privileged status, and in the end was unable to sustain life in the vacuum of support that existed. Nor were political elites ever actively involved in the promotion of Project Poshak, although they might have helped secure support for the study. This was due, in

[10] The politics of health care is discussed by V. Navarro, "The Underdevelopment of Health is the Health of Underdevelopment: An Analysis of the Distribution of Human Resources in Latin America," *International Journal of Health Services*, 4, No. 1 (1974), 5-27.

[11] *The M. P. Chronicle*, Bhopal, June 18-19, 1976, pp. 1, 5.

134

large part, to the participation of CARE, which was very reluctant to become involved in overtly political activities.

Administration

Reviewing the history of Project Poshak, one is constantly reminded of the central role played by CARE. To begin with, there would not have been a project without the ICSM which was supplied to the Madhya Pradesh government by CARE through the Food for Peace Program. The voluntary agency also prepared the project proposal and initiated dialogues with the governments of India and Madhya Pradesh, USAID, and UNICEF, to elicit their cooperation and support. After the scheme had become operational, CARE had "overall responsibility for administration of all aspects of the project, including finances."[12] Without this exogenous input, the system would not have operated as effectively as it did.

Yet, CARE's dilemma must be appreciated. On the one hand, the agency wanted a straightforward pilot project, while on the other hand, it was interested in conducting detailed and quite sophisticated research. The latter meant that certain things had to be done correctly and according to schedule, which required a high level of supervision. When it came time for the state to assume responsibility for the scheme, however, it is understandable that government officials felt both unfamiliar with its operation, since they were not intimately involved with the administration of the pilot study, and incapable of providing the same level of supervision to make the integrated take-home feeding alternative work.

Moreover, the CARE role in Project Poshak was directed mainly from New Delhi. Unintentionally, the feeling arose that the Madhya Pradesh government had little or nothing to do with running the project. The CARE-Delhi personnel directing Poshak would visit the state frequently, but most often it was to visit the research sites and not to meet with the senior officials in the government. In addition, the director of the project was not known to the government Secretariat. There was no one to serve as liaison between Poshak and the government who could explain the potential benefits that would be derived by the state's adoption of the scheme. Without this vital link, the program was adrift. Furthermore, the publicity generated by the Poshak team in New Delhi was of little benefit to the scheme in the capital of Madhya

12 *Project Poshak*, I, 11.

Pradesh where the continuation question ultimately had to be decided. Interest and a constituency in support of a project like Poshak can only be created by familiarization. Efforts to do this in Bhopal were lacking.

Even within CARE the administration of Project Poshak presented problems. The director of CARE-Madhya Pradesh had moved to CARE's country headquarters in New Delhi during the initial (Exploratory) phase of the project to become project coordinator. Two years later, however, he was transferred to Central America and no one in CARE-Delhi was appointed to replace him. Therefore, at an important point in the study, the Project Poshak team lost its established link with CARE-Delhi. The Poshak group was now a separate entity that operated independently of the rest of CARE. It had its own budget and personnel who were on contract for the duration of the study as opposed to being long-term CARE employees. The interaction and exchange of ideas between CARE-Delhi and the Poshak team, which could have benefited both parties, were reduced significantly.

As indicated above, the role performed by the secretary of health and family planning of the Madhya Pradesh government was of considerable significance. He had served as the secretary of the state's Tribal Welfare Department in the latter half of the 1960s and had been responsible for starting the school feeding program in Madhya Pradesh. He understood the importance of nutrition and was interested in doing more in the field as head of health operations. His experience with food programming had resulted in a close working relationship with CARE. For its part, CARE relied heavily on the secretary, an excellent and energetic administrator. At the same time, but in a less powerful position, the director of health services for Madhya Pradesh was dedicated to public health, believed in the Poshak concept, and promoted its cause. These two officials were responsible for getting the Department of Health and Family Planning to support the project and work on its behalf.

However, the secretary and director were not permanent fixtures in the Health Department. Their successors did not maintain the close personal interest in the project, and Poshak became "just another project" for them. With the new health secretary came a new chief minister and a new set of priorities. Predictably, the new secretary was eager to demonstrate his ability to his chief minister by establishing new programs. Moreover, the former secretary had alienated some of the departmental staff during his term in office. Therefore, once he departed, those who had cause and were in a position to do so, subverted or disregarded projects that the secretary had promoted. Finally, the highest state official associated with the project was a deputy director of health who served as state nutrition officer. He was the Project Poshak field leader, but because he did not hold an administrative position, he could make no decisions or take any action himself. His lack of rank meant he could only report his findings and recommendations to the secretary. If his superior were not interested in taking the necessary action, nothing would be done.

Coordination is yet another vital as well as difficult part of any integrated program like Poshak. The fate of many schemes has been adversely affected because of inter- and intraagency rivalry and lack of communication. Knowing the difficulty, it is naturally tempting for the leaders of the organization in charge of a project to take full control and limit the involvement of other parties that could be made active participants. The short-run advantages in administrative efficiency are gained at the expense of the long-run future of the scheme. In the case of Poshak, the government of Madhya Pradesh, not CARE, would be responsible for operating the project were Poshak adopted as a permanent feature of its feeding program. Poshak would have benefited, therefore, had the government been given greater administrative responsibilities, even at the expense of short-term goals. In fact, as indicated previously, the research-oriented objectives of Project Poshak determined the arrangements made, and the coalitions of interest that might have been nurtured within the government never materialized.

Another administrative peculiarity of Project Poshak was the involvement of different ministries at the state and national levels. The involvement with nutrition of the Health Department of the state government in the early 1970s was somewhat ahead of its time, mainly because of the personal interest of the secretary. The central Ministry of Health in those years had little or no involvement in the nutrition field. At the national level, interest in Project Poshak was confined to the Ministry of Social Welfare, where the Special Nutrition Program was administered. Consequently, when the national government's Ministry of Health became more concerned with nutrition during the drafting of the Fifth Five-Year Plan and was interested in having Poshak succeed and adopted on an extended scale, there were no established Poshak connec-

137

tions between the national and state health officials.[13] It was equally awkward to have the national funds come from the national Social Welfare Ministry through the Tribal Welfare Department for programming in Madhya Pradesh by the Health Department. It was impossible for any pressure for effective performance to be exerted along this broken chain of command.

At the implementation level there was the problem of morale among the state rural health workers. Discussions with medical officers and nurse-midwives in early 1976 made it clear that they were neither able nor willing to perform preventive health measures as called for in Project Poshak. The success of Poshak lay on the shoulders of the paramedical nurse-midwife, but she was responsible for approximately 10,000 people and was already overburdened with work.[14] For example, among other responsibilities she was supposed to attend every birth in her area. Given the annual birthrate of 35 per 1000 population, she would have to attend 350 births alone. This was almost an impossible task by itself and certainly left no time for any other assignments, such as immunization and pre- and postnatal surveillance. The midwives had such a herculean task that they saw no hope in accomplishing it and often assumed the attitude that since there was no possible way for them to do any more than a small fraction of what they were supposed to do, why do anything? The medical officers expressed much the same feeling. Even if the low echelon health workers did perform well, there was little chance for recognition or promotion.

The secretary of health who initiated and supervised the early phase of Poshak made a point of motivating the low-level personnel at their training session. He would explain the importance of the project while at the same time threatening to put negative remarks in their personnel files if they performed badly in Poshak

---

[13] Based on the Poshak experience there was a special mention of the take-home approach in the draft of the Fifth Plan and the National Ministry of Health adopted the concept in its small nationwide integrated scheme (Suraksha) for the children of accepters of family planning; the south Indian state of Karnataka has also launched a program similar to Poshak.

[14] This number is actually lower than the figure assigned to a nurse midwife in Madhya Pradesh. The number of health centers in 1974 was 3,000. Dividing the state's population by this number, one midwife must cover an average of almost 14,000 people. Figures on health centers taken from *Project Poshak*, I, 15.

assignments. As is clear, then, he maintained a close surveillance over the project's progress while he was in office, and the staff responded to his interest at the highest levels.

As is common in the Indian bureaucracy, the "order down" system was followed in which officials will do as instructed if they know that someone higher up cares enough to check on what happens. Once the secretary was replaced and different orders were sent down, Poshak was shifted to a back burner at the local level. New priorities were pursued because it became apparent to local health workers that there was nothing to be gained in return for doing a good job; nor would they lose anything or be reprimanded for doing nothing since no one above them really cared about the program.[15] Therefore, attempting to put additional responsibilities on these already overworked and demoralized workers made the chances for duplicating the Poshak concept very poor from the beginning.

Finally, in retrospect, it might have been an administrative error to choose Madhya Pradesh as the location for Project Poshak. The choice was a purposeful one—if Poshak could succeed in this underdeveloped tribal state, it could succeed anywhere. This suggests again that Poshak served as a demonstration project and exacerbated the "identity crisis" referred to earlier. The danger in this approach is that if the project did not succeed in Madhya Pradesh, the whole concept could be disparaged and similar efforts discouraged. Therefore, it might be risky to choose a less developed state in which to implement a pilot project. To start with, the planning ability of a state like Madhya Pradesh was severely limited. Similarly, its underdeveloped economy restricted the financial resources that were available for programming purposes. A more progressive state would have been better able, administratively and financially, to assume the burden of a project like Poshak. Once the Poshak concept had succeeded and had been adopted in a more advanced state, the poorer states like Madhya Pradesh would have stood a better chance of eventually benefiting from it.

[15] The bureaucratic tendencies exhibited in this case are found throughout India. S. Heginbotham has written of its effects on an agricultural project in south India. See his *Cultures in Conflict: Four Faces of Indian Bureaucracy* (New York: Columbia University Press, 1975), especially chap. 7 on bureaucratic compliance systems.

Timing

The element of chance is always a factor in large projects like Poshak that extend over a long period of time. Several important events over which none of the Poshak participants had any control occurred after Project Poshak had begun operation, and altered some of the basic assumptions made during the planning of the study. First, in 1972 and 1973 political problems between the United States and India arose following the Indo-Pakistani War of 1971. USAID was in the process of phasing down its programs and the Indian government adopted a strong self-sufficiency policy. As a result, there were discussions in CARE during the spring of 1973 about bringing the feeding programs to an end within a year or two. This situation coincided with a worsening world food supply problem and the likelihood of reduced allocations for the agency. Accordingly, CARE could not accept any new commitments for food and they drew up plans to reduce existing programs.

This was the state of affairs as the Extensive phase, the most realistic pilot study, came to an end in June of 1973. The Madhya Pradesh government was faced with the task of assuming responsibility for the more than 11,000 beneficiaries of the Extensive phase with no guarantee or even likelihood that CARE commodities would be available in the future. All of a sudden, the "free" food disappeared and the project was in trouble. The state government let the program lapse, and the Poshak beneficiaries no longer received their supplementary rations at the health centers. At this point momentum was lost, and the chances of the state ever accepting or adopting the program were greatly reduced.

Another factor presented itself in the 1973-1974 period when the draft of the Fifth Five-Year Plan was formulated. In this plan the strong emphasis on nutrition resulted in a considerable increase in the amount of money budgeted for it. However, the increase was to be borne by the states and not the national government, as had been the case up to that point. The financial responsibility for several large supplementary feeding schemes was to be shifted to the states. Although they had been warned that this would happen, states like economically underdeveloped Madhya Pradesh were terribly pressed by the increased financial burden.

The financial strain, coupled with the uncertainty of CARE supplies, caused the states to assume a cautious attitude in their planning. As it turned out, the problem of supply and resources was not as great as first imagined. Because of severe droughts in 1973 and 1974, the government of India moderated its self-sufficiency policy and continued to fund some state nutrition programs because the fifth plan was never formally adopted and fourth plan procedures remained in effect. For the national government, it seemed, the political importance of the feeding schemes was too great to risk discontinuation. However, by the time the situation was clarified, the damage to Poshak had already been done. The project fieldwork had been completed and as time passed Poshak became only a memory.

CONCLUSION

The Poshak case study provides an opportunity to identify some of the reasons why schemes of this nature rarely progress beyond the initial test phase. Generalizing from this case, it is possible to suggest several factors that should be taken into consideration in order to improve the chances for similar projects in Third World countries to be adopted and implemented on an expanded basis. As mentioned, certain problems are unavoidable. However, others can be avoided if proper attention is paid to details often overlooked in the pursuit of larger, more immediate, and impressive objectives. What is suggested here will not solve all the problems that pilot projects face in the transitional period—it is merely an effort to identify points that should be taken into consideration at this critical juncture.

To begin with, and to echo a theme in several of the chapters in this volume, each party involved in the project must have a clear understanding of what the project is to accomplish. There should be no confusion as to what function the scheme serves. Failure to define the project's objectives precisely will result in disillusionment and disenchantment on the part of one or more of the participants when they realize that their needs or goals are not being fully satisfied. Once this occurs, cooperation and the future of the scheme are in doubt.

If a scheme such as Project Poshak is to reach the broader implementation stage, careful and thoughtful planning must be carried out before the study is launched. Obviously, elaborate schemes that are heavily dependent on capital inputs, large recurring appropriations, and numerous highly trained personnel stand little chance of being duplicated in a Third World country. The planners of Project Poshak were conscious of this reality. But over and above these limitations, many other factors must be considered. Such matters as the involved personnel's workload, morale, and time constraints; the government's administrative structure and procedures, as well as its capacity to implement schemes on a large scale; local supply and transport facilities— all could negatively affect the ability of the government to carry out the scheme on a permanent basis. Planners must be realistic in their appraisal of the ability of the responsible agency to adopt the scheme.

Precautions must also be taken to limit the influence of exogenous organizations, personnel, equipment, and supplies in the operation of a preliminary study. Dependence on a foreign group or on imported, sophisticated commodities leads to a feeling on the part of the adopting agency that it will be unable to continue the scheme on its own. More success might be achieved if indigenous supplies and local administrators are used from the beginning, or at least phased in as the study progresses. In this way the problem of switching from foreign to indigenous inputs at the critical time of adoption would be eliminated.

But the best laid plans are of little value unless there is a genuine interest and commitment on the part of the agency that will eventually be responsible for operating the scheme. In general the latter group does not pay much attention to pilot projects, especially those in the social sector. A middle-rank bureaucrat is usually given responsibility for the scheme's progress, while the higher echelon officials concern themselves with more politically "important" matters. All too often the government's half-hearted involvement reflects a desire on its part to demonstrate that it is doing something about a problem, although in fact, nothing is being accomplished. The project is no more than a palliative effort; no significant progress is made toward a long-term solution.

The lack of interest in pilot projects results in two tendencies on the part of collaborating organizations. One is to form a close relationship with individual officials in positions of power who demonstrate interest in the same concerns as the sponsoring group. It is through this government contact that the project receives its official sanction or blessing. The project then becomes dependent on these few administrators for continuation. The other tendency is for the outside agency to administer its project virtually independent of the agency that is expected to do the implementing in the future. At times, for the sake of convenience and efficiency, this might be tempting. However, for the sake of the scheme's longevity, the practice must be discouraged. The project must become part of the government's normal operations and not merely an appendage to it.

Often it is a particular individual or "entrepreneur" in the organizing group who becomes indispensable. The project shows impressive results because of the intensive interest and the particularly efficient and effective work of the entrepreneur. However, once this dynamic person is replaced or the program expands to such an extent that his effect is diluted, weaknesses in the system appear to prevent successful execution. It is suggested that after a project has achieved a satisfactory level of success, an approach must be systematized and made part of the normal functioning of the governmental machinery.

But the problem remains concerning how to get the government involved and interested in the project so that it will consider adoption of the approach once the preliminary fieldwork has been completed. One way is to broaden the base of support within the government. Multidepartmental coordination is, of course, difficult, but it will reduce the overreliance on the single government official and greatly improve the project's chances to survive the precarious transition phase from pilot stage to implementation by providing a measure of administrative continuity. Broadening the administrative base will also improve the project's visibility. Because pilot projects do not receive much attention, this added support could be very important when it comes time to discuss the scheme's long-term future. But more in the way of publicity is required in order to build up a constituency for the scheme. Aggressive public relations efforts during the fieldwork are a necessary part of a pilot project's life if eventual adoption is an objective.

Finally, the project's future depends on skillful maneuvering during the transition period itself. Even if the scheme has been properly run up to this point—its objectives clearly specified, limitations realistically taken into account, outside inputs limited, base of support broadened, contacts with decision makers developed, reliance on a single person reduced, and public relations work carried out—there remains the job of "selling the concept." The approach must be packaged to make it appeal, very much the way a new product might be marketed.

Realistically, it is clear that political and economic elites are not

143

greatly concerned with the nutritional status of the lowest economic strata who are virtually powerless politically. Since malnutrition is almost wholly restricted to the poor, there is little likelihood of those in power either addressing the problem or even being able to comprehend its magnitude. Therefore, it would make sense to present the project in terms of programs in which the government has placed a high priority. If, for instance, the government had a great interest in family planning or increased utilization of health centers, program promoters would be advised to stress these features of the project. This means that what might be considered as spin-off effects of the nutrition scheme are emphasized because they coincide more closely with known governmental needs and, therefore, have greater appeal. Integrated schemes such as Poshak lend themselves very neatly to such maneuvering. It seems that more time will be required before policy makers realize the vital role of nutrition in development. In the meantime, program promoters should not put all their proverbial eggs in this one basket.

This chapter has demonstrated how Project Poshak suffered because critical factors were not given proper attention. Unfortunately, in the end Poshak was not judged on whether or not it had an impact or was cost-effective. It was simply dropped, a "nondecision" caused by a series of managerial problems and mistakes that might have been prevented through more careful planning and organization.

The ideas presented above are ways to help assure that valuable efforts such as Poshak are given a fair chance to be judged on their own merits. Most of the points are obvious, but nonetheless of great importance when carrying out a pilot scheme. They might be referred to as basic guidelines for pilot project management. The proper political management and implementation of a scheme like Poshak obviously deserve at least as much attention as the design of the intervention itself. Without recognizing the importance of wise management and implementation, the entire project will suffer. The work in question is much too important to fail because of such oversight.

SIX · Administrative Decentralization and the Implementation of Housing Policy in Colombia

IRENE FRASER ROTHENBERG

ADMINISTRATIVE decentralization probably is the single structural reform most frequently proposed for Third World countries. As Annmarie Hauck Walsh notes in her comparative analysis of urban politics and intergovernmental relations, the delegation of power to local policy implementors is being debated, demanded, and analyzed by legislators, local politicians, and administrative theorists throughout the world. Almost all of the thirteen countries covered by the Walsh study have proposed or actually taken some measure explicitly designed to deconcentrate governmental authority and strengthen local units of government.[1]

Note: The author is indebted to the Midwest Universities Consortium for International Activities for support for field research in Bogotá and Cali. This case study formed a part of the author's Ph.D. dissertation, "Centralization Patterns and Policy Outcomes in Colombia" (University of Illinois, 1973); an earlier version of this paper was presented at the 1975 meetings of the American Society for Public Administration and appeared as "Impacto de la descentralización en la política habitacional de Colombia" in the *Revista Latinoamericana de administración pública*, August 1975. The author is grateful to Dr. Pedro Pablo Morcillo, Dr. Hans Rother, Dr. Gustavo Espinosa, and Dr. Gerardo Simon, four Colombians who have both studied and contributed to housing policies in their country. The comments of Robert E. Scott, Phillip Monypenny, Peter Bock, and Mauricio Solaun, members of the dissertation committee, also were very valuable to the preparation of this revised version.

[1] A. Walsh, *The Urban Challenge to Government: An International Comparison of Thirteen Cities* (New York: Frederick A. Praeger, 1969), p. 154. For other discussions of the impact of decentralization on administrative efficiency, participation, policy outcomes, political integration, and economic development, see United Nations, Department of Economic and Social Affairs, Division for Public Administration, Technical Assistance Program, *Decentralization for National and Local Development* (ST/TAO/M/19) (New York, 1962); H. Maddick, *Democracy, Decentralization and Develop-*

Because support for the principle of administrative decentralization has been so widespread, debate in most countries has focused
on how to effect specific transfers of authority to local officials or
field offices. There has been little effort to determine whether
decentralization is desirable or even feasible in all organizational
settings, nor has there been an attempt to pose crucial questions
regarding the policy consequences of increasing the autonomy of
local and provincial implementors of public policy. For example,
administrative theorists imply that decentralization will encourage
flexibility and responsiveness in policy implementation by permit-
ting greater participation at the local level, yet "there is little evidence that local government consistently involves broader public
participation in decision making than does the central government."[2] Similarly, assumptions about decentralization presume a
division between politics and administration that is never perfect
and that is even less perfect in underdeveloped countries where
resources are more scarce, civil service employment less pervasive,
and political forces more divided. Finally, most proponents of decentralization do not account for the organizational and political
setting of local and provincial implementing bodies.

Failure to consider such variables in the context of decentralization has led to the perpetuation of three fallacies regarding the
deconcentration of administrative authority:

First, decentralization is viewed as a singular process, rather
than a multi-dimensional set of relationships. Second, decentralization and centralization are treated as opposites in a zero-
sum relation, although practical experience suggests that an increase in local roles does not necessarily entail a decrease in
central power, and vice versa. And third, futile attempts are
made to formulate optimum arrangements for all programs and

ment (New York: Asia Publishing House, 1963); J. LaPalombara, "An
Overview of Bureaucracy and Political Development," in J. LaPalombara,
ed., *Bureaucracy and Political Development* (Princeton: Princeton Univer-
sity Press, 1963); M. Levy, *Modernization and the Structure of Societies*
(Princeton: Princeton University Press, 1966), pp. 58, 488; F. Riggs,
"Bureaucrats and Political Development: A Paradoxical View," in La-
Palombara, *Bureaucracy and Political Development*; G. Almond and S.
Verba, *The Civic Culture: Political Attitudes and Democracy in Five
Nations* (Boston: Little, Brown & Co., 1965), pp. 235-244.
2 Walsh, *The Urban Challenge*, p. 21.

all times, without regard for variation in values, technologies and geography.[3]

The persistence of these fallacies may explain why in most countries decentralization measures have had little impact on existing patterns of decision making and control.[4] It also suggests the kind of research that must be done so that future plans for decentralization can be more successful. Assumptions regarding the virtues of decentralized implementation patterns must be questioned rather than assumed because potential reformers require information about the *real* impact of *particular* distributions of administrative authority within *specific* organizational settings.

This volume contains two such efforts. The present chapter examines one rather unsuccessful attempt to temper political centralization with administrative decentralization by bolstering the authority of local housing officials in the provincial city of Cali, Colombia. In the following chapter, Susan Hadden explores a much more successful effort to achieve controlled decentralization in the state of Rajasthan, India.

LOCAL AUTONOMY AND HOUSING POLICY IMPLEMENTATION IN CALI

As a centralized Third World country that is undergoing pressure to expand the power of local authorities and at the same time increase governmental responses to urban problems, Colombia provides a good opportunity for testing some fundamental assumptions about the virtues of decentralization. Beginning in the 1960s, the Colombian government became a strong advocate of administrative decentralization. As part of this general policy, the central government began to delegate greater administrative authority to local planning officials and to field offices of the national housing agency, the Instituto de Crédito Territorial, or ICT. As a provincial capital and one of the fastest growing metropolitan areas in Colombia, the city of Cali was a major target of such efforts. Our case study, largely consisting of field research conducted in 1969 and 1970, sought to determine the impact of this decentralization

[3] Ibid., p. 179.
[4] Ibid., p. 154.

program on the implementation of housing policies in Cali.[5]

By most standards, Colombia was a very centralized country in 1969. Although the legislative body at each level of government—municipal, departmental, and national—was elected by the constituents of each geographical area, the executive branch was hierarchical. The president appointed and could remove at will the governors of all departments and these provincial executives had similar powers over the mayors of all municipalities. Many implementation functions formally assigned to local units of government had been assumed at least partially by national ministries and centralized independent agencies such as the ICT. As a cause and consequence of this national assumption of local administrative functions, central officials controlled a large and increasing proportion of governmental revenues. Furthermore, the traditional Conservative and Liberal parties, as well as the newer Alianza Nacional Popular (Anapo) party, were very centralized.

As many Third World countries have discovered, however, vertical centralization does not ensure political unity, for it is often accompanied by structural and party divisions, particularly at the local level. In other words, vertical centralization and horizontal decentralization often coincide. At the time of the case study, Colombia suffered an extreme form of this tendency toward intragovernmental division, thanks to a peculiar constitutional arrangement called the National Front. Under this system, two bitter rivals—the Liberal and the Conservative parties—had agreed to rotate the presidency and to divide equally all other elected and appointed offices. The inevitable result was severe factionalism within both major parties, especially at the municipal level.

Even as they were lamenting one product of centralization—the weakening and fragmentation of local government—the Colombian people were experiencing centralization of a different sort, on a regional level. Like their counterparts throughout the Third World and especially in Latin America, Colombians were migrating from rural areas and concentrating in the large municipalities. The populations of the three major cities—Medellín, Cali, and especially the capital city of Bogotá—were growing at a rate grossly disproportional to that of the rest of the country. In the municipality of Cali, capital of the department of Valle del Cauca,

[5] Field research, partially consisting of 56 open-ended interviews with 43 different national and local housing officials in Bogotá and Cali, was conducted from September 1969 to August 1970.

the population had grown from 620,000 in 1964 to 950,000 in 1970, and projections indicated a population of 2.9 million by 1985.[6] This rapid urbanization posed new problems for the officials of Cali and other major cities. Urban housing deficits multiplied; unsanitary, unsightly, and often illegal migrant settlements lacked basic services; rapidly expanding slums were thought to be a potential source of urban unrest. According to one government report, approximately 55 percent of the people in Cali lived under "highly deficient" housing conditions.[7]

Because national concentration of power coincided with regional concentration of the population, the decentralist argument acquired a special meaning in these major urban areas. Cities such as Cali were seen as victims of both urbanization and national dominance. They witnessed a multiplication of responsibilities without a commensurate increase in legal authority or financial capabilities. The promotion of local autonomy was advocated as both a prevention and a cure for urban problems. In short, Colombian reformers assumed that a strong link existed between greater administrative autonomy and increased government attention to housing and other urban problems. The 1968 decision to delegate greater authority to local implementors of housing policies provided an excellent opportunity to determine whether this presumed link indeed would materialize.

[6] República de Colombia, Instituto de Crédito Territorial, *Apuntes sobre desarrollo urbano: Memorial al VIII Congreso Nacional de Ingenieros* (Bogotá, 1966), p. 15. For other studies of urbanization in Colombia, see R. Cardona, ed., *Migración y desarrollo urbano en Colombia* (Bogotá: Asociación Colombiana de Facultades de Medicina, División de Estudios de Población, 1970); República de Colombia, Departmento Nacional de Planeación, *El desarrollo socio-económico colombiano, diagnóstica y política* (Bogotá, 1970); H. Mendoza Hoyos, "Caracteristicas generales de la población colombiana," in *Urbanización y marginalidad*, 2d ed. (Bogotá: Asociación Colombiana de Facultades de Medicina, Division de Estudios de Población, 1969).

[7] A. Osorio and G. Cobo Losado, *Cali: Criterios sobre renovación urbana y la vivienda marginal* (Cali: Instituto de Vivienda de Cali and Oficina de Planeación Municipal, Sección de Renovación Urbana, 1968), p. 28. See also República de Colombia, Departmento Nacional de Planeación, *El sector vivienda: Descripción, desarrollo, y bases de política* (Bogotá, 1970); O. Vallderruten, *Mercadeo de vivienda en Cali: Unidad residencial Santiago de Cali* (Bogotá: Instituto de Crédito Territorial, n.d.); Valle del Cauca, Oficina de Planeación, *Area Metropolitana de Cali* (Cali, 1969); P. Morcillo, "El mercado de vivienda en Colombia," *Cabildo: Organo de la Asociación Colombiana de Municipalidades* (May-June 1966), pp. 15-17.

Prior to the period under consideration here, almost all governmental housing programs for low-income families in Cali were implemented by the ICT, a national independent agency affiliated with the Ministry of Development.[8] Although this agency had field offices in cities such as Cali, almost all administrative decisions regarding personnel, budgets, housing design, and construction contracts were made in the Bogotá office. Like other such agencies, the ICT operated with considerable autonomy at the national level. Presidential decrees regulating independent agencies reserved most controls for the executive, and congressmen seldom took advantage of their few opportunities to affect institute policy.[9]

This structural arrangement was advantageous to the ICT in many ways. Because implementors in the field had little power, local political factions and interest groups could not apply pressures at the local level. The high degree of national autonomy facilitated the development of a consistent central housing policy and insulated the institute from local attempts to influence the selection of particular housing projects or construction contracts through party leaders in Congress. These advantages enabled the agency to operate a massive and efficient housing program. Between 1939 and 1970 the ICT built or financed 150,000 dwelling units and helped renovate an additional 77,000 homes.[10] As the

[8] For information regarding the structure and functions of the ICT (Institute of Territorial Credit), see República de Colombia, Presidencia de la República, Secretaría de Organización e Inspección de la Administración Pública, *Manual de organización de la rama ejecutiva del poder público* (Bogotá: Imprenta Nacional, 1970); República de Colombia, Instituto de Crédito Territorial, Oficina de Organización y Métodos, *Manual de funcionamiento* (Bogotá, 1969); C. Perez et al., "La vivienda," II: "Estudio del problema," graduation thesis, Facultad de Arquitectura Universidad del Valle, 1968, 468-472; R. Pineda, "The Colombian Instituto de Crédito Territorial: Housing for Low-Income Families," in G. Geisse and J. Hardoy, eds., *Latin American Urban Research*, II (Beverly Hills, Calif.: Sage Publications, 1972).

[9] República de Colombia, Decreto 1050 de 1968; Decreto 3130 de 1968. Although this general legislation leaves open the possibility of direct or indirect congressional representation on the directing boards of such bodies, the president himself appoints all seven ad hoc and ex officio members of the ICT board. See República de Colombia, Decreto 3098 (1963) and Decreto 2168 (1968).

[10] Instituto de Crédito Territorial, *Informe al Señor Ministro de desorrollo económico, 1970* (Bogotá, 1970), p. 24. For details see other ICT reports including: *Informe al Señor Ministro de desarrollo económico, 1968* (Bogotá, 1968); *Informe al Señor Ministro de desarrollo económico, 1969* (Bogotá,

third largest city in Colombia, Cali was a major beneficiary of these efforts. The city acquired over 21,000 ICT housing units between 1960 and 1969 alone, and it was scheduled to receive an additional 4,615 in 1970.[11]

Although the national ICT was the only Colombian agency implementing large-scale public housing programs, municipalities had considerable formal authority over land use and housing even before the administrative decentralization program began. All municipalities of over 15,000 inhabitants had a legal obligation to allocate two percent of their revenues to the construction of "sanitary housing for the working class."[12] A 1936 law required that Cali and other large municipalities allocate five percent of their budgets for this purpose.[13] In addition, local bodies had many housing-related powers that were denied the ICT: only municipal officials could tax urban land, establish regulations regarding zoning, construction, and land use, and plan the physical development of Colombian cities.[14]

The agency specifically empowered to implement Cali's own low-income housing policy was the Instituto de Vivienda de Cali (Cali Housing Institute—Invicali). This local independent agency was created in October 1966 to replace the Personería de Ejidos y Vivienda Popular, a body whose sole function was the administration of Cali's *ejidos* (common public land belonging to the municipality).[15] With its new title the agency also acquired authority

1969); and *Vivienda y desarrollo urbano* (Bogotá, n.d.). As usually occurs with housing programs that produce finished housing rather than urbanized lots, most of these units served the middle class (see Rothenberg, "Centralization Patterns and Policy Outcomes in Colombia," pp. 299-311). For a discussion of the same policy problem in Kenya, see Frederick Temple and Nelle Temple, Chap. 9 in this volume.

[11] República de Colombia, Instituto de Crédito Territorial, Seccional Cali, Oficina de Relaciones Públicas, "Número de viviendas e inversiones realizadas en la ciudad de Cali en el período 1960-1969," mimeographed, July 1970, pp. 1-5.

[12] República de Colombia, Ley 46 (1918).

[13] República de Colombia, Ley 61 (1936); Decreto Ley 1465 (1953). Municipalities with populations of 25,000 or more also have the legal right to expropriate any land required for urban programs such as housing. See República de Colombia, Ley 1 (1943); Ley 81 (1960).

[14] See P. Morcillo, "Del deterioro de Cali a una política urbana," paper prepared for the "Seminario mundial sobre mejoramiento de tugurjos y asentamientos no controlados," Medellín, February-March 1970.

[15] See República de Colombia, Ley 41 (1948).

over many local housing functions, and Invicali became—at least in theory—the municipal equivalent of the ICT. The local agency, like its national counterpart, could plan, build, renovate, rent, and sell either individual homes or housing developments for the lower classes. It could purchase and sell land, and it was empowered to provide credit for the purchase of lots and homes. Furthermore, unlike the ICT, Invicali had the specific function of "gradually eliminating unhealthy or dangerous homes from the urban areas, through appropriate programs of slum clearance, construction, and rehabilitation."[16]

Although cities such as Cali had considerable responsibility and legal authority in the area of housing, until 1969 they lacked the resources to fulfill most of these obligations in a meaningful way. Because it did not have enough money to undertake major construction or renewal projects, Invicali limited its activity to more modest pursuits. It studied the needs of slum areas; it mediated squatter attempts to acquire legal ownership of occupied land; and it administered *ejidos*.[17] In short, all effective housing power was still vested in the central office of the national ICT because of its control over funds.

The administrative decentralization movement produced two measures designed to bring the implementation of national housing policy down to the local level. The first was a mild effort to deconcentrate the ICT itself by granting additional administrative authority to field offices in cities such as Cali. Part of this reform entailed the establishment of citizen advisory boards within each regional office. But the new ICT advisors, embroiled in controversies over contracts and other matters of material interest, very shortly proved intolerably disruptive to the formerly insulated and apolitical ICT field officers in Cali. When the terms of the original advisors expired, the ICT quietly shelved all plans for appointing a new group.

Our study focuses on the second, more ambitious effort to decentralize the implementation of housing programs. In 1968, the ICT decided to loan Invicali $540,000 (10.8 million pesos) for a massive and well-publicized slum clearance project in Cali. The program involved the removal of three centrally located and densely populated slums—Fátima, Berlin, and San Francisco—and

[16] Cali, Acuerdo 102 (1966), Art. 4.

[17] Cali, Instituto de Vivienda de Cali, "Invicali: Editorial," mimeographed; Instituto de Vivienda de Cali and Oficina de Planeación Municipal, p. 22.

the construction of new homes on the urban periphery. The remainder of the $900,000 project was to be financed by a $250,000 USAID loan, other loans totaling about $20,000, and $90,000 from the municipal budget of Cali.[18]

If the first reform effort was a disappointment, the second was a disaster. By the summer of 1970, Invicali and its project were totally discredited and the ICT had assumed complete responsibility for implementing the slum clearance project. Although the failure of this particular program caused considerable political embarrassment for individual power-holders in Cali, the real culprit was the very fragmented power structure within the city. As the following analysis of the Invicali experience illustrates, geographical or vertical centralization in Colombia coexists with local horizontal decentralization, a fragmentation of municipal power that undermines efforts to increase local autonomy and governmental activity at the same time. Because other Third World countries with a long history of centralization may share this same tendency toward local disunity, the painful experience of Invicali provides a valuable lesson for would-be reformers in other major urban areas.

Fragmentation of Administrative Roles

The local government of Cali can be described as a "council-dominated" system where "councilmen play a dominant part in the exercise of executive roles that are fragmented among specialized boards, committees, or individuals."[19] Although Colombian municipal councils clearly perform many legislative duties, they have considerable executive authority as well; in fact, the Colombian Constitution classifies these bodies as "administrative corporations."[20] In keeping with this formal designation, the Cali Council either performs or controls a wide range of administrative func-

[18] See Cali, Instituto de Vivienda de Cali, "Presupuesto del Instituto de Vivienda de Cali Invicali para la Vigencia de 1970" (November 1969). The text accompanying this budget points out that "if the subsidy from the municipality of Cali were appropriated in accordance with Ley 61 (1936) . . . it would reach 5,260,000 pesos." The budget also includes a projected transfer of more than one million pesos from Emsirva. According to Invicali officials, the Emsirva quota never was delivered—nor was it ever really expected. See also *El Pais* (Cali), October 16, 1969, p. 7. One peso equaled approximately US $0.05 in 1970.

[19] Walsh, *The Urban Challenge*, p. 103.

[20] See República de Colombia, *Constitución Política de la República de Colombia* (Serrano, 1969), Art. 196.

tions. Of the sixty-four local ordinances passed between 1966 and 1968, for example, nine were significant legislative acts—setting the municipal budget, establishing guidelines for independent agencies, and creating municipal offices or agencies. Forty-five, however, were acts involving minor budgetary alterations, the purchase and sale of public land, and other details of local management. Another ten ordinances focused on such symbolic gestures as designating street names and honoring civic leaders.[21] This council participation in the minutiae of local government inevitably fragments executive roles by limiting the mayor's control over local administration.

The establishment of semiindependent single purpose implementing agencies such as Invicali further atomizes local administrative authority. Organization charts of the municipality depict the mayor as the administrative chief; under him appear the Departments of Education, Government, Public Works, Public Health, etc. As at the national level, however, independent agencies provide most of the major services such as roads and sidewalks (Valorización), parks and sanitation (Emsirva), or water, sewage, electricity, and telephones (Emcali). By 1969, these newer bodies had acquired resources and powers that completely overshadowed those of the municipality itself. The expenditures of Emcali ($27.4 million), Valorización ($4.2 million), Emsirva ($2 million), and Invicali ($.6 million) accounted for over nine-tenths of the combined local agency budgets, while the $4.2 million spent by the municipality itself represented only one-tenth. Even more importantly, neither the mayor nor the council as a body had much control over these expeditures, for only the Valorización budget required council approval.[22]

But local independent agencies differ from their national counterparts in one very significant way. Central bodies such as the ICT are tied to the executive branch; most controls over local agencies emanate from the municipal council. In fact, councilmen often establish these agencies as a very deliberate device to take power away from the mayor.[23] The mayor lacks the extensive decree

[21] See Rothenberg, "Centralization Patterns and Policy Outcomes in Colombia," p. 226 for a more thorough analysis of these ordinances.

[22] P. Morcillo, "La nueva administración municipal: Bases para una reforma administrativa," *Cabildo: Organo de la Asociación Colombiana de Municipalidades* (September-October 1969), p. 54.

[23] V. Contreras, *Barrancabermeja: Estudio socioeconómico y administra-*

power accorded the president, for example, and thus the municipal council must pass all changes in the structure and functions of Invicali.[24] Similarly, because the local executive does not enjoy the budgetary prerogatives of his national counterpart, councilmen have a large role in determining the size of municipal grants to Invicali.

Domination of the board of directors undoubtedly is the most critical source of legislator influence over Invicali. While Congress names no ICT directors, councilmen provide, from their own ranks, four of the eight Invicali directors. The other four include the mayor or his representative, the manager of Emcali, the head of the Municipal Planning Office or his representative, and "a representative designated by the financiers of Invicali."[25] At most, the mayor can count on two votes in board deliberations—his own and that of his appointee, the planning manager. Councilmen, on the other hand, have four votes. This weighting of the board in favor of the local legislature is crucial because the directors personally make most of the major—and minor—decisions regarding agency staffing and administrative details in the implementation of particular housing programs.

Authority to select personnel was the most jealously guarded prerogative of the directors serving in 1969-1970. The board was authorized "to intervene in the appointment of Institute officials paid monthly salaries of 2,000 pesos [$100] or more."[26] This stipulation applied to fifteen of Invicali's forty-five employees in June 1970.[27] Interviews with board members indicated that this particular responsibility was taken most seriously because personnel questions provided a battleground for political rivalries among directors. The ordinance was vague about what this authority to "intervene" in personnel selection actually meant, particularly since the Invicali manager had the authority to "appoint and remove all employees."[28] In practice, however, this intervention was extensive, because the directors selected the manager. The ordi-

---

tivo del municipio (Bogotá: Centro de Estudios sobre Desarrollo Económico, Universidad de los Andes, 1970), p. 17. See also Morcillo, "La Nueva Administración," pp. 50-57.

[24] Cali, Acuerdo 102 (1966).

[25] Cali, Acuerdo 102, Art. 12.

[26] Cali, Acuerdo 102, Art. 15, sec. o.

[27] Information computed from Invicali personnel files.

[28] Cali, Acuerdo 102 (1966), Art. 17, sec. f.

nance solemnly noted that six board members must approve the selection of manager and that the latter is "elected for a two-year period," but the next sentence pointed out that this manager "may be removed freely by the same board."[29]

Directors also had—and exercised—many controls over the structure and policies of the agency. They were required to approve the budget and all contracts and other financial transactions; they organized and regulated the institution's structure; and they established the rent and selling price of all Invicali properties.[30] Invicali directors spent many meeting hours deliberating the details of such decisions. According to one director, they sometimes spent hours discussing what to do about the fact that someone had not paid the rent.

In short, councilmen exerted a strong influence on Invicali operations. As a member of the Invicali board and as the initiator of much local legislation, the mayor did have some housing powers, but the strength of council control over Invicali caused at least fragmentation—and probably council dominance—of both administrative and legislative housing roles. In other words, control over Invicali operations was divided between the mayor and the councilmen, and the latter probably had the upper hand.

Ironically, national (and international) subsidies or loans to local institutions often exacerbate this local fragmentation of power by channeling funds directly to local independent agencies instead of through the mayor. The situation of Invicali was somewhat exceptional because this housing institute was the only Cali agency receiving a subsidy from the 1969 budget and because the 1969 national grant to Invicali took the form of a loan. But even in this case, national funds were able to substitute vertical controls for horizontal ones. As stated earlier, Invicali received almost $90,000 from the municipality in 1969, but it also acquired an ICT loan of $540,000.[31] Because of the size of the ICT loan, the national agency became concerned about Invicali operations, and central housing officials became involved in many aspects of the local

---

[29] Cali, Acuerdo 102, Art. 16.

[30] Cali, Acuerdo 102, Art. 15.

[31] Cali, Acuerdo 005 (1968) (Presupuesto para 1969), p. 4. International loans can have a similar effect. The World Bank granted Emcali a $27.5 million loan in 1970. See *El Pais* (Cali), April 10, 1970. The municipality itself acquired only $50 in national or international funds that year.

housing project. If the local agency was answerable to the city administration, it was even more answerable to the ICT.

Partisan and Factional Divisions

The structure of local government and the distribution of budgetary resources combine to encourage the fragmentation of municipal power in housing and other policy areas. During the 1969-1970 case study period, the structure of the local party system ensured this fragmentation by fomenting divisions among councilmen and therefore inevitably politicizing the implementing agencies they controlled. Although the Colombian party system tends to be centralized geographically under the leadership of self-perpetuating national directorates, it usually is divided at each level of government. The historical polarization of the Colombian electorate around the Liberal and Conservative party labels divides the nation into two camps—often armed—recruited on the basis of "hereditary hatreds."[32] This mutual antagonism between the two parties has not brought unity in either of them, however. Party identification has been a given, and disputes over personalities, ideologies, jobs, and interests have occurred within the parties.[33]

At the time of the case study, Colombia was living under a unique constitutional arrangement designed to correct the excesses produced by the historical division between the two parties. Distressed over both the continuing violence and party exclusion from political life, Liberal and Conservative leaders had signed the Pact of Sitges on July 20, 1957, establishing a National Front government. This agreement, sanctioned by a 1957 plebiscite and broadened by later interparty negotiations, introduced three important constitutional changes. The first was the principle of parity, which established that Liberals and Conservatives should divide equally all seats in all legislative bodies. The Constitution required parity in appointed positions as well, from the Supreme Court down to the lowest positions in the local bureaucracies and inde-

[32] R. Dix, *Colombia: The Political Dimensions of Change* (New Haven: Yale University Press, 1967), pp. 205-216. One recent result was *La Violencia*, a period of civil war followed by Gustavo Rojas Pinilla's 1953-1957 military dictatorship.

[33] See Dix, *Colombia*, pp. 216-221; J. Martz, *Colombia: A Contemporary Political Survey* (Chapel Hill: University of North Carolina Press, 1962), pp. 33-147; J. Payne, *Patterns of Conflict in Colombia* (New Haven: Yale University Press, 1968), pp. 194-196.

pendent agencies. Probably by intent, the equal division of power between the two groups excluded challenging political movements, although new groups managed to evade this problem to some extent by tacking "Liberal" or "Conservative" tags on their party labels. A predictable but unintended effect of the parity arrangement was the increase of factionalism *within* the traditional parties. Each party was guaranteed half of the legislative seats. Because the determination of which individuals would hold these reserved seats followed a system of proportional representation, ambitious political groups drew up separate party slates, competing among themselves for shares of the fixed Conservative or Liberal quota.

To keep one party or another from single-handedly dominating any institution, the Constitution introduced a second requirement that most measures must be decided by a two-thirds majority vote. This provision obviously increased the ability of all legislatures to impede or delay governmental programs. A third amendment introduced the principle of alternation in the presidency, stipulating that this office alternate every four years between the two parties. This provision, like the parity arrangement, discouraged new political groups but promoted factionalism within the traditional parties.[34]

One of the most important consequences of the National Front was a multiplication and an escalation of conflict in the municipality. The fragmentation of the two vertically centralized and competitive parties encouraged conflict among councilmen and thereby imposed new bases for division on a fragmented governmental structure. National dominance of these factions further disrupted local government by accelerating turnover within local legislatures. Because councilmen played a vital role in local bodies such as Invicali, this atomization and discontinuity inevitably carried over to independent agencies as well.

The 1968-1970 Cali Council reflected both the constitutionally

[34] Most of these amendments remained in effect at the time of this investigation, although the 1968 constitutional reform provides for their gradual phaseout. In 1970 the parity principle did not apply to elections for the municipal councils or departmental assemblies; the 1974 elections required neither parity for Congress nor alternation for the presidency; and in 1978 the parity requirement was dropped for appointment of governors, mayors, and other administrative officials. The 1968 constitutional reform dropped the two-thirds rule for legislation, except in matters relating to the National Front phaseout itself. See *Constitución política de la República de Colombia*, Arts. 83, 114, 120, and 172.

supported bifurcation between Liberals and Conservatives and the attendant factionalism as well. The sixteen councilmen who served during the case study period represented six different factions, three Liberal and three Conservative. This factionalism continued despite the 1970 abandonment of the parity requirement for local legislatures. The 1970 elections saw nineteen slates for the twenty council seats and produced councilmen representing seven different factions.[35]

Central control of Colombian parties and their factions further eroded the unity of local government by ensuring continual rotation of councilmen. An examination of Cali's *Gazeta Municipal* reveals that 180 different individuals were councilmen or alternates between 1958 and 1972.[36] Since elections occur every two years, a legislator sitting continuously since 1958 would have served seven terms. As Table 6-1 indicates, however, no individual

TABLE 6-1
TENURE OF CALI COUNCILMEN AND ALTERNATES, 1958-1972

Number of Terms Served	Number of Councilmen
1	149
2	19
3	6
4	4
5	1
6	1
7	0
Total	180

Source: Computed from Cali, *Gazeta Municipal*, 1958-1970.

[35] The number of seats on the Cali Council was expanded prior to the 1970 elections. The distribution of seats among factions is determined by using an "electoral quotient." "The quotient is the number which results from dividing the total number of valid votes by the number of seats available. . . . The distribution of seats to each list will be done in proportion to the number of times which the quotient fits into the number of valid votes." (During the National Front, the number of valid party votes, rather than the total number of valid votes, was used as the base.) See *Constitución política*, Art. 172. The candidates whose names appear first on the faction lists are seated first.

[36] An alternate or *suplente* is a substitute who takes office if a councilman cannot serve. This substitution occurs quite frequently because the councilman often wins simultaneous election to a higher office. Legislators serving more than one term frequently alternate between councilman and alternate status. For this reason, these alternates are included in our calculations of turnover in the municipal council.

served seven terms, and 149 of the 180 sat on the council for only two years. Most of these single-term councilmen retired not through electoral defeat but because they lost or abdicated favored positions on the faction candidate lists. Incumbents seldom were nominated again; even those heading faction lists tended to be newcomers. The 1970 election, for example, produced seven winning slates for the Cali Council. Of the seven individuals heading these slates, only two were former councilmen. Similarly, only two alternates heading their lists had council experience. The Liberales Oficialistas had five council seats in 1968 and six seats in 1970, but only the head of the ticket served during both terms.

Because central party and faction leaders controlled the nomination process at all levels of government, municipal councils became appendages of the national parties; by nationalizing political rewards, vertical centralization in the party system exacerbated political fractionalization at the municipal level.[37] The position of local legislator in a city the size of Cali frequently was a trial run for aspirants to a political career; thus six of the ten senators representing Valle del Cauca in the 1970 Congress were former Cali councilmen. Three of the four senators lacking experience on the Cali Council became *new* councilmen in 1970.[38] This occurred because party and faction leaders, anxious to retain control over the legislatures of major cities, often chose prominent national figures to head local lists. In the 1970 Cali election, for example, the victorious council candidates represented seven separate lists, headed in every case by a nationally prominent individual. Three men topped lists for both the Senate and the Cali Council; one woman led her faction's slate for the House and for the Cali Council; presidential candidate Belisario Betancur headed a fifth council slate; the sixth was led by a past House member and unsuccessful Senate candidate in 1970; and a nationally prominent Communist headed the seventh slate.

As a result, parties and factions were so centralized that councilmen had neither the time nor the motivation to become involved with local issues or to forge policy-oriented alliances with their

[37] P. Morcillo and H. Castaño, "La Administración y financiamiento de los municipios y de los departamentos con referencia exclusiva al Valle del Cauca," *La nueva economía*, IV (June 1968), 112.

[38] See Cali, *Gazeta Municipal*, 1958-1970. The one senator who was neither an old nor a new councilman in 1970 was a former governor of Valle.

fellow councilmen. To succeed, a local legislator must advance the interests of his faction. He must oppose the mayor if their factions are in conflict; he must seek employment for local faction members; and he must limit the powers and activities of institutions headed by opponents.

The Politicization of Invicali

Independent agencies such as Invicali provide excellent sites for these partisan and factional skirmishes; they continuously award contracts, hire new employees, and undertake well-publicized public works projects. The division of executive roles in Cali ensured councilmen a strong voice in such decisions, but party divisions discouraged these local legislators from speaking in harmony. The National Front parity requirement escalated the level of conflict by guaranteeing the representation of rival groups on the Invicali board and thereby politicizing even the most mundane administrative decisions made by the agency.

Between 1969 and 1970, the frequency and intensity of such political conflicts virtually paralyzed the operations of Invicali. The board was riddled with personal antagonisms as well as bitter political rivalries. The urban renewal project was virtually stagnant, and the agency was discredited at both the national and local levels. Officials from the ICT, the council, the mayor's office, and Invicali itself charged that political intrigues always absorbed the energies of the local housing agency. Board members echoed this denunciation, although each director placed the blame on the others. According to the directors and the other Invicali officials interviewed, the agency had been a center for petty political quarrels since its days as the Personería de Ejidos. Board meetings became chaotic quarrels because factions opposed to the manager trusted neither his judgment nor his competence, and the various factions represented on the board were more concerned with personnel than with housing policy. These antagonisms among directors extended far beyond the political level. Some directors claimed they stopped attending meetings because of their intense dislike for other individuals present. Respondents frequently accused other directors and top Invicali officials of dishonesty, corruption, criminal activities, and sexual deviance. Whatever the truth of these charges, their frequency attests to the high level of politicization and conflict among the directors and staff of the implementing agency.

161

These bitter and intense divisions on the board created a direct
impediment to Invicali activity. Political rather than technical factors determined where the agency bought land, legalized squatter
settlements, or directed urban renewal efforts. For example, one
important Invicali function was to regularize illegal settlements
by mediating and arranging the purchase by squatters of the land
they occupied ("legalization"). As a past Invicali official pointed
out, however, the politically divided directors were unable to authorize a comprehensive solution to this problem.

> Legalization is a mess because each faction wants to get credit
> for it. When we were in Invicali, we studied the problem for a
> long time and presented a general plan for legalization of these
> squatter settlements. We would purchase the land with bonds
> and then sell the property to the squatters at a low cost. But the
> Board did not approve the proposal because two competing fac-
> tions united against it. They didn't want our faction to get credit
> for the plan. They were afraid we would make political capital
> out of it and use it in the next elections. They were correct, of
> course.[39]

Because antagonistic directors attached strategic value to policy
questions, discussion of these issues commonly produced deadlock
on the Invicali board. An even more significant deterrent to housing activity was the relatively low priority of these policy questions
themselves. In other words, directors did divide over issues, but
they focused most of their energies on other matters. According to
most respondents, personnel selection was the primary concern of
directors, and the major battles among directors involved the distribution of patronage jobs in the agency. During the National
Front, the parity requirement guaranteed equal representation of
Liberals and Conservatives, but the strength of each faction on the
board determined which particular groups of Liberals and Conservatives received Invicali positions.

The shifting strength of each faction on this patronage-oriented
board in turn produced an extremely high turnover of Invicali
employees. Table 6-2 shows that 36 of the 45 people working for
the agency in June of 1970 arrived less than a year before, while
only four individuals had over two years experience with the
agency. More importantly, new appointees filled all but one of the

[39] Personal Interview, April 15, 1970.

162

15 managerial posts, the positions paying over 2,000 pesos ($100) a month and therefore requiring board intervention. Although an expansion of the agency in 1969 accounted for some of these new faces, most of the arrivals were part of a very rapid and continuing pattern of turnover within the agency. The three years between June 1967 and June 1970 saw the arrival and subsequent departure of 53 employees. Thirty-one of these people served less than one year.[40]

TABLE 6-2
TENURE OF INVICALI EMPLOYEES AS OF JUNE 22, 1970

Monthly Salary in Pesos	Number of Individuals Employed						
	Under 1 Year	1 Year	2 Years	3 Years	4 Years	5 Years or More	Total
Under 1,000	6	0	0	0	0	0	6
1,001-2,000	16	5	0	1	1	1	24
2,001-3,000	3	0	0	0	0	1	4
3,001-4,000	3	0	0	0	0	0	3
4,001-5,000	0	0	0	0	0	0	0
5,001-6,000	3	0	0	0	0	0	3
6,001-7,000	0	0	0	0	0	0	0
7,001-8,000	3	0	0	0	0	0	3
8,001-9,000	1	0	0	0	0	0	1
9,001-10,000	0	0	0	0	0	0	0
Over 10,000	1	0	0	0	0	0	1
Total	36	5	0	1	1	2	45
Percentage	80.00	11.11	0.00	2.22	2.22	4.44	100.00

Source: Computed from Invicali personnel files. Figures include time spent by employees in the Personería de Ejidos before 1967. Percentages do not add to 100 because of rounding.

Turnover during the case study period reached dizzying proportions. In July of 1969, Alfonso Mora Rengifo became Invicali's fourth manager in two years. The very next month saw the departure of 11 employees, and September brought 23 new people to the agency. By June 22, 1970, Mora Rengifo had fired or accepted resignations from 31 employees and hired 42 people—a remarkable achievement, considering the fact that the agency's total June payroll included only 45 people.[41] Although the turnover rate had dwindled by April and May, agency officials already were packing their bags in anticipation of a new purge. The man-

[40] Computed from Invicali personnel files.
[41] Computed from Invicali personnel files.

ager faced a crisis on the board, and the council elections completed in April would put different factions in control of Invicali. Few
housing officials expected to survive.[42]

In Colombia, as in most Third World countries, high turnover
rates are very common in municipal governments. Low pay scales,
the lack of civil service regulations, and the higher prestige accorded national governmental bodies all contribute to this problem.[43] These factors, however, do not account for the exceptionally
short tenure of Invicali officials. At the beginning of 1970, less
than 10 percent of the total number of municipal employees in
Cali's departments had held their jobs for less than a year, but
new Invicali recruits accounted for 80 percent of that agency's
employees. As Table 6-3 reveals, the percentage of inexperienced
Invicali officials finds no equal in any dependency of Cali's executive branch or in the local office of the ICT.

TABLE 6-3
TENURE OF LOCAL EMPLOYEES IN 1970, BY INSTITUTION

		Percentage of Individuals Employed					
Institution	Number Employed	Under 1 Year	1 Year	2 Years	3 Years or More	No Data	Total
Mayor's Office	88	5.69	12.50	6.82	75.00	0.00	100.00
Planning	91	19.78	6.59	9.89	63.74	0.00	100.00
Assessor	93	24.73	21.50	9.68	44.09	0.00	100.00
Treasury	100	11.00	29.00	10.00	48.00	2.00	100.00
Controller	51	19.61	13.73	11.76	52.94	1.96	100.00
City Attorney	17	5.88	17.65	5.88	70.59	0.00	100.00
Government	267	8.99	10.86	10.49	69.66	0.00	100.00
Public Works	448	4.91	3.35	4.69	80.13	6.92	100.00
Public Health	424	8.25	6.13	5.19	80.20	0.24	100.00
Education	223	3.59	2.24	6.73	87.45	0.00	100.00
Revenue	82	25.61	8.54	3.66	62.20	0.00	100.00
Total Municipality	1,884	9.45	8.39	6.90	73.40	1.86	100.00
ICT (Cali)	141	22.70	18.44	3.55	55.32	0.00	100.00
Invicali	45	80.00	11.11	0.00	8.88	0.00	100.00

Sources: Invicali figures are computed from personnel files for the agency, June
22, 1970. ICT figures are computed from personnel files of ICT, Cali office, June
30, 1970. Others are from Eduardo Caicedo Ruiz, unpublished M.A. thesis research, Department of Industrial Administration, Universidad del Valle, 1970. Percentages do not add to 100 because of rounding.

[42] Mora Rengifo himself resigned in July 1970.
[43] See Morcillo and Castaño, "La administración," p. 118.

Only the agency's legislative ties can explain the extremely short tenure of Invicali employees. Municipal housing officials, in contrast to their colleagues in the regular city administration and in the ICT Cali field office, served at the whim of a very politicized and very divided board dominated by councilmen, and the agency was sensitive to any shift in the strength of alliances or factions in the legislature. Both the directors and the employees of Invicali recognized this. Board members frequently referred to "my secretaries" or "his bookkeeper," and employees measured their days by the power of their political patrons.

The Paralysis of Policy Implementation

Normal activity was impossible under these circumstances. By the time an employee had located his desk, it seemed he must begin to clean it out. Formal lines of administrative authority were ineffective because workers owed their positions to outside politicians rather than to their temporary superiors. Institutional loyalties failed to develop because there was not enough time and because employees resented the insecurity of their positions. At best, one wave of officials would manage to lay the groundwork for implementing a project, but the next group would be unwilling to follow through on plans bearing the signatures of predecessors.

Perhaps more importantly, personnel disputes and other patronage concerns left little time for policy implementation. A confrontation among directors in April 1970, illustrates this problem.[44] Several councilmen on the board were displeased because recent personnel shifts had favored rival factions, and these disgruntled legislators demanded the resignation of the manager, Mora Rengifo. Intrafactional rivalry between the mayor and Mora's supporters complicated this crisis. Directors spent the next two months circulating petitions, issuing press releases, and negotiating the factional representation of Invicali employees. Mora and several others resigned in July. The board then commenced meetings to elect a new manager, but by this time the councilmen elected in April were ready to replace the directors themselves. During this entire period, the political crisis took precedence over the work of the agency itself. The board was not discussing issues, and the employees spent their time reading help wanted ads. Because confrontations of this nature were very frequent, directors had little time or energy for implementing housing programs.

[44] See *El Pais* and *Occidente* (Cali), April-July 1970.

165

The recurring personnel crises, the high turnover of employees, and the extreme levels of politicization virtually paralyzed the agency during the period of the case study. The widely publicized slum clearance and relocation project experienced one delay after another. Since at that time Invicali was the only local body empowered to implement housing programs, and since this institution received all of the municipal funds designated for low-cost housing, stagnation of the agency meant immobilization of all municipal construction efforts.

The escalation of paralyzing political crises within Invicali coincided with mounting public pressures for action. The squatter settlements slated for clearance were located along the Cauca river; sewage flowing into the river posed a permanent health hazard and periodic floods exacerbated the problem. Nevertheless, a 1968 government survey revealed that residents of Fátima, Berlin, and San Francisco, like the Brazilian favela dwellers described by Janice Perlman in Chapter Ten of this volume, initially rejected the idea of relocation because they could not afford to pay for lodging or land and because their present homes were close to transportation and employment facilities. A concentrated effort by social workers in 1969 secured a reversal of this opinion, so that by the time of the case study it was reported that 80 percent of the affected residents favored the Invicali project.[45] This increasing acceptance of the project coincided with the decreasing ability of Invicali to deliver. Public pressures began to mount, no doubt fanned by political opponents of the Invicali manager. A severe flood in June of 1970 turned this grumbling into outrage. A short but powerful rainstorm caused polluted waters to rush through the squatter settlements, sweeping away seven makeshift homes and causing extensive flood damage to almost all of the others.[46] Four days later, over a thousand victims demonstrated before municipal offices, demanding official attention to this latest calamity, and the press reported rumors that residents of areas slated for clearance intended to implement the Invicali project themselves by taking over the land designated for their new homes.[47]

[45] Instituto de Crédito Territorial, Seccional Cali, "Resultados de investigación e informe sobre la zona de tugurios de los barrios Fátima, Berlin, y San Francisco de la Ciudad de Cali" (Cali, Colombia: República de Colombia, n.d.).

[46] *Occidente* (Cali), June 13, 1970, p. 3.

[47] Ibid., June 17, 1970, p. 3; *El Tiempo* (Bogotá), June 28, 1970, p. 19.

The result was inevitable. The ICT purchased the land acquired by the local agency for the housing plan and assumed total responsibility for the Invicali project.[48] This "nationalization" of the housing program encountered no local resistance. Municipal stalemate produced centralization by default and thus reinforced the traditional Colombian pattern of vertical centralization and horizontal decentralization. Just as national dominance of legal authority, financial resources, and partisan controls aggravated the atomization of local power, this municipal fragmentation in turn left national implementing agencies as the only alternative to inertia or chaos.

LOCAL AUTONOMY AND POLICY IMPLEMENTATION:
SOME CONCLUSIONS

The Invicali fiasco was extremely painful—to embarrassed local officials, to harried national housing experts, and, most of all, to the homeless of Cali. One hopes, therefore, that some benefit might be derived from this experience, that insights drawn from this case might provide a valuable and less painful lesson for officials in other Third World countries.

Is it possible to generalize from the Invicali experience? The particulars of the case certainly are uncommon: a history of bitter —often violent—party rivalry, a bizarre constitutional configuration that no longer exists even in Colombia, and an ill-timed flood. These factors combined to make decentralization a disaster. But the lesson of Invicali is much broader. Clearly there are circumstances under which decentralization is disadvantageous and would-be reformers well might examine some of these circumstances before leaping aboard the decentralist bandwagon. In particular, the Cali case suggests that one might look for the following danger signals:

1. *A structurally divided local government.* Devolution of authority from an executive-dominated central government to a less unified local administration inevitably will slow the pace of implementation, at least temporarily.
2. *A politically divided local government.* Factionalism may

[48] Instituto de Crédito Territorial, Seccional Cali, Oficina de Relaciones Públicas, "Programa de erradicación de tugurios de los barrios Fátima, Berlin, y San Francisco" (Cali, Colombia: Republica de Colombia, July 1970); *Occidente* (Cali), July 14, 1970, p. 15.

have reached unprecedented levels in National Front Colombia, but milder instances of local disunity are quite frequent in the Third World.

3. *A patronage-oriented party system.* In Third World countries with high unemployment and ineffective civil service systems, patronage concerns may be paramount to local leaders. The combination of patronage and intense party rivalry can be devastating, as we have seen.

4. *Historically unresponsive local agencies.* One could readily collect examples of local institutions that are not accountable to their constituencies or clientele groups. Yet there are other cities in which local officials traditionally are far more responsible. One explanation for such differences may be divergences in political culture from one city to the next, even within the same country. In Colombia, for example, the political structure and political culture of Medellín (capital of the department of Antioquía) differs dramatically from that of Cali. Residents of Medellín are said to be more hardworking, responsible, and civic-minded, more imbued with the "Protestant ethic."[49] It is interesting to note that the ICT was relatively pleased with its efforts to decentralize in Medellín. The political culture of Cali, unfortunately, probably is more typical of the country as a whole.

It is not likely that all of these danger signals will appear in most Third World cities—at least one hopes not—but it is quite possible that at least one will be present. The Cali case shows that these four factors in the aggregate can spell disaster for a decentralization effort. Even separately, however, they might prove troublesome.

In short, the lesson of Invicali is that increasing the autonomy of a fragmented local government almost inevitably slows the pace of implementation. Other Third World countries are not apt to encounter the same divisive forces faced by the Colombian municipality; in fact, the end of the National Front already is altering the nature of party competition in Cali itself. But it is likely that

[49] See for example D. Dent, "Oligarchy and Power Structure in Urban Colombia: The Case of Cali," *Latin American Studies*, VI (1974), 113-133; A. Portes and J. Walton, *Urban Latin America: The View from Above and Below* (Austin: University of Texas Press, 1976), chap. 4; L. Fajardo, *The Protestant Ethic of the Antioqueños: Social Structure and Personality* (Cali: Ediciones Departamento de Sociología, Universidad del Valle, n.d.).

many other local governments face comparable levels of institutional, budgetary, or partisan fragmentation. Ironically, this local disunity may be most prevalent in those countries needing decentralization the most, for vertical centralization and local fragmentation seem to be mutually reinforcing.

As Susan Hadden shows in the following chapter on controlled decentralization in Rajasthan, India, administrative decentralization is not always a disastrous political reform. The careful, selective, and controlled delegation of authority to a reasonably competent and politically unified local or provincial government undoubtedly can yield administrative efficiency rather than administrative inertia. In fact, even in Colombia there may be one or two cities such as Medellín which could use such powers wisely. In a politically fragmented city such as the Cali of 1969-1970, however, controlled decentralization was ineffective, for there was no power center to control and therefore no activity to channel. Even the ICT's substantial influence over the allocation of Invicali money could not defeat the forces of inertia. Although the ICT could have prevented the local agency from doing the wrong thing, it was powerless to prevent inaction.

Local autonomy may be pursued as an end in itself, as a value more important than substantive policy outcomes. If it is advocated as a means, however, decision makers must question rather than assume the relationship between administrative decentralization and successful implementation of public policy. The homeless of Cali probably receive little comfort from the knowledge that the public officials who failed to act live in Cali rather than in Bogotá.

SEVEN · Controlled Decentralization and Policy Implementation: The Case of Rural Electrification in Rajasthan

SUSAN G. HADDEN

DECENTRALIZATION is one of the most widely advocated reforms in public administration. Its major advantages are said to be that it increases participation, responsiveness, and efficiency in government.[1] Although decentralization is supposed to improve performance throughout the policy process, its major contribution comes at the stage of implementation. This is because decentralization allows officials to alter programs slightly to meet local needs and gives beneficiaries a chance to participate in implementation. Thus, decentralization minimizes the effects of many of the impediments to implementation such as unusual local conditions, strong opposition to means or ends by local groups, or the inability to predict and control multiple interacting decisions by a variety of groups.[2]

Note: The author is indebted to the National Defense Foreign Language Program for support for field research in India, 1969-1970. Lloyd I. Rudolph and Theodore Lowi commented upon this work when it was a draft of a dissertation. Later comments were made by Norman Uphoff, who also arranged for Cornell University's Rural Development Committee to publish a monograph based on the dissertation. Portions of this article are taken from that monograph: *Decentralization and Rural Electrification in Rajasthan, India*.

[1] This summary of the benefits and abuses of decentralization comes from E. Nordlinger and J. Hardy, "Urban Decentralization: An Evaluation of Four Models," *Public Policy*, 20 (Summer 1972), 359-396. Critics of decentralization tend to focus on the greater likelihood of tyrannies of the majority prevailing in small units and upon the difficulties of reconciling the goals of increased participation and increased efficiency.

[2] The phrase about multiple interacting decisions is from J. Pressman and A. Wildavsky, *Implementation* (Berkeley: University of California Press, 1973), p. 123.

Planners in Third World countries have been especially impressed by claims for increased efficiency through administrative reform, for acute scarcity of resources makes it essential to achieve maximum output. Indeed, when resources are scarce, the very stability of the political system may be dependent upon using every resource to the fullest. Development must occur quickly enough that the demands placed upon the system by newly mobilized groups can be met before they undermine the viability of the regime.

In India, the potential benefit of increased efficiency strengthens a predisposition toward decentralization dating from the colonial period and Gandhi's ideal of the self-sufficient village. Planning from below has been part of the official policy formulation process since 1959, when Rajasthan became the first state to initiate "panchayati raj." This "regime of village councils" consists of parallel political and administrative structures that begin in the village and pyramid vertically through the block to the district and then to the state level. The political structures at each level are composed of representatives of the next lowest level.

As in other countries, Indians found that the trouble with decentralization was that development goals often took second place to political ones in the implementation of policy. Political pressures that had previously been brought to bear on whole hierarchies of bureaucrats could be focused on individual administrators, who usually buckled and allowed political considerations to dominate administrative ones. If the effect of decentralization is in fact to render development administrators more vulnerable to increased political pressure, can it also increase efficiency? The preponderance of evidence suggests not. A large literature describes incident after incident in which decentralization is initiated with high hopes and ends in waste, disorder, and despair.[3]

This case study examines the effects of decentralization as a strategy for implementation on an important development program in India, rural electrification (RE). The emphasis in the study is on efficiency and its relationship to local participation and

[3] For example, see D. Potter, *Government in Rural India* (London: London School of Economics, 1964); M. V. Mathur et al., *Panchayati Raj in Rajasthan* (New Delhi: Impex, 1966); and N. Nicholson, "Panchayati Raj, Rural Development, and the Political Economy of Village India" (Ithaca, N.Y.: Rural Development Committee, Cornell University, Occasional Paper No. 1, 1973). Also see Rothenberg, Chap. 6 in this volume.

171

bureaucratic responsiveness. Contrary to the findings of most writers, in the rural electrification program in the state of Rajasthan, efficiency was not sacrificed to participation and responsiveness. The reason is that, in this case, decentralization was controlled. That is, higher level administrators established enforceable criteria for program participation that ensured that program goals would be met by not allocating funds to projects that did not fulfill the criteria. At the same time, the power to select direct program beneficiaries was delegated to lower level governmental bodies.

Controlled decentralization is a technique with widespread applicability that could be of considerable importance in improving the success with which the implementation of programs furthers policy goals. In this chapter, the general characteristics and uses of controlled decentralization are explored following a discussion of the implementation of the rural electrification program in Rajasthan, India, where the technique was employed. The study is preceded by a brief discussion of the analytical tools used to assess the success of program implementation.

CRITERIA, EFFICIENCY, AND IMPLEMENTATION

Rajasthan is a large state in northern India, just south and west of Delhi. It is distinguished by its colorful folk art, by the martial character of its dominant caste, and by its near-desert climate. Rich soil goes untilled despite India's need for food because of the general lack of rain. In such conditions, rural electrification provides a cheap means of lifting underground water to the surface, where it can be used for irrigation. A farmer with an electrified pump set can increase his production three- to eight-fold, because an assured supply of water allows him to make use of high yielding grain varieties and to raise two or three crops each year.[4]

Unfortunately, shortages of funds and materials available to the government mean that only two or two and a half percent of Rajasthan's 32,000 villages can be electrified in any one year. With minor exceptions, it can be assumed that all villages would like to

[4] On Rajasthan, see among others R. Sisson, *The Congress Party in Rajasthan* (Berkeley: University of California Press, 1972). Data and references on rural electrification in S. Hadden, "The Political Economy of Agricultural Policy: Rural Electrification in Rajasthan, India," Ph.D. diss. University of Chicago, 1972.

receive electricity to be used for irrigation, for lifting drinking water, for lighting streets, homes, and schools, and for powering machines for cottage industries. Thus, the selection of villages to receive electricity becomes a focal point for the pressures and counterpressures described above as being the typical context of development program implementation.

In distributive policies such as rural electrification, the formulation of criteria for selecting beneficiaries is a critical part of the implementation process. These criteria will embody or make concrete the goals of the policy by delimiting groups to whom the policy will apply. In using criteria for analyzing the implementation of public policy, the researcher must ask two major questions, each of which corresponds to a different part of the implementation procedure: 1) Do criteria in fact operationalize program goals? If not, the goals will clearly not be achieved, and the researcher must look at earlier stages of the policy process to see why.[5] 2) Are the criteria adhered to? If so, then the program is being executed as intended. Answers to these two questions provide a measure of program efficiency. When criteria are embodiments of program goals, increased adherence to criteria would indicate increased efficiency of program implementation.[6]

Equating increased efficiency with successful implementation yields a narrower definition of success than the one employed by Grindle in the introduction to this volume. "The capacity actually to deliver programs as designed" is a more general formulation of the second question posed here concerning adherence to criteria. Some programs will not lend themselves to analysis in terms of criteria, often because the programs are political compromises embodying multiple and/or conflicting goals that are not ranked by priority. Thus, criteria cannot be specified to operationalize one clear goal, and the only measure of success is whether the program is delivered as designed. The narrower definition linking efficiency and success is useful only for specific programs with well-defined goals. RE is such a program.

[5] This is similar to what Pressman and Wildavsky are saying when they note that the mismatch between means and ends is a cause of poor implementation of policies. See *Implementation*, xvii. See also the discussion of the relationship between formulation and implementation in Chap. 1 of this volume.

[6] Adherence to criteria does not ensure that the program will have the intended effects. In this case, however, problems cannot be attributed to poor implementation.

If success is to be measured by adherence to goals, then goals must be stated. In this study, not only economic but also political goals are distinguished. The existence of both types of goals is suggested by the discussion of efficiency in decentralization and the criticisms of programs, such as panchayati raj, that have been waylaid by political necessity. The economic goal of RE is clearly stated and follows from the history of the program: to increase agricultural production. The political goal we assume to be the maintenance of the incumbent in office or the maintenance of the Congress party in power.[7] We will compare the adherence to both economic and political goals of rural electrification policy in the state of Rajasthan before and after the policy of decentralization was established in 1969.

RURAL ELECTRIFICATION IN RAJASTHAN

In a federal polity such as India, program goals are rarely defined by one level alone. This is particularly true of rural development projects; although the national center has a near monopoly on funds, the states have formal constitutional authority over agriculture. The responsibility for electrification is similarly dispersed. Electricity was perceived by the writers of India's constitution as a critical part of the public sector's effort to enhance economic growth and, therefore, it was specifically mentioned in the document. Authority for electricity policy is vested in both the national center and the states in a uniquely Indian mechanism known as concurrent power.

The Electricity Supply Act of 1948 further defined the separate responsibilities of the center and of the states.[8] Central power is

[7] There has been much discussion recently of whether incumbents really do seek reelection regularly. See, for example, K. Prewitt and H. Eulau, "Political Matrix and Political Representation," *American Political Science Review*, 63 (June 1969), 427-441. Nevertheless, I believe that this goal is not unrealistic, especially if stated in terms of the various functional and other groups that also have political interests. This is another deliberate simplification that helps to define a consistent goal. On this problem, see W. Ilchman and N. Uphoff, *The Political Economy of Change* (Berkeley: University of California Press, 1969), pp. 29-30 and ff.

[8] For further details, see S. Hadden, "The Political Economy of Agricultural Policy" and S. Hadden, *Decentralization and Rural Electrification in Rajasthan, India* (Ithaca, N.Y.: Cornell University Center for International

largely limited to review of large projects and coordination of multistate projects. The states are directed to establish State Electricity Boards (SEBs), which must consist at a minimum of an administrator, an accountant, and an electrical engineer. The SEBs are autonomous technical bodies within the state governments, receiving some funds from them but also empowered to raise capital on the open market (which means primarily from central government-dominated banks and agencies). They are required to operate on a no profit-no loss basis. In most states, this has meant in practice that the boards pay the interest on their debts, but no more. The high cost of generating and distributing electricity in rural areas is one of the major reasons for the poor financial records of the SEBs.

In Rajasthan, the minister for power, who is a full member of the Cabinet, has a formal policy veto over State Electricity Board decisions, but he seldom if ever needs to exercise it because major policy changes are undertaken only after consultation with the state government. Nevertheless, the Rajasthan State Electricity Board, the RSEB, like its counterpart in other states, is very conscious of its autonomy. The attitude on the boards has typically been that the technical nature of the subject precludes effective understanding or control of policy by outsiders. This is true despite the fact that many SEB decisions concern labor relations and, of course, development planning. Rajasthan's full board of three full-time administrators and four part-time members, appointed from the business and labor communities, meets once a month or less, when recommendations of the full-time members are considered. Although labor matters and rate structure are debated, technical recommendations and selection of villages are usually ratified without much comment. The board obtains its information from its own engineers stationed in the various districts, but it tends to insulate itself from other state agencies and from the people it was intended to serve. It will be seen later that this isolation played a part in the way villages were selected to receive electricity and in the changes that occurred following decentralization.

Despite its lack of power over policy implementation, the center's electricity policy has influenced the states' programs consid-

Studies, 1974). (Hereafter referred to as *RDC.*) Much information in this section comes from the author's interviews with a variety of administrators at the state, federal, and local levels.

erably, in part because of the center's monopolies on funds and, until recently, upon skilled planners and development administrators.[9] Although central policy had other goals, from 1966 onward the primary object of RE was to increase agricultural output. After this goal was set, the center did not stint in providing resources and incentives to the states to implement the policy. Central expenditures on RE grew from Rs. 300 million (about $62.5 million) for the entire first Five-Year Plan (1951-1956) to Rs. 480 million in 1968-1969 (about $64 million at the new exchange rate) alone.[10]

Rajasthan and most of the other states were receptive to this goal; indeed, Rajasthan had attempted to provide RE for agricultural use as early as 1963. Rajasthan's farmers were also well aware of the utility of RE both as an agricultural input and as a means of improving the quality of village life, and they demanded this good regularly through the political process.

As interest in RE grew in the 1960s, pressure on the state mounted from below as well as from above to decentralize procedures for electricity planning in order to bring them into line with the rest of the rural development effort. District Agricultural Production Committees, which included local politicians, administrators, and technicians, were given the power to select the villages to receive electricity in 1969. In some places, decentralization has led to a reduced ability to implement development programs on the part of administrators open to political pressures. This has not been true in Rajasthan, as evidence from before and after the 1969 decentralization will suggest.

[9] On finances, see A. Hanson, *The Process of Planning: A Study of India's Five-Year Plan* (London: Oxford University Press, 1966), and S. Veeraraghavachar, *Union-State Financial Relations in India* (New Delhi: Sterling Publications, 1969). On administrators, see R. Taub, *Bureaucrats Under Stress: Administrators and Administration in an Indian State* (Berkeley: University of California Press, 1969).

[10] K. A. Venkataraman, *Power Development in India: The Financial Aspects* (Delhi: Wiley Eastern, 1972), p. 2. On lack of funds as an impediment to implementation, see Pressman and Wildavsky, *Implementation*, p. xii and throughout; also C. Van Horn and D. Van Meter, "The Implementation of Intergovernmental Policy," in C. Jones and R. D. Thomas, eds., *Public Policy-Making in a Federal System* (Beverly Hills, Calif.: Sage Publications, 1976).

176

Village Selection Criteria

In Rajasthan, selection of villages to receive electricity was the most salient aspect of policy to potential beneficiaries as well as the primary means of implementing the RE program. Criteria for selecting villages that are related to both political and economic goals are examined here. The economic criteria are to be found in publications of the RSEB and confirmed by interviews with board members and other administrators. The political criteria, like the goals they embody, are implicit, but were chosen as representative of the kinds of charges made by Rajasthani villagers and politicians, who believed that villages were selected to receive electricity because they were in the constituency of a person who needed to be rewarded or helped in his attempts to retain political office. In accord with the methodological approach outlined above, each criterion is examined first for its relation to stated goals and then for the degree of adherence to it. The entire period of 1964-1970 will be explored first, and then the effect of the 1969 decentralization will be considered more fully.

The three economic criteria for selecting villages that were stated publicly by the RSEB were size of population, distance from existing transmission lines, and agricultural productive potential. These are the economic or productivity criteria, since they were intended to have the effect of increasing agricultural production. These criteria are "economic" in somewhat different ways. The population criterion required that the largest villages (over 2,500 people) be electrified first, which would mean that a larger number of people would be affected for a fixed expenditure. In 1965, this criterion was replaced by the other two, which were more directly related to the goal of improving agricultural output.

Productive potential would ideally incorporate data about soil, groundwater, and farmer receptivity into an index of the increase in output that might be expected. In fact, the RSEB primarily made use of the data concerning the availability and nonsalinity of a village's underground water. Thus, only one of the factors affecting agricultural productivity was employed as a criterion—the one most directly related to rural electrification. The distance criterion called for electrifying villages within 2 kilometers of the existing transmission line. This criterion again minimized cost, which is directly proportional to distance, and maximized the number of

177

recipients for a fixed level of expenditure. Productivity considerations were only tangentially embodied in the distance criterion.[11]

Tables 7-1 and 7-2 describe adherence to the economic criteria. It will be seen that large villages were electrified first. The steadily falling proportion of the largest villages among those electrified in any given year reflects the decreasing number of such villages that remained without electricity. Since data about existing transmission lines is secret, the distance criterion is operationalized here by measuring distance from railroad stations, which must by law

TABLE 7-1

POPULATION AND DISTANCE CRITERIA: PERCENT OF VILLAGES ELECTRIFIED BY YEAR[a]

	1964-1965 (N=210)	1965-1966 (N=459)	1966-1967 (N=517)	1967-1969[b] (N=323)	Total 1964-1969 (N=1509)	1969-1970 (N=292)	Compared to all Villages[c] (N=595)
Population							
0-500	27.6	30.5	30.8	51.0	34.6	38.0	67.0
500-1500	41.4	39.0	41.8	38.4	40.2	45.2	25.8
1500-2500	14.3	14.8	16.1	5.3	13.1	11.6	3.0
2500-3000	16.7	15.7	11.4	5.3	12.1	5.1	2.7
Distance from Railroad Station[d]							
< 2 miles	23.8	17.2	15.7	23.0	18.8	16.0[e]	6.0
> 2 miles	76.2	82.8	84.5	77.0	81.2	84.0	94.0

[a] My calculations are based on a complete list of electrified villages and a 2 percent random sample of the 30,000 nonelectrified villages in Rajasthan.

[b] Only 5 villages were electrified in 1967-1968 due to delays in the program, so two years are combined. Fiscal years in India run from 1 April to 31 March.

[c] This distribution is based on a 2 percent random sample (see footnote a).

[d] Used as an approximation for distance from the existing 11 K. V. line since this information was not available. All railroad stations must be electrified.

[e] These are actual distance measures and thus not strictly comparable to the 1964-1969 data. In my judgment, the actual adherence to the distance criterion was greater in this year than previously.

[11] The cost of electrifying a village has two principal components: the transformer and the distribution equipment (poles, wires, etc.). Transformer costs are more or less proportional to the size of the expected loan, but returns are also higher when there are more customers. (Thus the original emphasis on the population criterion.) This leaves distance from the existing transmission line as the major variable in the cost of electrifying a village. Insofar as villages are more or less equal in productivity potential, maximizing the number of villages will also maximize production. This assumption is in fact tenuous.

178

be electrified. Although there are few railroad stations in the state, and this indicator underestimates adherence to the distance criterion, it is clear that villages fulfilling the distance criterion were electrified in significantly greater proportion than other villages. Finally, Table 7-2 shows that villages with good groundwater conditions received electricity disproportionately. The category "unsurveyed" applies only to villages contiguous to those for which a groundwater survey had been conducted; "poor" means that existing groundwater is scanty or saline. Although far from overwhelming, the data indicate general adherence to the economic criteria.

TABLE 7-2
THE GROUNDWATER CRITERION: PERCENT OF VILLAGES ELECTRIFIED BY YEAR

Category	1964-1965 (N=75)	1965-1966 (N=206)	1966-1967 (N=176)	1967-1969 (N=127)	Total 1964-1969 (N=584)	1969-1970 (N=192)	% of All Villages (N=206)
Not surveyed	48.0	57.3	44.9	34.6	47.4	48.9	59.0
Poor	22.6	19.4	21.1	44.1	25.7	25.0	22.9
Good	29.4	23.3	34.0	21.3	26.9	26.1	18.1

Political criteria fall into two major categories: those that ensure equal distribution of electricity, and those that reward districts with particular political characteristics. Equality of distribution is a political issue because of the strong regional loyalties of districts that were once separate princely states. Official policy was that no district should receive any additional electricity until at least 5 percent of the villages in each of the 25 districts were electrified. The effect of the distance criterion, however, was to concentrate electricity in previously electrified areas. A high correlation ($\tau = .545$) of rank orders of districts by numbers of villages electrified before 1969-1970 with districts receiving electricity in that year confirms that concentration was occurring. Other criteria of equal distribution called for electrification of the principal village of an area and for the electrification of villages inhabited primarily by disadvantaged groups, called Scheduled Castes and Scheduled Tribes. Table 7-3 shows that while principal villages (panchayat headquarters) were electrified, villages of disadvantaged sectors tended not to be. Political criteria calling for equal distribution of electricity were adhered to only in part.

179

TABLE 7-3

SCHEDULED CASTE AND PANCHAYAT HEADQUARTERS CRITERIA: PERCENT OF
VILLAGES ELECTRIFIED BY YEAR

Category	1964-1965 (N=75)	1965-1966 (N=206)	1966-1967 (N=176)	1967-1969 (N=127)	Total 1964-1969 (N=584)	1969-1970 (N=192)	All Villages (N=206)
Scheduled caste	14.8	14.4	15.1	12.7	14.2	17.5	16.7
Scheduled tribe	4.8	1.7	3.9	6.2	3.9	9.5	19.0
Others	80.4	83.9	81.0	81.1	81.8	73.0	64.3
Panchayat headquarters	58.1	55.3	54.2	35.0	50.9	47.3	about 20.0
Others	41.9	44.7	45.8	65.0	49.1	52.7	80.0

The other category of political criteria requires that villages or
areas with particular political characteristics be electrified more
frequently than others. Among the possible favorable characteristics are the location of a village in the district of a Congress legislator, in a competitive district, in the district of an influential state
politician, or in the district of the minister for power himself.
Tables 7-4 through 7-7 present evidence concerning such villages.
Table 7-4 shows that in most years, Congress villages were electrified in proportion to Congress representation in the state legislature, and Table 7-5 shows that in the period just after the 1967
election the *least* competitive districts tended to be electrified.

TABLE 7-4

COMPARISON OF ELECTRIFIED AND ALL VILLAGES BY PARTY OF PRESENT STATE LEGISLATOR
AND YEAR OF ELECTRIFICATION

Party of MLA	Electrified Villages Year of Electrification					All Villages		
						Share of Party Vote in 1967 Elections	Party's Share of Seats in Legislature	Percentage of All Villages Voting for Party
	1964-1965	1965-1966	1966-1967	1967-1968	1969-1970			
Congress	43.9%	40.5%	47.6%	47.0%	62.1%	41.4%	48.0%	46.7%
Swatantra	35.8	35.7	27.4	32.2	20.0	27.2	26.0	26.8
Jan Sangh	9.2	12.9	12.5	8.6	9.8	10.7	12.0	13.0
BKD	0.0	0.3	1.4	0.3	1.3	—	—	1.3
SSP and CPI	5.2	1.8	5.6	1.9	3.0	6.9	5.5	5.5
Independents	5.8	8.9	5.6	8.2	4.7	14.8	8.0	6.8
	99.9	100.1	100.1	99.2	100.9	101.0	99.5	100.1

Note: Columns do not total to 100 due to rounding.

180

Tables 7-6 and 7-7 provide convincing evidence that high-status legislators of both parties, and the minister for power in particular, were able to gain benefits such as electricity for their constituents.

TABLE 7-5
COMPARISON OF NUMBER OF VARIOUSLY COMPETITIVE VILLAGES RECEIVING
ELECTRICITY IN DIFFERENT YEARS

	Degree of Competitiveness		
	High (0-6% Difference)[a]	Medium (7-15% Difference)	Low (Over 15% Difference)
1967-1969	16.5%	22.5%	61.0% = 100%
1964-1967 and 1969-1970	23.5	31.3	45.2 = 100%
Nonelectrified	27.6	27.8	44.6 = 100%

[a] Difference between proportion of vote received by top two candidates in 1967 general election.

TABLE 7-6
THE STATE LEGISLATOR STATUS CRITERION, 1967-1970

Percent of	Very High Status	Notables	Others
Electrified villages	17.1	11.2	71.7 = 100.0
All villages	7.2	9.7	83.1 = 100.0

TABLE 7-7
DISTRIBUTION OF VILLAGES ELECTRIFIED DURING POWER MINISTERS' TENURES

Power Minister	H. H. Jhalawar	Harideo Joshi	Shiv Charan Mathur	Barkatullah Khan
Tenure	42 months	14 months	5 months	5 months[a]
Total number of villages electrified	1,240	64	1	327
% Power minister's district	5.2	12.5	0.0	4.0
% Other districts	94.8	87.5	100.0	96.0
	100.0	100.0	100.0	100.0
% Total Rajasthan villages in power minister's district	4.4	4.4	4.5	2.2

[a] Up to March 1970, when our last information on electrified villages was obtained.

In Rajasthan, both the political and the economic criteria for selecting villages to receive electricity were adhered to in part, although neither separately nor together do they provide a full explanation of the choice of beneficiaries.[12] In addition, the economic criteria do not fully operationalize the goal of increasing agricultural production, in large part due to the difficulty of obtaining reliable information. It is, of course, not unusual to find that goals cannot be made explicit enough for easy implementation, due to the complexity of most policy objectives and to the high cost of obtaining the information that would allow the program to be implemented fully. In the Rajasthan case, the problem can be simply stated: it was very costly and uncertain to measure a village's potential for increasing agricultural production. The State Electricity Board responded by emphasizing criteria that could be measured and ones that it felt comfortable with, such as quality of groundwater rather than soil conditions. Furthermore, by its own account the board relied most heavily on the distance criterion, which maximized internal board goals of electrifying large numbers of villages for a fixed cost, regardless of direct effects on productivity.

The goal that the political criteria were supposed to advance was that of retaining power for the Congress party or existing officeholders. The relationship between the distribution of a particular good and the success of a candidate or party is virtually impossible to determine, especially in a state where every resource, including the distribution of cabinet posts, is used as a political reward or incentive. There is evidence of the link between electricity and political success; one example is the village headman of Lalgarh, who recounted his difficulty in obtaining electricity for the village despite the fact that all the surrounding villages had transformers. When he switched parties and became a Congress supporter, the village was electrified.

In the data on village electrification, adherence to the political criteria that we inferred was moderate. However, there was strong evidence that the constituents of power ministers and other influential politicians did benefit disproportionately. This suggests that the centralized decision procedure followed by the state-level RSEB from 1964 to 1969 was accessible to a few very powerful legislators who had large resources at their command with respect to the

[12] Some of the inconclusiveness of the findings may be attributed to the fact that the political data are district level rather than village level, while the selection process affects individual villages.

board and the state. The overwhelming popular belief in the primacy of political criteria reinforces the statistical evidence.

DECENTRALIZATION

According to the previous discussion, the success of decentralization will be measured by its ability to increase efficiency as measured by increased adherence to stated selection criteria. Tables 7-1 through 7-6 provide the necessary data. Adherence to the economic criteria following decentralization of the village selection process in 1969-1970 is comparable to that of earlier years. A slight increase in the number of small villages being electrified is attributable to the principle of area coverage[13] or to the exhausting of the category of larger villages. Adherence to the distance criterion is still marked, although somewhat less than in earlier years; groundwater remains the same as well. Not reported above is an increase in the correlation between districts that received electricity and districts with high indices of potential productivity using soil and climate conditions as criteria. Also not reported is a regression equation that tends to confirm the incomplete explanatory power of the criteria but also shows a slight increase in the importance of the distance and party criteria for 1969-1970.[14] A final piece of economic evidence is the slight rise in the marginal revenues of RE for the RSEB, an increase that occurred despite the huge rise in overall expenditures for RE in the years following decentralization.[15]

[13] Area coverage is a criterion that capitalizes on the fact that returns are disproportionately large when all farmers in an area are using advanced agricultural inputs. If all villages in an area are electrified, naturally some of these villages will be small.

[14] The actual and potential productivities are taken from a survey by P. S. Sharma, reported in "A Regional Approach to Agricultural Development in India," *Indian Journal of Agricultural Economics*, 19, No. 1 (January-March, 1964), 176-192. Data were weighted in order to allow comparison among districts. Between the periods 1964-1969 and 1969-1970, rank order correlations between actual and potential productivity and proportion of electrified villages in a district increased from $\tau =$ about .225 to $\tau =$ nearly .400. The correlation of proportion of electrified villages with per horsepower returns to the RSEB increased from $\tau = .216$ to $\tau = .627$ in the same time periods.

[15] Marginal revenue is computed by dividing cumulative receipts through year x+1 by cumulative expenditures through year x. Its value in 1964-1965 was .76 with cumulative expenditures of Rs. 5.26 million. In 1967-1968, with

Along with these moderate increases in adherence to economic criteria, we observe in Table 7-4 a definite increase in adherence to the party criterion—a jump in villages in Congress constituencies from a maximum of 47 percent in earlier years to 62 percent in 1969-1970. Increased adherence to political criteria is now the expected result of decentralization; in the case of RE in Rajasthan, however, this increase was accompanied by only a slight increase or, at worst, no change in adherence to economic criteria. Thus, decentralization did serve to increase efficiency, using the same resources to achieve both political and economic goals. The remainder of this section is devoted to discussion of the mechanisms whereby this decentralization effort appears to have succeeded where others failed.

Our discussion of the criteria and the reasons for nonadherence to them focused implicitly upon four principal factors: 1) difficulties of making criteria congruent with (or operationalizations of) goals; 2) high costs of obtaining necessary information; 3) isolation of decision makers; and 4) goal conflicts. While an administrative procedure such as decentralization could not affect the relationship between criteria and goals, it did help to resolve the other problems—lowering costs of information, circumventing RSEB isolation, and minimizing goal conflicts by ordering priorities.

The effect of decentralization in decreasing the costs of obtaining information is best illustrated by contrasting the old and new procedures for engineers' surveys of villages. Under the old procedure, if a village fulfilled the distance criterion, engineers would question village farmers about their need for electricity. Potential productivity was ascertained, if at all, at the time the villagers spoke to the engineer. Under the decentralized selection procedure after 1969, the list of economic criteria was sent to each District Agricultural Production Committee. DAPCs were to provide the RSEB with a complete list of villages in their areas fulfilling the stated criteria; each year they also submitted a list of a specified number of villages ranked in the order in which they should be given electricity.

In short, information about adherence to criteria was cheaper

---

cumulative expenditures of Rs. 50.9 million, marginal revenue dropped to 42, but had risen again to .46 in 1970-1971, when cumulative expenditures had risen to Rs. 244.5 million.

under decentralization because it was obtained through officials who were likely to be familiar with village conditions, not strangers as were the RSEB engineers. This was especially important in ascertaining the number of potential users and their abilities to become producers of surplus food crops, since knowledgeable officials could discount the aspirations of those unaware of the problems involved in getting electricity. Moreover, the public nature of the lists of eligible villages provided a check on accuracy of information. Village headmen could be expected to ensure that their villages were placed on the eligible list if possible; the fact that DAPCs included both elected officials and bureaucrats prevented one group from interpreting information to its own advantage.

Conversely, the DAPC members were much more accessible to the concerned farmers than the RSEB, which had been accessible primarily to influential politicians. Previously, the only way open to most villagers to influence the board was through bribing the RSEB engineer or, more regularly, through joint letters most often written after consulting with state legislators or district headmen who had to be visited in distant places. Once the DAPCs became an integral part of the selection process in 1969, farmers could approach their block development officers, village-level workers, village headmen, and others to try to influence them to place their villages high on the priority list. They could use both their traditional influence and their votes. Thus, decentralization overcame the relative isolation of the RSEB and expanded its responsiveness to others besides the most influential of state-level politicians. At the same time, however, RSEB officials refused to fund projects in which economic criteria were not fully met.

As early case studies of decentralization have shown, the increased accessibility of decision makers usually tends to increase adherence to often implicit political goals. However, increased accessibility can also aid in adherence to economic goals if these are valued by the decision makers. Controlled decentralization as a strategy of implementation can ensure that economic goals remain primary when they are perceived as the legitimate bases for selection of beneficiaries. For example, in the case described here, groups or villages vying for scarce resources had to make the case for their respective claims in terms of productivity. Furthermore, villages of high potential productivity found it worthwhile in terms of their own resources and probable gains to exert pressure on

185

decision makers in the DAPC. Under centralized decision making, access to the isolated RSEB was so costly and random that even highly productive villages did not attempt to influence decisions; under decentralization, villages began to submit affidavits listing probable increases in food grain output if electricity were granted.[16]

Finally, by setting clear priorities, controlled decentralization minimizes problems of policy implementation caused by conflicting goals. In Rajasthan, DAPCs first ensured that all villages to be considered for electrification fulfilled the economic criteria; only afterwards were they allowed to rank these villages. Since many more villages qualified under the stated economic criteria than could be electrified in any one year, the DAPCs were able to impose additional criteria. As political bodies, they imposed political criteria, but they did not interfere with adherence to the economic ones.

The Rajasthan case suggests that controlled decentralization reduces the effects of three probable causes of poor implementation: high costs of information, isolation of decision makers, and goal conflicts. Such a powerful tool should not be limited only to one place or one policy. The following section describes the conditions under which controlled decentralization may be applied elsewhere and elaborates on how it succeeds where other forms of decentralization have failed.

CONTROLLED DECENTRALIZATION AND POLICY IMPLEMENTATION

There appear to be three basic characteristics of a program that make it amenable to administration under controlled decentralization: 1) It is a distributive policy, and demand for benefits under the policy exceeds the supply; 2) the policy has a technical component; and 3) there is widespread agreement that the program for implementing the policy is a good one.

It is obvious why demand for the benefits must exceed the supply in order for decentralization even to be necessary. If demand does not exceed supply, discussion of the policy will not enter the political arena in a meaningful way. No arguments need be made

[16] The author was allowed to see the RE file of an important district level official. The file contained numerous examples of letters from villagers, drafted with the aid of this and other officials, in which productivity data and irrigated acreages before and after electrification were presented.

186

over characteristics of beneficiaries or over how much to allocate to the program. It is also obvious that this condition of demand exceeding supply obtains for virtually every policy that one can think of.

Controlled decentralization as described here is an administrative procedure that is most applicable to distributive policies. Our discussion of criteria has been focused on the selection of beneficiaries, a topic of relevance primarily for distributive policies. Furthermore, the success of controlled decentralization is contingent in part upon the existence of enough potential recipients that relevant criteria can be determined and applied. Even at the stage where demands are placed upon officials, there must be a market-like system of access; the proper working of a market depends upon the existence of many small units. Distributive policies frequently apply to large numbers of individuals or small groups. Furthermore, distributive policies usually involve small-scale projects, allowing implementation with a small commitment of resources. Peter Cleaves amplifies this point in the concluding chapter of this volume.

The need for a technical component in order for a policy to be successfully implemented under controlled decentralization stems from the nature of administration itself. Controlled decentralization depends on the ability of some high-level policymaking body to specify conditions or criteria that will further the economic or technical goals of the policy. It is especially important in this context that the planning body pay close attention to the relationship between the criteria established and the goals of the program to ensure that they correspond. This is the area in which technical advice is most helpful to policymakers. In development policy, technical criteria are economic criteria.

The technical component also offers advantages to local administrators. They can blame the technicians for establishing restrictive criteria, reducing pressure on themselves while continuing to implement the desired policy. This also has the useful side effect of educating people about programs and techniques. When villagers understand that their most potent arguments for receiving benefits are to show that program goals will be furthered, they have learned about causality and about program goals, as well as learning that their government is trying to act in their interest.[17]

[17] On policies and programs as causal relations, see Pressman and Wildavsky, *Implementation*, p. xiv.

In Rajasthan, villagers were taught by politicians as well as administrators to couch requests for electricity in terms of additional acres irrigated and crops produced. Awareness of the value of electricity as an agricultural input was spread along with notions about the relationship between food production and economic development.

Finally, in order for controlled decentralization to work, there must be agreement among most people that program goals and means are good. This is not the stringent or tautological requirement that it might seem, for all that is required is that people be willing to pay lip service to the program. Observers have often described the obstacle to implementation created by lack of congruence between the goals of administrators at different levels as well as among different groups at any one level. Several chapters in this volume, especially those by Cynthia McClintock and David Pyle, document the need for congruent goals. However, controlled decentralization can remove much of the problem. Noncompliance at the lower implementation level means nonreceipt of goods; this hurts administrators, politicians, and constituents alike. Thus, for purely self-serving reasons, relevant goals become congruent. As we have seen, additional goals of lower level implementors are prevented from superseding development-related goals, but can still be encompassed by the development program.

The three criteria for instituting controlled decentralization are easily met by a wide variety of programs, especially development programs. In Rajasthan, control of agricultural policy was enhanced by decentralizing grants of agricultural credit; farmers were required to supply detailed crop plans and show how they intended to use electricity before local banks would approve loans for obtaining RE.[18] Similarly, inputs of the new agricultural technology including seed and fertilizer can be distributed under controlled decentralized programs. Promotion of small businesses, including distribution of limited supplies of imported goods and loans for capital development, fulfills the criteria for controlled decentralization. There are many other areas in which this technique can be fruitfully applied.

Controlled decentralization thus may retain the best features of centralization and decentralization. It employs the long-range per-

[18] See Hadden, "The Political Economy of Agricultural Policy," for a detailed description of this program.

spective of higher level bodies that set the technical criteria, while incorporating the short-range perspective of local officials who set additional political criteria. It may also make officials more accessible, thereby increasing participation, responsibility, and responsiveness. And whereas ordinary decentralization procedures have tended *not* to increase efficiency, controlled decentralization in this instance appears to have increased both economic and political efficiency by using the same resources to accomplish economic and political ends more effectively. The best use of controlled decentralization depends on effective use of technical advice by high-level officials in the setting of the criteria designed to operationalize the economic goals of the program. The ability to do this is increasing and is receiving explicit attention from many policy analysts and planners. Finally, controlled decentralization may lower the cost to higher levels of government of control over lower levels by making the granting of funds routinely contingent upon the fulfillment of certain conditions. The routinization of any procedure renders it less costly, and this is especially true in areas such as intergovernmental relations where any issue may be the subject of a power play.

I have discussed four problems of implementation and the way in which controlled decentralization minimizes them. Table 7-8 summarizes this information along with descriptions of several other problems of implementation.[19] As the table suggests, controlled decentralization can make an important contribution in facilitating the implementation process and especially the implementation of development policies. Some of its benefits accrue directly from the administrative procedure, in which control is exercised over lower level implementors by withholding funds from beneficiaries who do not fulfill related criteria. Other benefits accrue from the public nature of the procedure; criteria are clear and specified, so all can ascertain whether ineligibles are illegally benefiting. Some potential benefits come as a result of the centralized planning that remains possible under controlled decentralization; coordination of ends and means, coordination of several programs, and provision of sufficient funds are more likely (though hardly probable) when programs are meeting their objectives. Controlled decentralization permits some flexibility in

[19] Problems numbered 2 through 10 in Table 7-8 are discussed in Van Horn and Van Meter, "The Implementation of Intergovernmental Policy."

189

responding to local conditions, and, more importantly it greatly reduces the cost of acquiring information about adherence to criteria. It makes officials more accessible and responsible without sacrificing adherence to program goals. Finally, it is a tool that is applicable to a wide range of development programs.

TABLE 7-8
CONTROLLED DECENTRALIZATION AND PROBLEMS OF IMPLEMENTATION

Problem	*What Controlled Decentralization (CD) Does*	*Does CD Help?*
1. Interlevel goal conflicts among administrators	Establishes direct controls through criteria and money	Yes
2. Same-level goal conflicts among interested groups	Establishes public criteria difficult to avoid	Yes
3. Directions unclear	Criteria are less ambiguous than many other types of directives	Yes
4. Requirements incompatible	CD cannot aid this; planners must control. But decentralization of criteria choosing could help this problem	Yes
5. Implementors must understand what is expected	Again, criteria generally clear	Yes
6. Staff overworked and/or incompetent	Fixed criteria reduce time and ability needed by staff	?
7. Impossible time constraints	Might reduce decision time	?
8. Insufficient information	Again, criteria should be most pertinent information. Cost of obtaining information about adherence to criteria lowered	Yes
9. Implementors unwilling to abide by policy	Controls inherent in process if maintained	Yes
10. Insufficient resources	Centralized planning could help here—criteria applied to limit of resources only. Additional criteria may be added to limit potential beneficiaries	Yes
11. Large number of decision points	Criteria reduce decision points	Yes
12. Mismatch between goals and programs	This is a planning (preimplementation) problem	No
13. Lack of flexibility of program to conform to local peculiarities	Decentralized administrators given enough power to respond	Yes

Controlled decentralization does not overcome entirely those problems of local factional control that have been so clearly addressed by Norman Nicholson and others.[20] The fact that the DAPCs were a long-standing part of community development

[20] Nicholson, "Panchayati Raj."

190

rather than a new institution for RE suggests that they have been part of the general trend in this respect. However, controlled decentralization does reduce the area in which these local factions have discretion or influence, and therefore helps to leave the way open for more democratic decisions. In Rajasthan, the public nature of the technical criteria and the mixed elected-administrative nature of the DAPCs, as well as the fact that DAPC members come from different levels (state legislature, block, village, and district), helped to reduce the impact of any one group of influentials.

Implementation is perhaps the central stage in the policy process in Third World countries. Any addition to the understanding of the implementation process, therefore, has the potential for being translated into improved policy output. Controlled decentralization has long been practiced, but its mechanisms and benefits have not before been made explicit. It does appear to have potential for aiding economic development by increasing the congruence between program goals and program output. Further experimentation is now necessary in order to confirm or disprove the utility of controlled decentralization as an aid to implementing economic development in the Third World.

Part Three · DECIDING WHO
GETS WHAT

THE site of program delivery is a third stage at which crucial decisions are made. As indicated in Chapter One, political participation in the Third World is particularly likely to be oriented toward individual or group demand making at the output phase of the policy process. This means that much participation will occur at the local level and will be directed toward influencing the allocation decisions that fall to administrative personnel at this level. At the same time, whose demands are acceded to and whose are rejected may have much to do with the overall structure of the political regime itself in terms of its goals, its locus of support, and its capacity to deal with opposition.

The determination of who is to receive government goods and services and the degree to which they will benefit from them is crucially affected by political factors. For example, the commitment of national, regional, or local officials to the project under consideration may be of utmost importance. These officials provide legitimacy, visibility, and rationale for the program, and this support may influence the degree of resistance met by the implementors in the field. By the same token, when program goals are not congruent with regime goals in terms of changes that they envision in the distribution of power at the local level, the commitment of political officials is likely to be lacking, and the amount of conflict engendered by allocation decisions may be greater.

The determination of who gets what is similarly affected at the local level by responsiveness on the part of the political regime to the needs and demands of the intended beneficiaries. When these groups or individuals are considered by the political regime to be crucial sources of support, it is more likely that they will in fact receive the goods and services as planned than if they are marginal political groupings whose support need not be courted assiduously. Whether or not the recipients play an active role in soliciting and utilizing program resources may also influence outcomes, and participation may be encouraged or discouraged by the political context at the local level where implementation is taking place. Thus, a vital input at the delivery stage is the utilization of payoffs for compliance with policy directives. These can be selected and used by bureaucratic officials seeking diligent performance from their subordinates, by politicians seeking to influence decision makers, or by implementors seeking to induce

195

behavior changes in recipients. But the availability of such pay-offs, once again, may be conditioned by the commitment of the political regime to the distributive or redistributive program.

Inputs are also made when individuals and groups are in a position to report on the conduct of bureaucratic officials in the field, the specific impact programs are having on particular communities, or the process by which goods and services are delivered. As is made clear in Part Three, the capacity to make such reports depends upon the political power of the groups or individuals involved and the sensitivity of the political regime to their demands and complaints. This kind of political feedback may result in a redefinition of policy objectives or in a redesign of delivery procedures. If the feedback about a program comes from those who object to the impact it is having, the result may even be a decision not to implement further. Additional demands may result from the publicity received by a program or the informal communication about its existence. Thus, a village that does not have a health clinic or school may become aware of a neighboring community that has been selected to receive government funds to build these facilities. Village leaders may then mount a campaign to pressure government health or education officials into providing their community with the facilities also. This increased pressure may result in a decision to expand a program even beyond the capabilities of the resources allocated to the program, jeopardizing the feasibility of the program delivery system.

In Part Three, then, we see that program content is considerably affected by the political context of implementation in the Third World. In case studies from Mexico, Kenya, and Brazil, the local political environment is used as a means to explain administrative actions in rural development and housing programs. While purely organizational, administrative, and management factors are also considered in these chapters, the primary focus is not these, but the complexities of power, influence, manipulation, and coercion that condition who gets what in terms of the benefits of distributive and redistributive policies.

EIGHT · *The Implementor: Political Constraints on Rural Development in Mexico*

MERILEE S. GRINDLE

CENTRAL among the actors involved in executing government programs in the Third World is a type of official who can be dubbed the "implementor." While this term is often applied to administrators at different levels of the bureaucratic hierarchy, it is used here to refer to a corps of middle-level officials who have responsibility for implementing programs in a specific, relatively constricted area—a state, a district, a province, or an urban zone—and who are held responsible for program results by their superiors. This corps of individuals—the first and second ranks of the field administration—maintains frequent contact with national or regional superiors, but also has occasion to interact with the clients of government agencies and with opponents of the programs at local levels.[1] These middle-level officials may have considerable discretion in pursuing their tasks and, even when it is not defined as part of their formal duties, they may have a decided impact on individual allocation decisions. Thus, they may select sites for new installations, the recipients of minor or local contracts, the eligibility of those who wish to participate in a program, or the beneficiaries of goods and services offered by the government. If not granted formal authority over these decisions, their advice on such matters to national or regional officials may be carefully considered.

The implementors are charged by their national-level superiors with performing duties in accordance with overall policy or program goals—goals that have generally been enunciated by political leaders, enshrined in legislation, or encapsulated within specific program plans. Thus, the implementors are key actors in achieving program success, as this was defined in the introductory chap-

[1] This may, in fact, include two or even three hierarchical levels of bureaucratic officials.

197

ter. At the same time, however, national bureaucratic chiefs often expect their agents in the field to resolve conflicts that arise at the subnational level. The fulfillment of this task is important to bureaucratic leaders because conflict resolution and accommodation may be part of the role assigned to them, implicitly or explicitly, by the national political elite in both civilian and military regimes. It also accords with their personal interest in maintaining the appearance of presiding over a smoothly run organization and in protecting themselves from undue problems, stress, and the demands or disapproval of their political superiors.

A consequence of the need to resolve or avoid conflict is that frequently those with the greatest potential for creating a disturbance will have the greatest success in eliciting a positive response from bureaucrats who make allocation decisions. Often, those able to make themselves heard are the political leaders and economic elites at the local level who may have access to national-level protectors, money to offer the bureaucrat, force to intimidate those who oppose them, and a variety of other economic and political sanctions. There may exist an imbalance of power such that it is always expedient for the implementor to meet the demands of the wealthy and the powerful rather than to serve the interests of low-status clienteles. Added to the problem is the fact that those programs stressing redistributive goals are those most likely to cause conflict over resource allocation. Responsiveness to demand groups other than the intended recipients is a factor accounting for the failure of many programs to produce the expected results. The implementors are obviously implicated in these failures but so, too, are their superiors—both bureaucratic and political—who place a high value on the avoidance of conflict. In short, it is frequently the case that maintaining the political peace has a higher priority than achieving developmental advances in Third World countries.

This chapter describes how and why program resources are often allocated at the local level by presenting a model of the political and administrative context in which middle-level bureaucratic implementors make decisions.[2] Then, an attempt by

[2] The model presented is an attempt to generalize from four bodies of empirical and theoretical literature. The first is a group of recent studies that has called attention to implementation as a problem in the policy process. Included in this group are general considerations of implementing processes such as those of E. Hargrove, *The Missing Link: The Study of the Implementation of Social Policy* (Washington, D.C.: The Urban Institute,

1975); D. Van Meter and C. Van Horn, "The Policy Implementation Process: A Conceptual Framework," *Administration and Society*, 6, No. 4 (February 1975); and D. Van Meter and C. Van Horn, "The Implementation of Intergovernmental Policy," in C. Jones and R. Thomas, eds., *Public Policy Making in a Federal System* (Beverly Hills, Ca.: Sage Publications, 1976). Other works are case studies of policy delivery such as M. Derthick, *New Towns In-Town: Why a Federal Program Failed* (Washington, D.C.: The Urban Institute, 1972); M. Derthick, *Uncontrollable Spending for Social Services Grants* (Washington, D.C.: The Brookings Institution, 1975); A. Heidenheimer and M. Parkinson, "Equalizing Educational Opportunity in Britain and the United States: The Politics of Implementation," in W. Gwyn and G. Edwards, III, eds., *Perspectives on Public Policymaking*, 15 (New Orleans, La.: Tulane Studies in Political Science, 1975); J. Murphy, "The Education Bureaucracies Implement Novel Policy: The Politics of Title I of ESEA, 1965-1972," in A. P. Sindler, ed., *Policy and Politics in America: Six Case Studies* (Boston: Little, Brown & Co., 1973); J. Pressman and A. Wildavsky, *Implementation* (Berkeley: University of California Press, 1973). Finally, included in this group are general considerations of responsiveness and control in bureaucracy such as A. Downs, *Inside Bureaucracy* (Boston: Little, Brown & Co., 1967); and H. Kaufman, *Administrative Feedback: Monitoring Subordinates' Behavior* (Washington, D.C.: The Brookings Institution, 1973).

The study of development administration is also relevant to the model. G. Heeger, "Bureaucracy, Political Parties, and Political Development," *World Politics*, 25, No. 4 (July 1973) provides a general discussion of the literature of development administration. See also W. Ilchman, *Comparative Public Administration and "Conventional Wisdom"* (Beverly Hills, Ca.: Sage Professional Papers in Comparative Politics, No. 01-021, 1971).

A third series of sources for the model is that which focuses on descriptions and analyses of subnational political systems in Third World countries, providing information on the context in which the implementor pursues his responsibilities. See R. Bates, "Ethnic Competition and Modernization in Contemporary Africa," *Comparative Political Studies*, 6, No. 4 (January 1974); W. Cornelius, *Politics and the Migrant Poor in Mexico City* (Stanford, Ca.: Stanford University Press, 1975); S. Kothari and R. Roy, *Relations Between Politicians and Administrators at the District Level* (New Delhi: Indian Institute of Public Administration, 1969); H. Tinker, "Local Government and Politics, and Political and Social Theory in India," in M. Swartz, ed., *Local Level Politics* (Chicago: Aldine, 1968).

A final source of previous scholarship is composed of empirical case studies of policy implementation that highlight variables specific to the Third World context. In addition to the chapters in this volume, see B. Ames, *Rhetoric and Reality in a Militarized Regime: Brazil After 1964* (Beverly Hills, Ca.: Sage Professional Papers in Comparative Politics, No. 01-042, 1973); P. Cleaves, *Bureaucratic Politics and Administration in Chile* (Berkeley: University of California Press, 1974); M. Grindle, *Bureaucrats, Politicians, and Peasants in Mexico: A Case Study in Public Policy* (Berkeley: University of California Press, 1977); R. Gurevich, "Teachers, Rural Development, and the Civil Service in Thailand," *Asian Survey*, 15, No. 10 (October 1975).

national-level officials in Mexico to implement a policy for the development of the subsistence sector of the agricultural population is recounted, focusing attention on the field administrator whose actions were considerably influenced by local political events. This chapter attempts to provide insights into why the content of policies in terms of the allocation of resources may change significantly during implementation at the local level.

━ Because most Third World political systems are based on more or less fragile coalitions of elite groups, the need to utilize government goods and services to cement bargains for loyalty and support is a common characteristic. This may be true whether political leaders are wedded to the preservation of the economic and political status quo or are more reformist in orientation. Therefore, the analysis presented in this chapter may be relevant for understanding administrative behavior in a wide variety of Third World political systems. Political leaders in Mexico, for instance, consciously distribute resources at the local level to individuals and groups in order to coopt dissidents and accommodate varying interests, in spite of the fact that they oversee an unusually strong state apparatus and a dominant party system. ━ Many of the military regimes that are increasingly in evidence in the Third World are also supported by political, social, and economic elites whose allegiance must be courted nationally and at the local level. Similarly, many competitive electoral systems are based on elite coalitions and are maintained by the allocation of resources to those groups most crucial to the durability of the regime. These elites then use state resources to maintain followings whose votes they deliver, machine-fashion, in return for broader protection of their interests. In all of these systems, the implementor will tend to be most responsive to those groups considered essential to the regime in power, whether or not they are the intended beneficiaries of the programs for which he is responsible. By the same reasoning, the analysis in this chapter is probably not appropriate for revolutionary regimes that attempt to alter power relationships in the society. These regimes tend to maintain their support through the very redistributive programs that are so difficult to implement elsewhere.

The Mexican case study is based on field research conducted in Mexico in 1974 and 1975, when national policymakers, program managers, and implementors assigned to the state and local

200

levels were interviewed.[3] It demonstrates the political problems faced by programs with redistributive goals, and it indicates the constraints on administrators charged with ensuring that low-status recipients actually benefit from government goods and services. In Mexico, the limits of explicit policy goals were reached when the implementation of the rural development program threatened to infringe on the power and the prerogatives of groups and interests whose support was vital to the continued stability of the political regime.

THE CONTEXT OF ALLOCATION DECISION MAKING

In addition to the principal implementors, a number of other actors are involved in any attempt to implement a program through the bureaucracy. There are, for example, the national or regional bureaucratic chiefs who are charged with producing program results and overseeing the activities of the implementors. Other important individuals in any implementation process are the local, district, or regional political or military officials and party leaders who hope to see government goods and services directed toward themselves or their support groups. They are the governors, the delegates from the area to the national or provincial legislatures, the party officials, the tribal leaders, the village presidents, the mayors, and the military administrators whose constituencies fall within the jurisdiction of the implementor. Local elites who may find their interests threatened by a program are others with whom the implementor must deal. Landowners, merchants and other businessmen, clergy, doctors, commercial middlemen, and local aristocrats fall into this category.

The clients of government organizations are also involved in efforts to implement programs. However, the large number of policies and programs that have distributive or redistributive goals in Third World countries means that many of the intended beneficiaries are low-status actors—peasants, the young, urban squatters, the unemployed, villagers. They may be ill-prepared to understand or benefit from the programs offered by the government;

[3] The research was supported by a grant from the Social Science Research Council and the American Council of Learned Societies. This case study is drawn from chap. 5 and 6 of M. Grindle, *Bureaucrats, Politicians, and Peasants.* I am grateful to the University of California Press for permission to reproduce parts of that work.

201

peasants may not be economically or psychologically prepared to employ relatively expensive technology on their subsistence plots, for instance.[4] A reason often cited for the failure of development programs is the disinterest, apathy, or outright rejection of them by low-status groups. Therefore, the implementors in many development plans are expected to mobilize or create a constituency for the programs that are their responsibility. In other cases, the clients may be competing with each other for access to the resources that they perceive to be—generally correctly—in short supply. Others who compete for the attention of the implementor are the potential beneficiaries of construction, transportation, or production contracts.[5]

The implementor is the focus of the frequently conflicting demands and expectations of these sets of actors.[6] Within his own organization, he is obliged to fulfill the broad and long-term expectations of his superiors and subordinates. National- or regional-level chiefs, for example, generally make two kinds of demands on the implementor. On the one hand, they expect him to use the resources at his disposal to achieve the goals and objectives of the programs that have been designed. At the same time, these officials generally expect the implementor to maintain a jurisdiction that is relatively free of open conflict in areas affected by the organization. These two expectations may provide divergent guidelines about how best to allocate public resources, as will be evident in the case of rural development in Mexico. In addition to his superiors, the implementor's subordinates also have expectations about his behavior. Their demands upon him tend to be manifested in large numbers of individual requests for resources and support of specific projects. However, these particular requests are based on more generalized expectations about proper administrative behavior, career aspirations, long-term commitment

---

[4] See J. Montgomery, *Technology and Civic Life* (Cambridge: MIT Press, 1974); J. Scott, "Exploitation in Rural Class Relations: A Victim's Perspective," *Comparative Politics*, 7, No. 4 (July 1975).

[5] See, for instance, Cleaves, *Bureaucratic Politics and Administration in Chile*, chap. 7.

[6] A. Frank, "Goal Ambiguity and Conflicting Standards: An Approach to the Study of Organization," *Human Organization*, 17 (1958-1959) and J. Phelan, "Authority and Flexibility in the Spanish Imperial Bureaucracy," *Administrative Science Quarterly*, 5 (June 1960), elaborate on the idea of conflicting standards for performance and their impact on the behavior of bureaucratic officials.

to policy or organizational goals, or those of friendship and personal loyalty.

Outside the organizational context, the implementor is the focus of a variety of specific demands from groups and individuals. For instance, influence may be exerted by local politicians. Their demands tend to be highly specific and individualized; they are generally not concerned with the overall or long-term performance of the implementor, but simply his reaction to individual requests. They may, however, be interested in befriending, coopting, or rewarding him to such a degree that he repeatedly complies with their requests. Similarly, local elites make highly specific demands for the allocation of resources or the hindrance of program objectives. They may wish to see low-cost government farm inputs sold to them; they may be concerned that they *not* be sold to peasants who would consequently not have to deal with local merchants; they may expect to be given priority in acquiring credit or access to health and educational facilities. They may seek to coopt bureaucratic officials in order to ensure that they do not even attempt to implement programs that might threaten their interests. Included here may be elite clients of government programs, such as those who receive construction and supply contracts, often as a result of a "special understanding" with the implementors.

Finally, there are the clients of particular programs or agencies. If the clients are of low status, they may not make demands for government resources; if the programs offered are not perceived to be relevant to these clients, if local political and economic elites have managed to intimidate or coopt them, or if the bureaucratic officials are perceived to be too remote and aloof from them, low-status actors will probably not be among those actively demanding a share of the resources. In other situations, clients may demand, on an individual or group basis, consideration for their special needs, prompt execution of official duties, and instruction in utilizing effectively the goods and services offered. This behavior, however, presupposes a knowledge of what the program and the implementor have to offer, as well as an attitude on the part of the individual or group that they have a right to demand these benefits. These conditions are generally conspicuous by their absence in the Third World. The demands of low-status clients, when they are forthcoming, tend to be highly issue-specific, concerned with immediate and localized problems that are perceived to be subject to amelioration through governmental activity.[7]

Another factor that influences the outcome of the development program is the organizational context in which implementing administrators operate. This context includes cultural aspects that may condition the interaction between superior and subordinate, the extent of the delegation of authority, the type and effectiveness of oversight and control mechanisms in the bureaucratic organization, the tradition of service established, the range of the agency's responsibilities, and the size of the bureaucratic staff charged with such functions. The variables in this organizational context affect the manner in which implementors respond to the demands made upon them.

A simplified diagram of the context in which allocation decisions are made indicating the demands and constraints on the administrator is presented in Figure 8-1. The implementor is situated in a horizontal rectangle representing his decisional jurisdiction. At the same time, he finds himself within a vertical rectangle representing the organizational context that directs and constrains his behavior. The demands directed toward him are represented by the arrows that converge upon him. Solid arrows indicate the generalized expectations that superiors and subordinates have for his performance; broken arrows represent the more specific and particularistic demands made by clients and local political and economic elites.

Each of the actors has control over incentives or sanctions to influence the behavior of the implementor and to gain from him a favorable response. National policymakers, for instance, usually are able to back up their performance expectations with the incentive of career mobility or the threat of job deprivation. Related to these are incentives such as monetary rewards, prestige within the organization, the capacity to assign the official to various geographical locations, and the benign or hostile attention that is given to other aspects of the official's job or behavior. National policymakers can also attempt to influence the behavior of the implementor through training courses, and by requiring periodic reports and inspection tours. Additionally, they can assign greater amounts of resources to those implementors whose behavior they

---

[7] See W. Cornelius, "Urbanization and Political Demand Making: Political Participation Among the Migrant Poor in Latin American Cities," *American Political Science Review*, 68, No. 3 (September 1974).

Figure 8-1. The Context of Policy Implementation

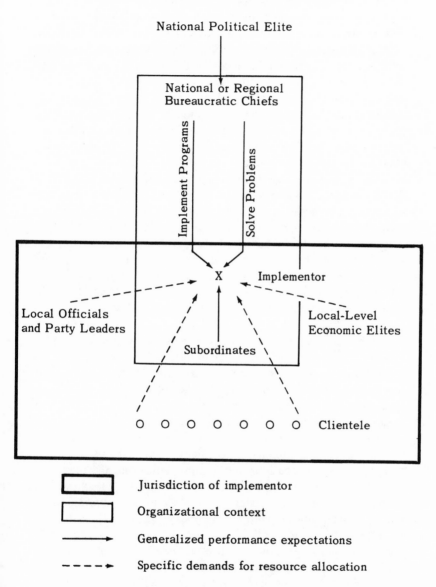

National Political Elite

National or Regional Bureaucratic Chiefs

Implement Programs

Solve Problems

X   Implementor

Local Officials and Party Leaders

Local-Level Economic Elites

Subordinates

O O O O O O O   Clientele

Jurisdiction of implementor

Organizational context

Generalized performance expectations

Specific demands for resource allocation

approve. The implementor's subordinates may respond to a positive reception of their demands by offering more effective performance or greater diligence in their activities. They may also supply their superior with information relevant to his own job and seek to protect him from the pressures of the clients they serve.

The politicians or military personnel who have responsibilities or followers at the local level also have a number of incentives they can apply in making their demands on the implementor. They can, for example, be helpful to him in carrying out his duties— offering official support, the cooperation of other public agencies in which they have influence, and help in maintaining cordial relationships with the wealthy and the powerful at the local level. Conversely, they can threaten noncooperation and obstruction if the official displeases them. They can additionally offer opportunities for personal enrichment. In many cases, they may be able to hold out the possibility of alternative jobs or careers—appointments to lucrative party positions, for example. They may also be able to influence the behavior of the bureaucrat by reporting favorably or unfavorably on his performance to agency leaders or appealing to them over the head of the administrator for favorable action. Similar incentives are available to the local economic elites. They can offer bribes and payoffs, social status, and acceptance. Their most powerful resource, however, may be the negative incentive to make things uncomfortable for the implementor if he does not bow to their demands. Their ties to the members of the local press, to local and national politicians, and to other members of economic elites can be exploited to bring to bear great pressure on the implementor.

Other incentives can be offered to the implementor from the agency's clientele. The intended beneficiaries may be able to offer bribes and other pecuniary inducements that might be attractive to him. On some occasions and in some environments, they may have the capacity to create a public disturbance—a demonstration in front of his office, for instance—which may be embarrassing to him or cause problems with his superiors. Or, the recipients may have personal ties to politicians who could be mobilized on their behalf. By and large, however, low-status clienteles must rely on cultivating personal ties with the administrator, offering him the opportunity to be their benevolent patron and protector in return for their loyalty, deference, and public support. Very frequently, the resources available to this demand group are so meager that they are dependent upon the activities of national administrators to represent their interests. In Figure 8-1, this proxy influence is represented by the arrow labelled "implement programs."

The demands made on the implementors mean that they are under pressure to "spend" government resources in a variety of ways. There are, of course, limits on their ability to allocate available resources as they wish: bureaucratic chiefs may reject their initiatives, and the constraints imposed by bureaucratic routines and regulations limit their autonomy to make decisions. But the implementors are not simply passive recipients of demands nor are they always prisoners of the organizational context in which they operate. Rather, their responses to expectations and demands are frequently deliberate, conscious choices among available alternatives. The alternative chosen is that one which will maximize the achievement of goals, whether these goals be striving for personal enrichment, maintaining a job, anticipating a brighter career future, amassing a personal following, or conforming to professional ideals of the "good public servant." Thus, the choices made by an implementor may well vary from decision to decision, depending upon how he perceives the situation and his best chances for achieving personal goals. In part, the decision he makes is a function of the tactics available to him for justifying his position. In most cases, the implementor, in allocating scarce resources, can rarely avoid situations in which he complies with the demands of some actors to the detriment of others, but a number of strategies are available for protecting him from the increased pressure or retaliation of those whose demands he ignores.

When seeking to evade demands from his superiors, for instance, he may be able to falsify reports to the "home office," ignore communications from them, or outline a multitude of problems he encounters in his job that prevent him from pursuing national program goals. Alternatively, he can play upon the fears of higher level officials that a public disturbance will occur by emphasizing the explosive nature of the demands made by particular individuals or groups. To deflect the demands of politicians and economic elites, he can invoke the authority of "technical studies" or "technical requirements" that indicate the inappropriateness of meeting their demands; he can disclaim authority over decisions or blame the straightjacket of rules and regulations imposed upon him. He can attempt to intimidate low-status clients with imperious behavior; he can fail to appear at his office for long

207

periods of time or not be available when certain actors seek him out; and he can comply with some demands in order to refuse others. These tactics prevent him from constantly suffering the opprobrium of the demand makers and increase his capacity to respond independently to demands made upon him.

This context in which implementation decisions are made means that allocation decisions tend to be highly adaptive to local-level and immediate political issues. Indeed, it is possible that because of their immediacy, decisions to avoid or ameliorate conflict situations will take precedence over those to implement programs as they are envisioned by policymakers. This was the outcome of an attempt to implement a rural development program in Mexico, for example. This program placed the state representative of a federal agency, CONASUPO (National Staple Products Company), at the vortex of attempts to influence allocation decisions at the state level and forced him to choose carefully how agency resources would be distributed.

THE AGENCY AND THE POLICY

CONASUPO is a large federal agency in Mexico charged with regulating the price of "basic necessities," broadly interpreted to include foodstuffs, clothing, agricultural implements, school and household supplies, construction materials, toys, and other items. Its primary duties are to regulate the prices of important agricultural products such as corn, beans, wheat, and rice; to process a number of staple products such as milk, flour, tortilla dough, and pasta products; and to sell these and other staples through a variety of commercial outlets, including CONASUPO's own chain of 2,500 fair price stores. At the time of the research, the agency employed over 8,000 people and was organized into a parent company with 16 subsidiaries, each of which was responsible for an important operation such as purchasing and storing agricultural products, retailing foodstuffs, stimulating the development of construction materials production, processing flour, processing and dispensing milk, and so forth.

In accordance with Mexican practice, there was an almost total turnover of high- and middle-level officials in CONASUPO when President Luís Echeverría assumed office in late 1970.[8] After

[8] Of the 78 agency officials interviewed, only twelve had served in CONASUPO immediately prior to the inauguration of Echeverría and none of

208

careful study of the agency and government records, the new cadre of officials became convinced that the major thrust of the agency's activities should be in rural areas and in stimulating the development of productivity in the subsistence agricultural sector. Their studies indicated that the subsistence sector was actually declining in productivity because the peasant in Mexico was a victim of unequal economic exchange relationships in the rural areas; he was exploited by middlemen, by local economic bosses, by government policies for credit and pricing, and his low economic level made it impossible for him to compete successfully in the market.[9] The CONASUPO officials therefore proposed that the agency become involved in a major effort in rural development to help the subsistence peasant escape from poverty, low productivity, and exploitation. This would be achieved by offering him a package of programs: higher prices for agricultural products and direct purchasing of them; access to low-cost transportation, fertilizers, insecticides, and farm implements; training in marketing and agricultural practices; installation of rural retail outlets for basic necessities; provision of consumer and production credit; and agency collaboration in the establishment of health centers and industries in rural areas.

The State Representatives and Resource Allocation

This policy was developed within CONASUPO between early 1971 and 1973. By mid-1973, a package of feasible programs had been designed, the director of CONASUPO was firmly committed to the policy, and, most importantly, presidential support had been acquired and was reflected in a much expanded budget. The stage was thus set for implementing the policy through CONASUPO's existing network of rural grain warehouses. A primary means to achieve this was to be through the state offices that CONASUPO established in November of 1973. In every state, a representative appointed by the agency director was empowered to coordinate all local activities of the agency. He had the authority to correct abuses of official function locally, to hire staff, and to deal with

---

these occupied the same positions before and after the administration change.

[9] See CONASUPO, "Esquema general para la transformación de la agricultura de subsistencias," unpublished manuscript, 1972; and CONASUPO, "Programa de acción para la agricultura de subsistencias," unpublished manuscript, 1972.

state representatives of other federal government agencies. He was also charged with the duty of establishing close working relationships with the state government and, specifically, of seeing that CONASUPO programs did not cause conflict or political problems with the governor. Finally, in the event of natural disaster in the state, such as flooding, drought, or earthquake, the representative was to have extraordinary powers to coordinate CONASUPO's relief efforts. It was hoped that the personnel in the state offices, in touch with local conditions, would aid the agency in selecting locations where effective programs could be implemented and in designing the most efficient mix of programs to meet rural community needs. The representative was expected to be able to identify problem spots early and to correct them rapidly.

The new offices of CONASUPO consisted of the representative and agents of the various subsidiaries that had operations in the state. According to central office managers, the ultimate goal of the state office was to "become a sort of mini-CONASUPO with the same administrative organization" as in the center. The representative was to be the local counterpart of the director of CONASUPO. Setting up the mini-CONASUPOs, however, was to stop short of initiative in policy matters, according to the same officials in national headquarters. The state offices were established for the purpose of removing some of the burden of day-to-day problem solving from Mexico City. "What this means now is that the solutions to local problems can be found locally, while still maintaining policy control from the center." Another national official reported, "We feel our principal goal in the State Offices Division is to make sure that the programs put in motion here in Mexico City actually reach the people they are designed to benefit."

The representatives themselves were aware that their function was to be implementing and problem solving rather than policymaking. One explained the purpose of the program: "The state offices were really set up as a tonic. . . . It was . . . an effort to decongest the problem solving system and to see if some things couldn't be resolved right here in the state." It was made clear to the representatives when they assumed their posts that an important criterion by which they were to be evaluated was their ability to find solutions to such problems. In regular reports to the central offices, they were to keep Mexico City informed of the local situation, but preferably *after* they had reached a satisfactory resolution of the difficulty. Thus, one national coordinator of

210

the state offices program stated, "The more problems they send through to us, the worse we know their performance is. . . . The best state representatives solve problems at their own level." The evaluation of their performance was important to the representatives. Since all middle- and upper-level officials in Mexico occupy appointive positions, the state representatives could be "released" from public service at any time that their superiors or protectors found their performance lacking. In addition, many were concerned with performing acceptably because they hoped this might gain them an appointment to another position in the next administration, to assume office in late 1976.[10]

Problem solving generally involved making decisions about the allocation of CONASUPO resources. There were, of course, limits to the ability of the state representative to allocate the resources as he wished. The hierarchies of the subsidiary companies in some cases determined how their own resources were to be allocated, and national authorities in the agency itself might approve or reject the representative's initiatives. In addition, constraints imposed by bureaucratic routines and regulations limited the autonomy of the representative to make decisions as he wished. Nevertheless, in most cases he had an important if not decisive voice in determining the use of agency resources: he had direct access both to the director and to the state governor; his decisions and support influenced when and where stores and warehouses were to be constructed, when training courses would be given, which merchants would receive regulatory supplies of important foods, which trucking companies would be hired to transport CONASUPO products, which communities would receive development promoters, and how extensive the range of auxiliary CONASUPO services would be in the state.

The representative used his influence to deal with difficulties that were likely to arise on different fronts. The private sector and the state government especially presented the representative with demands that required his constant attention. An important duty

[10] For the effect of the presidential succession on the behavior of public officials in Mexico, see F. Brandenburg, *The Making of Modern Mexico* (Englewood Cliffs, N.J.: Prentice Hall, 1964), chap. 6; M. Grindle, *Bureaucrats, Politicians, and Peasants in Mexico*, chap. 3; M. Greenberg, *Bureaucracy and Development* (Lexington, Mass.: Heath Lexington, 1970), chap. 7; R. Fagen and W. Tuohy, *Politics and Privilege in a Mexican City* (Stanford, Ca.: Stanford University Press, 1972), chap. 2.

assigned to the representative, for instance, was to maintain non-hostile relationships with local businessmen, generally through the chambers of commerce in the state. The task was a sensitive one; relationships with the private sector were strained under the Echeverría administration and frequently, at both national and local levels, CONASUPO was threatened with serious opposition.[11] Businessmen, identified with the political right in Mexico, had waged vigorous propaganda campaigns against CONASUPO in the past. The private sector in general tended to view CONASUPO's activities as an interference in the free market and as unfair competition. More specifically, installation of CONASUPO outlets and programs was perceived to be a real economic threat to merchants in the area serviced by the program. Attacks on the agency most commonly impugned the honesty and efficiency of the organization and its officials.

In the state offices, the goal of the representative was to keep the discontent or hostility of businessmen from escalating to a public level. He generally dealt with the problem presented by the private sector by using his influence over agency programs to benefit businessmen when they were willing to take a sympathetic view of CONASUPO's activities. For example, one representative explained his strategy.

> I also try to improve relations with the Chamber of Commerce. I try to overcome the problem we have of lack of understanding. And I recently showed them a new contract we have in which CONASUPO undertakes to sell them rice so they can sell it at reduced prices. I'm trying to help them get supplies of more CONASUPO products to distribute this way. When I first came here they attacked us in the newspapers.

Regulatory reserves of foodstuffs maintained by CONASUPO could be assigned to friendly merchants and perhaps denied to hostile ones when they were distributed to private commercial establishments for retail sale at government established prices. Contracts for transporting agricultural products could also be given to those who were amenable to CONASUPO activities. The agency had a policy of purchasing merchandise, whenever feasible,

---

[11] For the relationship of the private sector with the regime in general, see S. Purcell, *The Mexican Profit Sharing Decision* (Berkeley: University of California Press, 1975); R. Shafer, *Mexican Business Organizations: History and Analysis* (Syracuse, N.Y.: Syracuse University Press, 1973).

through local and regional manufacturers or processors, a practice that was used to elicit cooperation from local industrial elites. In the event that a particular CONASUPO action, such as the installation of a fair price store, threatened influential private interests, the representatives could halt the project or relocate it in a less offensive area. In exchange for these accommodations, the state representatives expected a more friendly acceptance of the agency's activities from the businessmen and, not infrequently, some personal token of gratitude.

Perhaps more importantly, local problem solving for the state representative meant establishing and maintaining cordial relationships with the state government, particularly with the governor.[12] Theoretically, the requirements of federal programs, such as the ones established by CONASUPO, and those of state political actors are not necessarily in conflict. A state governor might be every bit as convinced as CONASUPO officials that rural development depended upon creating the conditions to liberate the subsistence farmer from his cycle of backwardness. In reality, however, governors found it necessary to make many compromises with competing interests in order to maintain their base of political support in the state. They were frequently dependent on the state organization of the National Peasants' Confederation (CNC), which in turn relied on local bosses to organize and manipulate political followings of peasants; CONASUPO policies that threatened the instruments of control used

[12] In Mexico, state governors can be selected to occupy their positions for a variety of reasons. Some are important figures in national politics who are sent to the provinces by the president as his personal emissaries. Others are *caciques* (or their henchmen) whose extensive political machines within a state have earned them impressive bargaining power when dealing with the president and national political leaders. Still others are individuals typified by both national elite membership and strong local machines. Finally, a few are those who have been "burned" at the national level and have been retired, at least temporarily, to the relative ignominy of a powerless governorship. Whatever the reason behind their official appointment as PRI candidates and their subsequent election, governors are not often in a position to challenge presidential leadership openly.

Generally, relations between the federal and the state governments are characterized by mutual attempts at manipulation and accommodation. For example, state governors may attempt to acquire influence over federal programs in the state while federal officials may seek to gain the political support and aid of the governor, but without unduly jeopardizing the objectives of their programs.

213

by the political and economic bosses were often subject to modification by the governor.

Nevertheless, the governors could be useful to CONASUPO when the agency attempted to carry out its activities at the state level. The governors, through their ties to the CNC, could mobilize peasants to cooperate with CONASUPO; they could make it convenient for other federal agencies to collaborate; they could use their legal powers to close state borders to shipments of grain and foodstuffs in order to prevent speculation and hoarding; and they could smooth relations with the private sector. They could also provide individual CONASUPO officials with opportunities for more lucrative jobs at the state level or could facilitate the accumulation of private fortunes. At the same time, the governors found CONASUPO to be a particularly useful agency. It had not escaped the attention of state governors, for example, that the opening of a CONASUPO store or rural warehouse in some areas might reflect well on their administrations and be valuable in solidifying support for the official party, the PRI (Institutional Revolutionary Party). In other cases, it might be helpful for the governors to be able to halt the installation of a store or warehouse that was inconvenient for certain local interests, sometimes their own. In addition, disaster relief, emergency food programs, pork-barrel, and patronage opportunities could all be made available through CONASUPO.

It is evident, then, that collaboration between the CONASUPO representative and the governor could be mutually beneficial. The state representatives were very aware of their responsibilities to cooperate effectively with him, and friendly relationships were considered necessary to elicit the governor's support in solving local problems. The style of collaboration was vividly described by one representative: "I have made it a point to become good friends with the governor. I slap him on the back, shake hands with him and go over often to talk with him. . . . I try to do what I can for him, to improve relations between the agency and him." Another corroborated the need for mutually beneficial exchanges: "Relations with the governor couldn't be better. Actually, most of the communication we have with the governor is initiated by him—requests that we open a store here or look into such and such a problem. But then he reciprocates . . . it was the governor who gave the order to close the state border."

However, such close relationships could actually jeopardize the ability of the representatives to implement the policies of CONA-SUPO. In the spring of 1975, three state representatives were relieved of their official responsibilities. The explanation for their removal circulated within the agency was that each had been demonstrating "excessive enthusiasm in collaborating with the governor" in his activities. Evidently, the extent to which these administrators were enbling the governor to determine the distribution of CONASUPO resources had passed beyond the limits acceptable to central office management. Nevertheless, it was frequently stressed that the governor's interests—both political and economic—should be given careful consideration by the representatives. In the words of one CONASUPO official, "The job of the state representative is basically a political one. His main function is to maintain relations with the governmental apparatus at the state level. He is here to see that CONASUPO does not intrude or interfere with the interests of the governor. Most of the state delegates are not technical people but people who have had long political experience."

The goal of all the problem-solving activities, as defined by the representatives interviewed, was the maintenance of CONASUPO operation without public conflict or scandal. Avoidance of scandal meant, in part, keeping unfavorable information about the agency from appearing in the local newspapers. One representative, for example, explained that the press in his state, controlled by the private sector, "would seize upon the slightest statement or failure and make a big scandal of it." Moreover, the representatives interviewed all indicated awareness that their performance was being judged in Mexico City by their ability to solve problems without public discontent or attacks on the agency. They were also aware that some individuals at the state level might have influence in national politics and be in a position to complain of the performance of the agency or of the representative to officials in Mexico City.

The job of the state representative, therefore, required considerable political sensitivity and skill, in addition to a certain amount of administrative experience. Not surprisingly, the individuals chosen for this position were noted for their political rather than their administrative backgrounds. Most were selected by the agency director on the basis of personal friendship or political connections. Typical among them was Miguel Rivera, CONASUPO representative in one of Mexico's more important coastal states.[13] Rivera was a native of the same state as the agency director and a longtime political ally of his. The two became friendly at the university where they both received degrees in economics. Rivera then began a 25-year career in government and politics in his home state. He served in a state ministry, was manager of the state agricultural bank, and was head of the association of cattlemen, a position that solidified important linkages to local elite politics. He complemented these positions with work for the party, culminating in the chairmanship of an influential committee at the state level. In 1974, the director of CONASUPO contacted him personally to ask if he would serve as representative in a state with a reputation for being politically difficult.

Rivera was aware that his political experience was an important qualification for his job. In an interview, he expressed a sense of self-confidence in his command of important skills. "I have a great deal of experience in politics. I've been involved with the PRI in various capacities for 25 years in my state. I think it's been a help to me because I know how to operate in this atmosphere. I know how to handle myself and avoid problems. I understand how it works. I know how to adapt myself because of the politico-administrative experience I've had." He was also well aware that he had been sent to the state to facilitate CONASUPO's activities and to solve problems at their source. When asked how his superiors would be able to evaluate him, he was candid in admitting that his actions would be monitored through various channels.

> Putting myself in the place of those in Mexico [City], I think I would notice if, for example, there was a great influx of problems to the central offices and then all of a sudden the problems stopped coming. This I would take as a symptom that the office was working well; I'd know that something had changed. The other way I'd judge would be from information I received from other sources. For example, if everytime the governor went out he heard that CONASUPO's representative was a thief and a liar and a no-good, he would get on the phone to Mexico and say to [the director], "Look, your man out here is causing me problems." That's how they'd find out. These are the criteria they are using to evaluate me.

[13] The name of the representative is fictitious.

216

Interestingly, he felt he would be judged by his reputation and his ability to solve problems, not on the basis of how competently he was able to achieve program goals, measured in some objective fashion.

Nevertheless, he seemed sincere when speaking of his commitment to the policies and programs of the agency.

I'm from the country myself—one of eleven children—and I know what it's like to be poor and hungry. I think, then, I identify with the peasants and their problems. In all my actions, I try to see that the real benefit of CONASUPO reaches the most needy classes. Also, I'm a very honest man; people have approached me with propositions but I have let them understand that I'm not interested. This has to be done carefully so as not to create problems or offend people. I think it is a shame when positions in CONASUPO, in the Ministry of Agriculture, or in the official banks are used for private ends of profit, because when this is done the peasant is corrupted also and he loses faith in his government.

Still, the goals of CONASUPO programs had to be pursued with caution, and Rivera was fully aware that local elites would be watching the agency and its employees and assessing actions that might threaten their interests. While speaking of the problems he encountered in his job, Rivera stated,

This is a very politicized state. There are many groups that are very strong and they have direct ties to people in Mexico [City]. There are many [people from this state] working for the government in Mexico City because two presidents were from [here]. The CNC is very strong and so is the milling industry. They can pick up the phone and talk directly to Mexico City if anything happens. Because of this, it's an agitated state and a difficult one; it takes a certain amount of delicacy to handle it.

He reported that he had achieved good relations with the governor and that this aided him in his work. "I have no problems with the governor. We have very good working relations and good personal relations, although we are not close friends. . . . I have helped the wife of the governor a number of times." However, some problems might be anticipated from local merchants.

217

Sometimes, as you probably know, the organized merchants can cause us some problems. Fortunately, their reaction to us has not been very strong lately. When I first came, the head of the Chamber of Commerce launched a strong attack on CONASUPO in a meeting, but instead of trying to fight with them, I have attempted to reason with them and to explain CONASUPO's function as an economist, a professional. . . . This way, they have to accept us. Just recently the head of the Chamber of Commerce was sitting in the same chair you're sitting in and we were discussing things as friends. I asked myself how this could happen. . . . We also have a policy of trying to buy as many products as possible from local sources for our stores.

Other problems that threatened the reputation of the agency needed to be dealt with carefully. One case that was explored during the course of an interview again demonstrates Rivera's sensitivity to the local political environment and the need for him to exercise his judgment wisely in resolving problems.

[An employee] made a statement to the press about the closing date of a purchasing program and this was used as the basis for an attack on CONASUPO. The press will use the slightest thing and turn it against us. I must inform Mexico [City] about it but I think the best thing to do is to pretend it never happened. A clarification from Mexico would only confuse things and make it a bigger deal yet. And I don't think it would be a good idea to dismiss [the employee] because he might then go to the press and say that he had been fired for telling the truth.

It seems clear from his remarks that Rivera's job was not so much that of an administrator, empowered to direct state activities in accordance with agency goals, as that of a local troubleshooter, responsible for adjusting CONASUPO activities to enhance the agency's reputation and maintain local tranquility. These adjustments, of course, could seriously endanger CONASUPO's ability to enhance the welfare of the most needy peasants. In fact, Rivera acknowledged the limits of the agency's redistributive efforts: "More attention should be given to the areas that are most inaccessible. In those areas the *cacique* [boss] really rules and has his *tienda de raya* [company store]. If CONASUPO could penetrate these areas, it would really be fulfilling its social function."

218

In the case of Rivera and other representatives interviewed, it was significant how infrequently they mentioned direct pressure from peasants, the intended beneficiaries of CONASUPO's rural development policy. The peasants' failure to act effectively on their own behalf can be credited to their lack of power within the Mexican political system. Since the Revolution of 1910, peasants in Mexico have been gradually integrated into the political institutions of the regime. In the 1930s, the support of President Cárdenas encouraged some independent peasant political activity, but currently, the rural poor are organized and represented by the most docile and least rewarded of the three sectors of the official party, the CNC.[14] Typically, local power wielders such as *caciques* and *ejido* officials mobilize peasant followings through the use of economic rewards and sanctions and then deliver their support to municipal and state officials of the National Peasants' Confederation, which represents the peasant sector in the PRI.[15] As a consequence, the votes of rural Mexico have long provided the regime with its most stable and reliable base of support. At the same time, however, government activity toward its agrarian population has generally been characterized by neglect and exploitation. Understandably then, peasants have had limited political or organizational resources to use in pressing their claims on government agencies like CONASUPO. Among those who could benefit from the use of agency resources—merchants, middlemen, local political leaders, medium and large landowners, truckers, caciques, and peasants—clearly the most powerless were the peasants.

Therefore, it is not surprising that CONASUPO's state offices were not always effective in ensuring that programs designed in Mexico City would actually be realized at the local level. While

[14] On the position of peasants in the Mexican political system, see R. Hansen, *The Politics of Mexican Development* (Baltimore: Johns Hopkins University Press, 1971); Instituto de Investigaciones Sociales, *Caciquismo y poder político en el México rural* (Mexico: Universidad Nacional Autónoma de México, 1976); J. Reyna, *Control político, estabilidad y desarrollo en México* (Mexico: Cuadernos del Centro de Estudios Sociológicos, El Colegio de México, 1974) and *An Empirical Analysis of Political Mobilization: The Case of Mexico* (Ithaca, N.Y.: Cornell University, Dissertation Series No. 26, 1972); R. Stavenhagen et al., *Neolatifundismo y explotación* (Mexico: Nuestro Tiempo, 1968).

[15] *Caciques* are local or regional strongmen, traditionally the informal leaders of Mexican communities who may at times serve in official capacity. *Ejidos* are officially recognized corporate communities of peasants in Mexico.

219

they were capable of achieving a degree of state-level coordination and reducing some of the upward flow of decisions, the local offices were not able to guarantee that CONASUPO programs always reached their intended beneficiaries in the peasant communities. Competing hierarchies within CONASUPO, the requirements of local problem solving, in addition to the temptation to use agency resources for personal advancement were factors that often prevented the faithful execution of the rural development scheme. The following statements, made by state office officials in answer to the question, "How do you determine where CONASUPO installations will be located?" indicate the variety of pressures placed upon them in day-to-day decision making about resource allocation.

> The primary criteria for locating installations are political. Once a place has been suggested by the governor or someone, then a study is done. I choose the sites mostly on the criterion of knowing the people involved. Of course, we carry out socioeconomic studies to set up the stores—to select the most adequate places —but really, the selection of sites is mostly a political question. A municipal president or even the governor or the representative will determine where a store is to be opened.

> We get probably five or six applications for stores a day. Some arrive even from the president of the Republic, some from the general director, some from the governor. . . . My criterion is whether I can supply a store.

> One store we are working on now is a case resulting from the presidential campaign. When Echeverría came to this particular place during the presidential campaign, he promised the people a CONASUPO store. Later, the director came and confirmed this.

One official summed up the position of the chief local agent of the company.

> The state representative is often sandwiched between his responsibilities as a direct representative of CONASUPO or the director in the state and the political pressures which are exerted on him by the governor and local political forces. Many times he might be in a position of wishing to ignore or "not hear about" the malfunctioning of CONASUPO programs because of other pressures upon him.

Unfortunately, the data do not exist to assess how much of CONASUPO's rural development program was rechanneled to individuals other than subsistence farmers or how much of it went unimplemented at the local level because of political pressures brought to bear on the representative. Nevertheless, it is clear from this description of the context surrounding the decisions made by the agency's chief state-level administrator that demands were made upon him and he found it expedient to respond to the powerful, the wealthy, and the important. It was much to expect that individual representatives would become vocal and effective champions of subsistence farmers; such activities on their part could easily result in public conflict and dissention, conditions that are anathema to Mexican officials and that generally result in the loss of their jobs.[16]

CONCLUSIONS

Among a variety of factors that determine whether or not programs formulated at the national level will reach their intended beneficiaries is the performance of the field administrator-as-implementor. Whether or not he responds to the expectation that he execute programs depends upon the force of other demands made upon him as well as his own perceptions of how best to achieve his personal goals, whatever they may be. Numerous studies of bureaucracies in the Third World indicate the counter-productivity of imposing rigid constraints and controls on this bureaucrat in order to force him to implement programs as they are designed: he becomes overly concerned with fufilling the letter rather than the spirit of the law; he becomes an ineffective and aloof administrator; he does not provide his superiors with adequate or useful feedback.[17] As an alternative strategy, the study of rural development policy implementation in Mexico suggests that national administrators may have an opportunity to manipulate the decisional environment of the implementor so that pursuit

[16] See Fagen and Tuohy, *Politics and Privilege in a Mexican City*, chap. 6.

[17] See, for example, N. Abedin, *Local Administration and Politics in Modernising Societies: Bangladesh and Pakistan* (Dacca: National Institute of Public Administration, 1973); S. Heginbotham, *Cultures in Conflict: The Four Faces of Indian Bureaucracy* (New York: Columbia University Press, 1975); A. Kuper, *Kalahari Village Politics* (Cambridge, England: Cambridge University Press, 1970); F. Riggs, *Administration in Developing Countries: The Theory of Prismatic Society* (Boston: Houghton Mifflin Co., 1964).

of his own goals coincides with implementing the program goals of the center.

One such method to achieve the implementation of programs over the long run would be to seek to improve the capacity of the intended recipients for effective demand making. Thus, the objective would be to strengthen low-status clienteles in relation to the political and economic elites who generally have the capacity to subvert program goals. As a strategy, an alliance of development-oriented national or regional administrators and low-status beneficiaries might thus encourage better preformance from implementors such as the CONASUPO state representative. This might mean encouraging the clienteles to organize and aggregate their demands at the local level. It might also imply encouraging them to threaten or create public disturbances so that their demands are dealt with, a tactic not likely to be favored by any but the most open and secure of political regimes.[18] If such a strategy is chosen, however, the national administrators must be willing and able to provide local agents with incentives for responsive behavior and with protection from the potential disgruntlement and retaliation of those threatened by their activities.

If such a strategy is successful and national administrators are able to strengthen the position of the clientele vis-à-vis the other demand makers, then it may be possible to introduce measures to delegate or devolve more authority to the implementor and thus relieve some of the administrative bottlenecks that are frequently decried in studies of the bureaucracy in the Third World. If delegation or devolvement of authority precedes the institutionalizing of effective implementation, however, the result is not likely to be an increase in the responsiveness of the implementor, given the lineup of powerful inhibitors at the local level.

For such a strategy to work, there obviously must exist a national administrative leadership that is sincerely committed to achieving the objectives of the policies, particularly those that stress redistribution. As we have seen, the devotion of administrators to the pursuit of policy goals is often qualified by the need to be responsive to broader regime goals. If, however, there is an administrative cadre dedicated to developmental goals, the policies it supports must also be realistic in terms of their implementa-

[18] On the problems involved in protest activities by low-status actors, see M. Lipsky, "Protest as a Political Resource," *American Political Science Review*, 62, No. 4 (December 1968).

bility, and there must be available to them sufficient resources in the form of goods and services to make the objectives more than empty promises. Perhaps most importantly, these administrators must be able to count upon the support of national political leaders when conflict arises at the local level. This is the ingredient most frequently missing, due to the overriding concern of leaders of Third World countries with creating and maintaining coalitions of supporters to ensure the continuity of the political regime. Often, the resources that are needed to achieve policy goals are also the resources needed for building and maintaining political support or for resolving elite or subelite conflicts. The capacity of low-status clienteles to benefit from government policies may therefore ultimately depend on the congruence of their needs with broader regime goals.

NINE · The Politics of Public Housing in Nairobi

FREDERICK T. TEMPLE and NELLE W. TEMPLE

EXAMINATION of the provision of public housing in Nairobi during Kenya's first decade of independence, 1963-1973, reveals a considerable discrepancy between officially stated policy preferences and actual results. In spite of a professed commitment to produce a massive number of units to serve the city's low-income residents, government agencies supplied only a moderate number of houses, mostly for middle- and upper-income families. This chapter argues that as general housing policy goals were translated into real buildings allocated to specific individuals in Nairobi, the closed nature of the Kenyan political process led politicians and officials to respond more to the preferences and needs of the city's better-off residents than to those of the poor. Not only were many of the policymakers personally sympathetic to the needs of more affluent residents because they themselves belonged to the society's higher strata, but the political pressures exerted on them by the better-off were much stronger than the influence exercised by the poor. This is similar to the experiences in Brazil, Mexico, and elsewhere documented in other chapters of this volume. For local officials and politicians with responsibility for housing program choices in our study, there were few rewards for advocating low-income housing schemes and potentially great personal and career rewards for controlling access to middle-income housing.

This chapter will document the bias toward the better-off in Nairobi's public housing programs and then explore reasons why official goals of low-income housing construction were not achieved in practice, and why the programs can be judged to be

Note: The research on which this article is based was carried out by the authors in 1971-1973 under a grant from the Center for International Studies at the Massachusetts Institute of Technology. The opinions expressed in this chapter are the authors' alone and do not represent the views of MIT or any of the institutions with which the authors have been or are currently associated.

224

failures in terms of the definition of success adopted in this volume. One general factor was that bureaucrats and politicians perceived high quality construction to be less susceptible to public criticism and economic default than low-budget techniques afford-able by the poor. More significantly, however, poorer segments of the population lacked the channels of political influence to compel attention to their needs. As in many other countries, the middle- and upper-income groups possessed disproportionate amounts of the resources that sway policy choices and influence allocational decisions in Kenya.

The information in this study was gathered in 1971-1973 from records of the Nairobi City Council and other agencies involved in housing, from interviews with their staff members and with politicians, and from monitoring the daily press and housing con-cerns of Kenyan friends during two years' residence in Nairobi. In the following pages, housing conditions in Nairobi will be described, as well as government policy statements directed toward ameliorating these conditions. Subsequently, we document the bias in housing built by the government and provide both attitudinal and political explanations to account for the change in the content of housing policy during implementation.

NAIROBI AND ITS HOUSING CONDITIONS

The city of Nairobi was a colonial creation, founded during the late 1890s. It was developed to serve as the administrative and commercial center of a British colony expected to become a "white man's country" by its European (i.e., white) settlers.[1] Access to economic opportunities, residential patterns, and social patterns was racially stratified, with Asians occupying an inter-mediate position between Europeans and Africans. Africans were not viewed as permanent town dwellers and were at one time required to carry passes in town. Their presumed temporary urban residence was used to justify low wages and provision of minimal workers' quarters intended only for single males. Euro-peans typically occupied private homes on spacious lots in the higher, cooler, northwestern section of the city; Asians lived in large, extended-family homes near the city center; and Africans

[1] E. Huxley's biography of Lord Delamere, an influential early settler in Kenya, is entitled *White Man's Country* (London: Chatto and Windus, 1935).

225

(other than household servants) were relegated to cramped rental quarters in the lower lying, hotter "Eastlands."

In spite of their socioeconomic and political subjugation during the colonial period, Africans have always been numerically dominant in Nairobi. Table 9-1 indicates the growth and racial composition of Nairobi's population. During the period under consideration, 1963-1973, the city's population roughly doubled, growing from about 350,000 to about 680,000.[2] The main source of growth was in-migration into the city by Africans. At the beginning of the 1970s, Nairobi's African population was estimated to be growing at about 9 percent per annum, 3 percent of which was due to the birthrate and 6 percent to in-migration.[3] The Asian

TABLE 9-1
NAIROBI'S GROWTH, 1901-1969

Year	Total	Europeans	Population Asians (Percentage)	Africans	Land Area (Square Miles)
1901					7.0
1906	11,512	4.9	31.1	64.0	
1919					9.8
1926	29,864	8.9	30.8	60.3	
1936	49,600	11.3	32.3	56.5	
1944	108,900	9.6	31.5	59.0	
1948					32.4
1962	{ 266,794	8.0	32.4	59.5	35.0
	{ 347,431	8.3	25.0	66.7	266.0ª
1969	509,286	3.8	13.2	83.0	266.0

ª In 1963 Nairobi's boundaries were expanded to include 266.0 square miles.

Sources: L. White, L. Silberman, and P. Anderson, *Nairobi: Master Plan for a Colonial Capital* (London: His Majesty's Stationery Office, 1948), p. 43; D. Halliman and W. Morgan, "The City of Nairobi" in W. Morgan, ed., *Nairobi: City and Region* (Nairobi: Oxford University Press, 1967), p. 100; A. Vukovich, "National and Nairobi Population: Structure and Growth 1962-69. Population Estimates 1970" (Nairobi: Nairobi City Council, Nairobi Urban Study Group, 1970); and A. Vukovich, "Technical Appendix No. 1—Population and Employment" (Nairobi: Nairobi City Council, Nairobi Urban Study Group, 1971).

[2] These estimates are based on the 1962 census figures for the 1963 city boundaries and a projected rate of net increase in Nairobi's population from the 1969 census to 1973 of 7.5 percent per annum as contained in A. Vukovich, "Technical Appendix No. 1—Population and Employment" (Nairobi: Nairobi City Council, Nairobi Urban Study Group, 1971).

[3] Ibid.

226

population has been declining as a result of the precariousness of its economic status in Kenya. The European population has remained at roughly the same level, for while the white "settler" population has declined, Nairobi has increasingly become an international commercial city.

Contemporary Nairobi is a city of sharp contrasts. The town center is modern and clean, with attractive offices, shops, hotels, and restaurants catering to affluent Kenyans and tourists. Kenya's economy has grown relatively rapidly and a rising number, but still tiny proportion, of African Kenyans now enjoy an urban standard of living comparable or superior to that of most "Europeans." On the other hand, population growth has considerably exceeded the expansion of economic opportunities and public services. Consequently, many urban families suffer from unemployment or intermittent low-wage employment and live in increasingly overcrowded housing in neighborhoods lacking even basic services and amenities.[4]

Housing conditions for Africans in Nairobi were already officially considered appalling at the beginning of the 1960s. One assessment for 1961 is contained in a housing study prepared by the city council's town planning section.[5] Of the roughly 46,000 dwelling units found within the city's boundaries at that time, 60 percent were considered to be in "poor condition" and were designated for redevelopment. In the eastern section of the city where 71 percent of Nairobi's African population lived, 88 percent of the dwelling units were designated for redevelopment. In 1964, a United Nations team, asked to prepare a report on the nation's housing needs, stated that less than 3 percent of Nairobi African families owned their own homes; 52 percent rented accommoda-

[4] The best overview of employment, incomes, and living conditions in Kenya is contained in International Labour Office, *Employment, Incomes and Equality: A Strategy for Increasing Productive Employment in Kenya* (Geneva: 1972). Informative community studies of Nairobi neighborhoods are D. Etherton, *Mathare Valley: A Case-Study of Uncontrolled Settlement in Nairobi* (Nairobi: Housing Research and Development Unit, University of Nairobi, 1971); J. Bujra, "Pumwani: The Politics of Property—A Study of an Urban Renewal Scheme in Nairobi, Kenya," unpublished ms., 1973; and N. Temple, "Urban Commitment, Neighborhood Politics and Political Demand-Making in Nairobi," Ph.D. diss. M.I.T., 1979.

[5] The results of this study are summarized in J. Thacker, "The Housing Stock in the 'Old City' Area" (Nairobi: Nairobi City Council, Nairobi Urban Study Group, 1971), pp. 2-9.

tion, while 45.5 percent lived in employer-supplied housing.[6] Overcrowding was especially prevalent among African households. Eighty-one percent of Nairobi Africans lived in one-room dwellings, and 57 percent of these dwellings housed three or more people. Overall, 52 percent of African households had three or more people per room. Basic services were often lacking; one quarter of the African households were served by buckets or pit latrines.[7]

HOUSING POLICY AND THE PROVISION OF PUBLIC HOUSING IN NAIROBI

The housing conditions for Nairobi Africans inherited from the colonial period and a slump experienced by the private sector housing industry during the political changes of the 1960s encouraged the government to attempt to play a major role in solving Nairobi's housing problems. While housing was in short supply at all income levels, official government statements indicated that low-cost housing construction would be the top priority of public housing policy. The government's sessional paper, in response to the U.N. housing mission, emphasized that "funds voted by the Government will be used mainly in providing low- and medium-cost housing and to support rural housing improvement."[8] According to the *Development Plan 1970-1974*, the principal housing agency of the central government, the National Housing Corporation, was supposed to lend money only to projects in which housing units cost less than K£ 1,200 [$3,396].[9] Public officials reiterated the commitment to low-cost housing in their speeches. The following newspaper report is typical: "While houses should

[6] L. Bloomberg and C. Abrams, *United Nations Mission to Kenya on Housing* (Nairobi: Government Printing Office, 1965).

[7] The figures in this paragraph are taken from Bloomberg and Abrams, *United Nations Mission*, pp. 64, 72.

[8] Republic of Kenya, *Sessional Paper No. 5 of 1966/67: Housing Policy for Kenya* (Nairobi: Government Printing Office, 1966), p. 7.

[9] Republic of Kenya, *Development Plan 1970-74* (Nairobi: Government Printing Office, 1969), p. 514. All monetary values in the text and tables are given in U.S. dollars. Kenya's monetary unit is the Kenya Shilling (KSh). Although the Kenya Pound (K£) is not an official monetary unit, values are often expressed in K£s, with K£ 1 = KSh 20. During the period when this research was conducted, the official exchange rate was U.S. $1 = KSh 7.11 and U.S. $2.83 = K£ 1.

lend themselves to dignity and good health, priority had to be
given to low-cost houses which were within the reach of the lower-
income groups who form the majority of the people, the Minister
for Housing, Mr. Ngei, said yesterday."[10] As will be demonstrated
later, low-cost housing did not receive top priority in fact.

Three governmental organizations have been given primary
responsibility for responding to Nairobi's housing needs: the National Housing Corporation, the Housing Finance Company of
Kenya, Limited, and the Nairobi City Council. The National
Housing Corporation and the Nairobi City Council are supposed
to concentrate on building low-cost housing appropriate for the
bulk of Nairobi's population, while the Housing Finance Company
is designed to provide mortgage finance for more expensive houses.

In 1967, the Central Housing Board was transformed into the
National Housing Corporation (NHC) on the basis of the United
Nations housing mission's recommendation that a national housing
authority be created. The NHC lends money to local governments
for housing construction and can also build housing on its own,
without working through a local government authority. In specifying the NHC's role in meeting Kenya's housing needs, the
Development Plan 1970-1974 stated that, "because four-fifths of
the urban demand is for dwellings costing under K£1,200
[$3,396], it has been decided that all Government lending through
NHC will be for projects designed to produce houses at that
figure or below."[11] The NHC is designed to be the main government agency responsible for low-cost housing throughout the
country. In Nairobi, the NHC loaned the Nairobi City Council
about $11.5 million between 1967 and 1971.[12] It also spent almost
$8.5 million on its own housing schemes in Nairobi during this
period. Part of the money provided to the city council was used
for units costing more than $3,396, and almost 80 percent of the
units constructed by the NHC itself were more expensive than the
$3,396 target.[13]

[10] "Mr. Ngei Calls for Priority in Low-Cost Housing," *East African Standard* (Nairobi) March 29, 1972.

[11] *Development Plan 1970-74*, p. 514.

[12] Nairobi City Council, *Loan Repayment Schedule Book*, Accounts Section, City Treasurer's Department.

[13] The figures come from *Annual Reports* of the National Housing Corporation for the various years and are summarized in F. Temple, "Politics, Planning and Housing Policy in Nairobi," Ph.D. diss. M.I.T., 1973, p. 199.

The Housing Finance Company of Kenya, Ltd. (HFCK) was incorporated in 1965 to provide mortgage finance to assist eligible individuals with the construction of new homes or the purchase of already existing units. The HFCK acquires its funds from several sources: repayments from borrowers; loans from the Kenya government and the Commonwealth Development Corporation (CDC); and deposits by small investors and institutions. The company's board of directors consists of three appointees of the CDC, two government officials, and one outside member; the government appoints the chairman. According to the *Development Plan*, HFCK financing is to be used for units costing more than $3,396, thereby complementing the efforts of the NHC and local authorities in the low-cost housing field.[14] During the period between mid-1966 and late 1971, 77 percent of the total mortgage commitments and loans of the HFCK were made in Nairobi. The agency financed roughly 1,500 units, of which the vast majority cost $5,660 or more.[15]

The Nairobi City Council (NCC) is the agency with primary responsibility for low-cost housing within Nairobi itself. In addition to borrowing money from the NHC, the council also raises money for its housing program by issuing stock on the local market and negotiating loans with international agencies, such as the Agency for International Development and the Commonwealth Development Corporation. Since independence, it has spent a large proportion of its total capital expenditure on housing. During 1964-1970, 48 percent of the council's total capital expenditure was devoted to housing; in 1968-1970, the proportion was 62 percent (see Table 9-2).

Table 9-2 also indicates the types of schemes for which the council used its housing expenditure during the period 1964-1970. The table demonstrates the growing importance in the council's program of tenant purchase schemes in which the tenant obtains title to the property after the prescribed course of payments. By 1970 this type of scheme accounted for two-thirds of total capital expenditure. Tenant purchase schemes have been favored over rental schemes because expansion of home ownership among Africans is assumed to contribute to the creation of stable, urban-based families. Rehabilitation and redevelopment projects ab-

[14] *Development Plan 1970-74*, p. 511.

[15] Statistical data supplied by the HFCK are summarized in F. Temple, "Politics, Planning," p. 203.

TABLE 9-2

PERCENTAGE OF NAIROBI CITY COUNCIL CAPITAL EXPENDITURE ON DIFFERENT TYPES OF
HOUSING PROJECTS, 1964-1970

Type of Project	1964	1965	1966	1967	1968	1969	1970	Total 1964-1970
Tenant Purchase Schemes	0.0	0.0	19.8	2.2	31.9	66.3	70.7	41.1
Rental Schemes	50.9	0.0	9.3	33.7	22.5	9.5	14.6	19.6
Rehabilitation & Redevelopment Schemes	24.6	69.3	10.6	24.7	35.8	21.1	11.5	25.4
Site and Service Schemes	11.4	6.1	9.1	0.5	5.2	1.1	0.1	3.1
Completion, Alternation, & Upgrading of Preindependence Schemes	4.1	22.8	18.7	23.5	1.9	1.8	1.8	6.1
Staff Housing	8.9	1.2	20.1	14.9	2.7	0.1	0.0	3.9
Miscellaneous	0.1	0.6	12.3	0.0	0.0	0.1	1.2	0.8
Total NCC Capital Expenditure on Housing ($)	1,079,155	613,821	486,290	1,946,808	4,096,431	4,075,990	3,074,772	15,373,267
Housing as percentage of total capital expenditure	34.9	36.4	15.1	33.4	55.9	66.3	65.3	48.0

Source: Analysis of data on housing expenditure from the Nairobi City Council's annual *Abstracts of Accounts*.

sorbed roughly a quarter of total NCC housing expenditures; 75 percent of this was used for a single scheme in the oldest central city residential area. During the first few years after independence, about a fifth of the annual housing expenditure was devoted to upgrading or completing old schemes inherited from the colonial government. Much of this money was used to modernize pit latrines or bucket sanitation facilities. Recently such expenditures have accounted for less than two percent of the total. Over the whole period, expenditure on site and service projects (in which lots serviced with sanitation units are allocated to individuals so that they can construct their own houses) represented only three percent of total expenditure.

As Table 9-3 shows, the average cost-per-unit of public housing construction by the city council has been rising over time. Almost all of the most inexpensive council housing in use at the beginning of 1972 was inherited from the preindependence period. Thus, of

231

the 13,751 units that had charges of less than $15.28 per month, 12,934 or 94.1 percent were built prior to independence. Among the 5,066 units built between 1964 and 1971, 41.6 percent had monthly charges of $15.28 to $26.60, 21.6 percent fell in the $26.74 to $38.06 range, and 20.4 percent cost more than $38.20 a month. Naturally, the pre- and postindependence units are not directly comparable because of the rise in building costs, and because the colonialists emphasized the provision of minimal accommodation for African laborers rather than family units. Nevertheless. it is clear that the units built at different times are serving different segments of Nairobi's population.

TABLE 9-3
NAIROBI CITY COUNCIL STOCK OF CONVENTIONAL HOUSING BY TYPE, COST, AND PERIOD BUILT (PERCENTAGES)

Monthly Cost of Units[a]	Rental Units Built Before 1964	Rental Units Built 1964-1967	Site & Service Plots 1964-1967	Rental Units Built 1968-1971	Tenant Purchase Units Built 1968-1971	Total Units in Use, December 31, 1971		
						Site and Service	Rental	Tenant Purchase
Up to $7.50	46.8		74.3			3.9	34.5	
$7.51 to $11.32	11.2				1.7		8.2	0.3
$11.33 to $15.14	33.1						24.4	
$15.15 to $18.96	0.8			21.8	17.2		5.2	3.6
$18.97 to $26.60	2.2				12.9		1.6	2.7
$26.61 to $38.06	2.5	24.1		9.7	11.3		5.2	2.4
$38.07 to $53.35	3.3			5.0	11.1		3.4	2.3
$53.36 to $76.27	0.1				3.8		0.1	0.8
over $76.27	0.0	1.7		0.8	3.8		0.5	0.8
Subtotal		25.7	74.3	38.2	61.8	3.9	83.1	13.0
Period total	100.0	100.1		100.1			99.9	
(Number of housing units)	(14,203)	(1,010)		(4,056)			(19,269)	

[a] The monthly rent for rental units; the monthly repayment, assuming the maximum 20-year loan, for tenant purchase schemes; and the monthly plot and service fee for site and service plots.
Source: Nairobi City Council, Department of Social Services and Housing.

The growing inadequacy of the volume of the public sector housing program is reflected in the declining ratio of city council units to Nairobi's population. In 1963, Nairobi's population was 342,764 and the city council had 14,203 units of rental housing, yielding a ratio of one unit per 24.1 people. By 1971, the population had risen to 585,191, while the council's housing stock grew to 19,269; the ratio thus climbed to one unit per 30.4 people. During the eight-year period, the population grew by 242,427 and the council's housing stock by 5,066, changing the ratio to one unit for every 47.8 people. Clearly, the activities of the city council and other government agencies in the housing field have not been keeping pace with Nairobi's rapid population growth.

BIASES IN NAIROBI'S PUBLIC HOUSING PROGRAM

Evidence that recent public housing construction in Nairobi is strongly biased in favor of those in the middle- and high-income brackets is found in Table 9-4. It presents a cumulative index of housing built by the government between 1968 and 1971 in Nairobi, and an estimation of the proportion of Nairobi's African households in a position to afford publicly built housing of various costs. Of the units in Table 9-4, 83 percent were built by the city council, 15 percent by the NHC, and 2 percent through a civil servants' mortgage scheme.[16] It is apparent that virtually nothing was built by the public sector between 1968-1971 that fell within the means of the poorest third of the African population, that the middle third of African households was disproportionately favored by the public sector program, and that the top third was only very slightly underserved. In numerical terms, the roughly 42,000 African households (containing over 175,000 people) with incomes under $76 per month saw only 67 units they could afford built during this period. This represents one unit for every 627 households. The middle third of the households, falling in the $76 to $191 monthly income range, were in a position to afford slightly more than two-thirds of the units. Thus, one unit of appropriate housing was built for every 12 households in this group. Finally, a third of the units were appropriate for only the African households with monthly incomes over $191, or one unit for every 25 households in this group.

The preponderance of tenant purchase housing has been another way in which Nairobi's public sector housing program has served the city's middle- and upper-income groups better than the poor. Better-off people have generally preferred to buy homes if

16 Ibid., p. 209.

233

TABLE 9-4

HOUSING DEMAND BY NAIROBI AFRICAN HOUSEHOLDS, 1971, COMPARED TO
PUBLIC SECTOR RESIDENTIAL CONSTRUCTION, 1968-1971

Monthly Cost Category[a]	Percentage of Public Sector Units, 1968-1971[b]		Percentage of African Households Able to Afford This Housing[c]	
	%	Cumulative	%	Cumulative
Up to $7.50	0.0	0.0	5.4	5.4
$7.51 to $11.32	1.4	1.4	16.7	22.1
$11.33 to $15.14	0.0	1.4	13.1	35.2
$15.15 to $18.96	32.8	34.2	9.4	44.6
$18.97 to $26.60	11.3	45.5	14.5	59.1
$26.61 to $38.06	24.1	69.6	9.4	68.5
$38.07 to $53.35	14.6	84.2	10.4	78.9
$53.36 to $76.27	6.5	90.7	10.4	89.3
over $76.27	9.4	100.1	10.6	99.9

[a] Monthly rental and tenant purchase payments.

[b] Includes Nairobi City Council and National Housing Corporation units as well as civil servants' mortgage houses in Nairobi.

[c] Assuming that 20 percent of household income is devoted to rental or tenant purchase payments. The income distribution was estimated on the basis of data for 1968-1969 reported by the International Labour Office in *Employment, Incomes and Equality: A Strategy for Increasing Productive Employment in Kenya* (Geneva, 1972), p. 346. The 1968-1969 figures were increased to reflect the 10.6 percent per annum growth of Nairobi's Gross Domestic Product estimated by the Nairobi City Council's Urban Study Group.

possible while poorer people have preferred rental units.[17] Table 9-3 indicated that 62 percent of the housing units built by the Nairobi City Council during the period 1968-1971 was for sale on a tenant purchase basis; almost all of the housing handled by the National Housing Corporation and the Housing Finance Company was also for purchase rather than rental.

These data argue strongly that the publicly stated priorities of the government's housing program were not implemented in that

[17] Data from a 1972 survey in a mixed income neighborhood of Nairobi showed that members of the middle- and upper-income groups had a strong preference for buying a house rather than renting one. In a survey of tenants' preferences for renting versus buying a house, the preference for renting had a strong inverse relationship to income. The higher the income of the respondent, the more likely he was to prefer buying a house. Whereas two-thirds of those with monthly incomes under $35 preferred to rent again, over two-thirds of those with incomes of $105 or more preferred to buy or build. N. Temple, "Housing Preferences and Policy in Kibera, Nairobi" (Nairobi: Institute for Development Studies, University of Nairobi, 1974), table VIII.

234

the program served the middle- and upper-income groups rather than the low-income sectors. If it were not for the inexpensive city council rental housing inherited from the colonial period, the public sector would have had almost no housing to offer to the poorest third of the urban population.

The middle- and upper-income bias in Table 9-4 is so marked that even if there were distortions in the data on housing demand, they would probably not be of enough magnitude to change the conclusion. In fact, since the survey on which the table's income distribution data are based probably undersampled poor households, the bias may even be understated.[18] Moreover, for reasons to be discussed below, the housing allocation process also tends to favor the middle- and upper-income groups, so that poorer people do not receive many of the units appropriate for them, except as subtenants paying market rents several times higher than the official monthly cost.

The remainder of this chapter will explore more fully the reasons why the announced goals of public housing policy were not implemented in practice. The next section examines elite attitudes that affected housing outcomes, while the following section focuses on the politics of housing policy and allocations.

EXPLAINING THE BIASES IN NAIROBI'S PUBLIC HOUSING PROGRAM: OFFICIAL ATTITUDES

Many national government officials and prominent politicians as well as city councillors and council staff have had a preference for high quality, and therefore costly, public housing construction, and their attitudes were reflected in the kinds of housing programs actually promoted. The question of housing standards, particularly in Nairobi, is a sensitive political issue, and in a country very concerned with its progress toward modernity, public housing is often treated as a visible symbol of Kenya's achievements.[19] President Kenyatta himself took the lead in touting the virtues of modern

---

[18] The survey was conducted by the Nairobi Urban Study Group of the Nairobi City Council in 1971. Biases in the sampling frame which resulted in undersampling low-income households are discussed in F. Temple, "Politics, Planning," p. 210.

[19] Cf. R. Stren, "The Evolution of Housing Policy in Kenya" in J. Hutton, ed., *Urban Challenge in East Africa* (Nairobi: East African Publishing House, 1972), p. 81.

housing and castigating those who would build dwellings reminiscent of the quarters provided by the colonialists for Africans. When he inspected a new city council estate with apartments that rented for $63.68 and $73.58 a month, he is reported to have commented that it was adequate, but should have included servants' quarters.

The president's strongest statement came in 1972 when he was opening some new houses at Thika, a town about 25 miles from Nairobi. According to a *Daily Nation* account entitled, "No More Shabby Houses for Our People—Mzee,"

> President Kenyatta warned at the weekend he will sack any of his Ministers who continue to treat Kenyans as the colonialists did by building them "native-type" houses not suitable for human habitation.
>
> He said all those charged with the responsibility of building houses for Wananchi [the common people], especially in towns, must ensure that the houses built are suitable for a family to live in.
>
> Mzee Kenyatta recalled that in the olden days Africans were provided with poor quality houses known as "native houses" not fit for human beings to occupy. The houses were not adequate to accommodate families and lacked such amenities as water, sanitation or light.
>
> "I will sack any of my Ministers who continues to treat Wananchi of independent Kenya in this manner," the President said.
>
> Saying that the time has gone when the people of Kenya should be treated in such a manner, Mzee Kenyatta also said that his Government would vigorously engage itself in clearing slums throughout the country.[20]

This speech had a profound effect on city council officials; months later, when asked why the council did not build cheaper housing, they still recalled it. The atmosphere created by such statements encouraged government officials to treat city council proposals for low-cost housing gingerly.

Far from compelling conformity with its enunciated low-cost housing goals, the national government sometimes acted as a restraining force on efforts by the city council to build homes for

[20] "No More Shabby Houses for Our People—Mzee," *Daily Nation*, (Nairobi) July 24, 1972.

Nairobi's less well-off inhabitants. Although the *Development Plan* stipulated that low-cost site and service schemes in which residents build their own houses and gradually improve them "will be a significant part of the housing programme in urban areas," a meeting of high-level national government decision makers decided in February 1972 that this approach was unsuitable for Kenya's cities.[21] Although this decision was later effectively reversed, the government withheld approval for approximately a year on a proposal for a site and service scheme in Nairobi which the World Bank had tentatively promised to finance. It appears that one of the reasons why approval was eventually forthcoming was that the government did not want to refuse finance for a project that the World Bank, which provided Kenya with much development finance, had indicated it thought was in the best interests of the country.

The attitudes of the city councillors also affected the design of houses. Their criticisms often not only delayed the design and construction of housing estates, but when taken into account, increased the cost of the units considerably. The councillors frequently complained that the houses designed by council staff were not good enough. This view was expressed in its most general form at a meeting of the Social Services and Housing Committee in 1970:

> A member informed the committee that the layout plan of certain City Council houses did not provide maximum conveniences to the tenants and suggested that in future, officers should consider housing layout plans which would afford maximum conveniences for the occupiers. . . .
>
> A member of the committee reported that the tenant-purchase houses at Uhuru and Kariobangi Estates were too close together and each house should have been built on its own plot. Consequently, these houses did not provide maximum conveniences to the occupiers.
>
> The City Engineer reported that the layout and designs of these houses were in accordance with designs approved by this committee. The prices charged to the purchasers were most reasonable and if the houses were constructed on separate plots the price would have been considerably higher.[22]

[21] *Development Plan 1970-74*, p. 519.
[22] Nairobi City Council, *Minutes*, 37 (1969-1970), 1656, 1658.

The committee then advised the staff to take its criticisms into account when designing estates in the future.

On many occasions, council staff had to modify proposed designs to incorporate councillors' criticisms. The result was invariably an increase in the cost per unit of the dwellings, and often the total number of units in the scheme was decreased because the money allocated to the scheme was not sufficient to build as many units as originally planned.[23] In their efforts to explain behaviors such as these on the part of councillors, council staff tended to emphasize their lack of technical understanding. It was thought that they had a difficult time appreciating the cost implications of the changes they proposed and their significance for the types of people who could afford such units.

While this point undoubtedly has some validity, it assumes that the primary goal of the councillors was to provide the least expensive housing possible. But since the councillors were by and large an upwardly mobile group who shared the middle-class consumption aspirations of Nairobi's elite, and benefited politically from allocating council housing mainly to other members of this elite, they naturally preferred the council to build the type of housing in which they and people like them would want to live.

The attitudes of officials responsible for the council's finances also contributed to the tendency to build more expensive housing. These officials were naturally concerned that the council should only invest in sound projects, and they were always wary of low-cost schemes. Much of the council's capital finance was obtained on a long-term basis. When money was borrowed from the National Housing Corporation to build rental units, for example, it was repayable over a forty-year period, and rents were set so that the scheme would be self-financing over that time span. The spectre that haunted officials in the City Treasurer's Department was that a low-cost scheme would become obsolescent before the end of the repayment period. The council would then be left with outstanding financial obligations and an estate that it deemed unsuitable for habitation. Whenever a low-cost scheme was proposed, therefore, officials concerned with finance were often the first to voice the fear that it would turn into a slum. In an inter-

[23] For examples, see Nairobi City Council, *Minutes*, 36 (1968-1969), 1042, 1057; 37 (1969-1970), 487; 38 (1970-1971), 584-585, 832, (1954-1955), 2169-2170, 2782-2783, 2788-2789; and 40 (1971-1972), 294-295.

view, for instance, one of the city's senior financial officials questioned the reasonableness of the definition of low-cost units as those that could be built for $3,396 or less. He expressed the opinion that $4,245 might be a more appropriate ceiling.

In addition to the complex of attitudes and practices discussed above that relate directly to housing, images of Nairobi and its role in the nation held by decision makers also indirectly affected decision making with regard to housing. Many of the city's residents take pride in Nairobi's visible modernity, a pride that was reinforced in 1972 by its selection as the site for the First All-African Trade Fair and for the headquarters of the United Nations Environmental Program. The *Sunday Nation* newspaper affirmed that "Nairobi is now being recognized and acclaimed all over the world as one of the most progressive and beautiful world capitals," and the city's provincial commissioner expressed the opinion that "with the political stability prevailing in the country as a whole, the growth of Nairobi was proceeding at an accelerated rate and, in a few year's [sic] time, if all goes well, Nairobi will undoubtedly rank among the world's best cities and compare favourably in standards with the old established cities of the world."[24] The concomitant of this civic pride was often the belief that inexpensive housing would mar the city's image and that any manifestations of poverty should be eradicated, usually by repatriating the poor to the countryside.

The way in which these attitudes could affect thinking about housing in Nairobi is amply illustrated by the minutes of a meeting to discuss the redevelopment of an old city council estate relatively near the tourist-saturated city center:

> Concern was expressed by [one officer] about the type of housing to be erected at Shauri Moyo. The estate is so close to the City centre that visitors to the City are likely to see this area and in addition the value of the land is quite high. Therefore it might not be possible to house people in such income bracket [$42.50 to $85 per month] at Shauri Moyo.
>
> [Another officer] suggested that instead of thinking in terms of retaining the present site for low income housing, an effort

[24] "Nairobi Wins More Praise" and "PC Sees Nairobi as One of World's Top Cities," *Daily Nation* (Nairobi), December 3, 1972 and September 11, 1971, respectively.

should be made to avoid creation of modern slum neighbor-hoods.[25]

Similar sentiments were expressed virtually every time a housing project near the city center or a main road was discussed.

This climate of elite opinion also discouraged the kind of technical and social experimentation that might have helped surmount the obstacles to housing poorer sections of the population posed by rising building costs. When, for example, timber was used in an experimental project, the object was not to build the least expensive units possible, but to see whether it was an appropriate material for medium-cost houses. The councillors' general attitude toward the houses built in the experimental scheme was that they were nice, but would have been better if they had been built of more expensive concrete blocks. These attitudes also prevented the government from relying more heavily on low-cost site and service schemes.

Given the prevailing attitudes described above, it was obvious to most African staff members of housing agencies that advocacy of low-cost housing was not the best channel for upward career mobility. Those Africans who were interested in fostering inexpensive housing tended to adopt a low profile, being reluctant to push very hard or very visibly. Many of the African staff members shared the prevalent attitudes about housing and, therefore, had little inclination to promote inexpensive housing.

Expatriate staff of the city council and other agencies, on the other hand, provided much of the initiative behind low-cost housing proposals. They did not have to worry about long-term futures in Kenya. Most came to Nairobi on two- or three-year contracts and obviously had no ambitions in the local career structure. Also, many of the expatriates attracted to work in Kenya brought with them some concern for the poor, and they were troubled by the biases in the urban public housing program. They tended, therefore, to be particularly enthusiastic about low-cost housing and were the authors of many of the statements on housing policy in official government documents.

However, there was considerable reserve on the part of many of the African staff for the schemes to "help the poor" proposed by expatriates. The situation is well illustrated by the history of the

[25] Nairobi City Council, "Redevelopment of Shauri Moyo—Notes of a Meeting held at County Hall on 22nd October 1970."

240

city council's involvement in the Mathare Valley slum area. During the late 1960s, this area mushroomed into Nairobi's largest concentration of uncontrolled informal sector housing. The initiative behind the council's program to ameliorate the appalling conditions there came particularly from five expatriates: three city council staff members, an American working with the National Christian Council of Kenya (NCCK), and a Peace Corps volunteer. One council official, noting the religious convictions of one of the staff members and the presence of the NCCK worker, said that the program was launched "with the aura of a missionary crusade." The program was designed to supply services in the area and to assist residents in improving their housing. In 1972, however, partially on the initiative of President Kenyatta, the government declared its dissatisfaction with the approach and ordered the city council to stop all work in Mathare Valley. By then, four of the five expatriates mentioned above had left Kenya, and the fifth was no longer working for the council. As a consequence, the council's African staff were left with responsibility for the ill-fated program—in this case, with the blame.

Experiences such as this made many of the council's African staff wary of the well-intentioned ideas of expatriates with regard to low-cost housing. The usual response to such ideas was not to criticize or oppose them, but, intentionally or unintentionally, to stall. This may have reflected the low priority accorded to inexpensive housing, the relatively long time it could take for proposals to move through bureaucratic channels, and the inexperience of expatriates at prodding the bureaucratic machine; or it may have reflected a conscious strategy. The expatriate staff tended to come and go with relative frequency, and there were few who remained with the council long enough to learn how to have their ideas implemented. The result was a virtually constant undercurrent of discussion about low-cost housing, but relatively little achievement in practice.

Explaining Biases in Nairobi's Public Housing Programs: Political Pressure and Allocation Decisions

In addition to official attitudes that established a bias in favor of expensive rather than low-cost housing, Nairobi's public programs were also affected during their implementation by the types of political resources available to the intended beneficiaries—the

241

poor—compared to those available to the actual beneficiaries—better-off individuals. The politics of allocation in Kenya indicate the absence of effective channels through which the city's poorer inhabitants could affect policy formulation and implementation.[26] According to the general manager of the National Housing Corporation, one of the major reasons why "a very large percentage of these [publicly built] houses are occupied by people in the medium and sometimes also in the high income groups" was the "inability of the poor to create effective pressure groups which can force housing authorities to allocate rental housing to members of the lower income groups."[27]

Thus, one of the most significant characteristics of politics in Nairobi is the limited role played by formal organizations that express the interests of various groups in the city. Instead, most of the demand making is done on a particularistic basis through personal contacts with politicians or bureaucrats. Groups and organizations that play important roles in American urban politics are therefore relatively insignificant in Nairobi. This is true in the case of business groups, the press, labor unions, voluntary associations, and political parties.

The larger businesses in Nairobi are predominantly foreign-owned, and many of their senior executives are not Kenyans. Therefore, many businesses are reluctant to play a formal, public role in politics in Nairobi lest they appear to be interfering illegitimately in local affairs. Similarly, Nairobi's two most prominent newspapers, the *East African Standard* and the *Daily Nation/ Taifa Leo*, are also predominantly foreign-owned, and this may contribute to their reticence in taking strong stands on contro-

---

[26] The political ineffectiveness of the urban poor is not unique to Kenya, of course, as indicated in Janice Perlman's study of Rio de Janeiro in this volume. For a broad review of the political roles played by the urban poor, see J. M. Nelson, *Access to Power: Politics and the Urban Poor in Developing Countries* (Princeton: Princeton University Press, 1979). Two specific Latin American studies which also deal with housing policy and the urban poor are W. A. Cornelius, *Politics and the Migrant Poor in Mexico City* (Stanford, Ca.: Stanford University Press, 1975); and A. Portes, "Housing Policy, Urban Poverty and the State: The Favelas of Rio de Janeiro 1972-76," paper prepared for the Burg Wartenstein Symposium No. 73 on Shantytowns in Developing Nations under the auspices of the Wenner-Gren Foundation for Anthropological Research, July 1977.

[27] Speech of S. G. Ayany, general manager, National Housing Corporation, given at the United Kenya Club, Nairobi, September 15, 1971, typescript.

versial issues in Nairobi.[28] The government does not control the press directly, but the newspapers practice self-censorship. Much of the news about the Nairobi City Council in both papers, for example, is taken directly from press releases and the monthly *Minutes*; critical commentary on council actions is rare and tempered when it does occur.[29]

As in many other Third World countries, Kenya's postcolonial political leaders have been suspicious of the trade union movement's potential as a base of political opposition as well as a threat to the stability of the economy. The government's regulation of the trade union movement has discouraged it from assuming a political role either on the national or local level. In addition, the number of voluntary associations in Nairobi is comparatively limited, and few of them have participated actively in politics. Some of the tribally based associations that have Nairobi branches, such as the Luo Union or Gema (the Gukuyu, Embu, Meru Association), are well organized, but they are primarily concerned with the welfare of their tribes' rural home areas rather than with Nairobi affairs. The political role of voluntary associations has been further restricted by the government's regulation that they avoid politically threatening activities in order to become and remain legally registered. Permission to hold public political meetings or meetings of nonregistered groups must be obtained from the provincial administration, which provides the government with a further curb on the political activities of associations.[30]

In Nairobi, the disorganization of the country's single political party, KANU, and the characteristics of recent elections have meant that the city's only political party has not been a major channel for demand making. KANU has essentially ceased to function at the local level in most places in Nairobi, and it is certainly not organized to dispense rewards to common members. In fact, in single-party elections in which several party candidates run

28 See *Who Controls Industry in Kenya?*, Report of a Working Party, set up under the auspices of the National Christian Council of Kenya (Nairobi: East African Publishing House, 1968), p. 108.

29 This point, which is evident from reading the newspapers, was confirmed during discussions with two local journalists.

30 The principal exception to the generalization that voluntary associations have not been able to influence political decisions in Nairobi is the National Christian Council of Kenya, which has initiated a number of projects to help poor people in the city and played an active role in trying to shape the city council's policy toward the Mathare Valley slum.

against each other, the logic of rewarding voters for supporting the party breaks down. Furthermore, the administrative manipulation of the last regular election in 1968, the low turnouts in by-elections since then, and the postponement until 1974 of city council elections scheduled for 1972 have all combined to reduce the incentives for politicians in Nairobi to be particularly sensitive to the demands of their constituents.

In the absence of organizations through which they can express their demands, people who wish to obtain help from the government must resort to direct contacts with politicians or bureaucrats. In order to understand why this political style should favor Nairobi's better-off residents over poorer people, it is instructive to examine the potential resources that members of each group can use to influence decision making. In many political systems, the primary resource of the masses is their numbers. In systems in which competitive elections are held regularly, the poorer urban residents can often derive benefits from supporting a particular candidate or party. This is the typical pattern of "machine" politics: a political party provides tangible rewards, such as jobs or favors from the city bureaucracy, in return for regular support at the polls.[31] In the United States, political machines provided an important organizational mechanism for integrating immigrants into urban life. In Nairobi, however, the characteristics of the electoral system have not been conducive to the establishment of machine politics. Politicians have not had to rely primarily on the periodic mobilization of voters to succeed politically, and the incentives for developing strong local party organizations have been weak. Of the forty elected councillors serving in 1972-1973,

---

[31] There is substantial literature on machine politics in the United States. E. C. Banfield and J. Q. Wilson, *City Politics* (Cambridge: Harvard University Press, 1963) provides a chapter-long overview of American urban machines, while E. C. Banfield, ed., *Urban Government* (New York: Free Press, 1969) presents a variety of perspectives on machines and efforts to reform them. The evolution of the Chicago machine is particularly well described in H. F. Gosnell, *Machine Politics Chicago Model* (Chicago: University of Chicago Press, 1937); M. Meyerson and E. C. Banfield, *Politics, Planning and the Public Interest* (New York: Free Press, 1955); and E. C. Banfield, *Political Influence* (New York: Free Press, 1961). A perceptive analysis of the conditions under which machines emerge and atrophy in developing countries is presented in chaps. 6-9 of J. C. Scott, *Comparative Political Corruption* (Englewood Cliffs, N.J.: Prentice-Hall, 1972).

244

twenty-nine had been elected unopposed in 1968 when the opposition KPU candidates were administratively disqualified. Seventeen of these entered the council for the first time that year, with the result that 43 percent of the councillors in 1972-1973 had not been elected in competitive elections. The eleven councillors who entered the council between 1968 and 1972 were chosen in elections characterized by very small turnouts.

Under these circumstances, many councillors may justifiably feel more obligated to members of the local political elite who helped them secure their nominations than to their constituents. The observation of one council officer during an interview that "most of the councillors don't know any houseless people" is probably not too much of an exaggeration. These factors help to explain why none of the councillors tried to turn the bias in the council's housing program into a political issue.

In addition, however, poorer urban residents lack the qualitative characteristics that permit Nairobi's better-off inhabitants to take advantage of personal contacts to secure benefits, such as public housing units, from the city's governing agencies. Among the more important resources are education, wealth (even if it is quite modest), contacts made at school or work, and any prerogatives that might be associated with jobs. Education, for example, is important because it bestows status and improves one's ability to deal with the bureaucracy. Most official forms are written in English, and a person who is illiterate or who only knows Swahili in addition to his tribal language can easily be intimidated by bureaucratic procedures. Of course, education is also important because it opens up job opportunities.

Friendships developed at school can be useful in providing a network of contacts in various government agencies and private businesses throughout the city. Secondary school ties can be as important as those developed at the university level. Kenya's educational pyramid is narrow (and was even narrower when the current adult generation passed through the system), and most of Kenya's better secondary schools are boarding schools. Attendance at these schools breeds close ties with fellow students and an awareness of having progressed further than most of one's peers.

Wealth and a job that might permit one to do favors for other people are useful because they enable an individual to enter into reciprocal relations with other members of his network of con-

245

tacts. Money can, of course, be used to bribe people for favors, but, more prosaically, it is also important because it permits a person to cultivate contacts with potentially helpful people. For example, informal drinking sessions after work are an important means of communication in Nairobi, but only those with a steady income can afford to participate in them regularly.

Ethnic ties are one important resource available to the poor as well as to the better-off Nairobi residents. Requests for assistance from governmental agencies are often made through members of one's own ethnic group, and this helps to explain the concern with "ethnic representation" in employment decisions in the city council. Hiring a member of a particular ethnic group is not only a form of patronage, it is also a way of increasing the likelihood that members of that ethnic group will be treated sympathetically when they make requests to bureaucrats. Nevertheless, although a poor person may be able to rely on ethnic ties to establish contacts with influential people, his chances of actually obtaining favorable responses will be less than those of other members of his ethnic group who can also use the other resources described earlier.

Many people in Nairobi believed that housing allocations were especially vulnerable to personal influence. Even when low-cost housing was built, many units intended for the poor apparently were allocated to better-off people with "good connections." Since housing allocations provided a very tangible means of rewarding supporters, relatives, and friends, it was not surprising that the city councillors endeavored to preserve as much personal control over allocation procedures as possible. Council staff members were also tied into Nairobi's network of personal influence and obligation, and many of them tried to use their positions to influence allocations. Furthermore, many city council employees desired council housing for themselves, and given Nairobi's long tradition of employer-supplied housing, they felt that the council had an obligation to provide it for them. When medium-cost estates came up for allocation, council employees often constituted a powerful internal lobby.

The city council's handling of its tenant purchase scheme drew sharp criticism from the Parliamentary Public Accounts Committee in 1972:

> This Committee is very concerned that the administration of
> Tenant Purchase Schemes in the City Council and the selection

of those to benefit from them leaves much to be desired. The Committee is further concerned that in general the houses in these schemes may have been used for speculative purposes by some individuals and that the allocation of the houses may not always have been fair. . . .

The processing of the applications in respect of these schemes leaves much to be desired. The register does not record adequate details of applicants, neither does it show the action taken on each application. As for the required deposits, cases have been noted where although the initial deposits were not in accordance with the prospectus, houses were allocated to the depositors. Further, arrears of principal and interest do not appear to have been pursued vigorously enough by Council while outstanding balances are not reconciled regularly.[32]

It is hardly surprising, given the nature of the allocation process, that when the architect who designed one of the city council's medium-cost estates did a user-reaction study, he discovered "there was reason to believe, within weeks of the first dwellings being handed over, that a higher income level of tenants were moving in than those that the Estate was originally designed for."[33]

The quotation from the Public Accounts Committee's report hints at one of the reasons why the housing allocation process is so politically charged: a great deal of money can be made through the illegal subletting of these units. Since the market rents are so much higher than the monthly charges for public housing, an individual can make large profits by renting out his public housing rather than moving into it. The units are, in fact, often internally subdivided and rented to several households. This can be a profitable business for a person whose good fortune and political connections enable him to be allocated several units of public housing. It is not unknown for influential individuals to secure public housing in more than one city in Kenya.

The individual demand maker seeking a desirable house was not really concerned with redirecting overall housing policy toward the better-off, but only with getting a good house or apartment. Thus, public housing policy, in practice, seems to have evolved as a result of these myriad individualistic pressures from

[32] Republic of Kenya, *Report of the Public Accounts Committee on County Councils for the Period 1967 to 1971* (Nairobi: National Assembly, 1972), pp. 32, 34.

[33] Menezes and Partners, "Outer Ring Road Estate, Nairobi" (Nairobi: 1971), paragraph 1.00.

247

NINE · *Temple and Temple*

better-off people, rather than from explicit deliberations by policy-makers about alternative housing programs. Theorizing and elaboration of "official" government policy positions went on at one level, while the actual policy was created in daily decisions on lot size, unit size, building materials, housing standards, and last but not least, allocation of the units.

CONCLUSION

Publicly supplied housing has several intrinsic characteristics that affect the nature of the political pressures brought to bear at the implementation stage. It is visible, divisible, desirable, and tangible. Public housing can be an extraordinarily visible symbol of the government's accomplishments on behalf of the people. Provision of "modern" housing superior to the minimal quarters erected for local people by the colonial regime is one way a newly independent nation's government can demonstrate that it is delivering the fruits of independence to the people. Conversely, building low-cost settlements that visually resemble "slums" is not a source of pride for the government. It is often more politically rewarding to blame poor housing conditions on others—the colonial government, illegal squatters, unscrupulous landlords, the unsanitary habits of slumdwellers—than to take responsibility for providing improved housing conditions that are affordable by the poor. Thus, ironically, efforts to build modest low-cost housing often prove vulnerable to criticism that they show a "colonial mentality" or a lack of concern for the poor because the housing is not good enough. The fact that officials frequently equate "cheap" with "unsound" also leads to fears that inexpensive housing will not last long enough for the government's development costs to be recouped.

Because it is a divisible rather than a collective good, competition for public housing is usually individualistic, with the competitors keenly aware that the supply of units is limited. In rapidly growing cities, all housing is in short supply, and public housing is especially coveted because it is usually priced at cost or lower, rather than according to market demand. Moreover, in many cities, public housing can be a capital asset or an income generating asset as well as a benefit to be consumed. Given the fact that public housing is the type of program in which widely desired benefits are to be conferred on only a few, it is not surprising to find that individuals and groups with greater political power seek

248

to acquire these benefits for themselves. In the Kenyan political context, as in the Mexican case discussed in Chapter Eight, the poor generally lack effective channels for affecting policy formulation and implementation, while individuals of higher status have a disproportionate share of the resources that can be translated into political influence. This political context is another reason why a public housing policy ostensibly directed to serving the poor was redirected during its implementation to benefit higher-income groups.

Nairobi has not one housing problem, but many. Roughly a third of the city's residents live in uncontrolled, illegal housing. In many areas of the city, the level of amenity is low and there is overcrowding. Many dwellings, especially in the center of the city, are old, run-down, and were targeted for redevelopment in the early 1960s. Rents, building costs, and land prices have been rising. Too few units of new housing are being built to house the city's rising populace at desired standards and at costs that they can afford.

The *formal* response of Nairobi's governing institutions to these problems—reiterated in a variety of reports, plans, and public statements—is a commitment to build inexpensive public housing intended primarily for the city's poorer residents not served adequately by the private market. In practice, this goal has been subverted, and the public sector housing program in Nairobi has emphasized medium- and high-cost houses. Nairobi's government has behaved as though the city's primary housing problem were a shortage of housing for purchase by middle- and upper-income groups.

The bias toward medium- and high-cost housing found in Nairobi is typical of many cities in Third World countries. Some of the characteristics of politics in Nairobi are shared by other cities and may help explain this bias. Since political leaders, and especially public officials, are usually members of the economic elite in developing countries, they may well be more attuned to the interests of that group than to other sectors of the society. To the extent that decision making for housing is insulated from pressures brought by low-income people, the biases of politicians and bureaucrats that arise from their status are free to operate, and the tendency toward expensive public housing becomes more understandable, if not more acceptable, to those who would prefer to see greater attention given to the poor.

TEN · The Failure of Influence: Squatter Eradication in Brazil

JANICE PERLMAN

MANY of the chapters in this book demonstrate how public policy is modified as it proceeds from *idea* to *implementation* to *impact*. In an open society, a well-organized constituency can often affect programs or policies that have direct bearing on them either through representation, negotiation, or confrontation. In an authoritarian regime, however, this is rarely if ever possible. Access to decision makers is severely limited, and attempts at influence are dealt with not through responsiveness but repression. As Juan Linz has pointed out, it is in the nature of authoritarian regimes to require a population that is quiescent and obedient.[1] When the populace does not acquiesce, severe sanctions are brought to bear.

This chapter describes an attempt by one constituent group within an authoritarian regime to prevent the implementation of a policy that would have totally destroyed its way of life. Not only did the group fail to influence the outcome in the one instance, but sanctions employed against it were so severe that any future attempts at influence were entirely abandoned.

The irony of the situation is that the policies implemented created a self-fulfilling prophecy, giving rise to precisely those problems and destructive tendencies they were intended to control and incurring significant social, political, and economic costs for the system.

The case in point is Brazil, and the specific issue is that of housing policy for the one million squatters living in the *favelas*

Note: This chapter is adapted from my book, *The Myth of Marginality: Urban Politics and Poverty in Rio de Janeiro* (Berkeley: University of California Press, 1976). I am grateful to University of California Press for permission to reprint part of that book.

[1] J. Linz, "An Authoritarian Regime: Spain" in E. Allardt and Y. Littunen, eds., *Cleavages: Ideologies and Party Systems* (Helsinki: Transactions of the Westmark Society, 1964). See also A. Stepan, ed., *Authoritarian Brazil* (New Haven: Yale University Press, 1973).

(shantytowns) of Rio de Janeiro in the years 1968-1969. Brazil has one of the highest rates of urban growth in Latin America. A fifth of the entire population of the nation became cityward migrants in the decade of the 1960s, and there is no indication of a decrease in either absolute numbers or rates of migration in the 1970s. Recent official figures estimate rural-urban migration at the rate of 1,300,000 people per year. Of the nine major metropolitan areas of the country, Rio de Janeiro is among the fastest growing and demonstrates in most striking form the problems referred to as "hyperurbanization." The coup of 1964 established a military dictatorship and created an institution, the National Housing Bank, with enough centralized power, financial resources, and back-up military force to implement a policy of massive squatter eradication.

The first target was Rio de Janeiro, which by the mid-sixties had some 300 favelas containing one-seventh of the total population of the metropolitan area. While the city itself was growing at 2.7 percent a year, these favelas and the peripheral dormitory towns ("suburbios") were growing at 7.5 percent a year. They were considered an eyesore, a blight on the urban landscape, and an irrational use of valuable and well-located land. The people living in them were considered to be "marginal," i.e. to be a parasitic drain on the urban economy, to pose the threat of political disruption, to cling to parochial rural values, to be isolated from mainstream urban life, and to suffer from all forms of social disorganization—family breakdown, crime, and prostitution.

The evidence, however, strongly indicates that the favelados are not marginal but in fact integrated into the society, albeit in a manner detrimental to their own interests. They are certainly not separate from or on the margin of the system, but are tightly bound into it in a severely asymmetric form. They contribute their hard work, their high hopes, and their loyalties, but they do not benefit from the goods and services of the system. In short, the favela residents are not economically and politically marginal, but are exploited and repressed; they are not socially and culturally marginal, but are stigmatized and excluded from a closed social system. Rather than being passively marginal in terms of their own attitudes and behavior, they are being actively marginalized by the system and by public policy.

A prime example of this active marginalization is the policy of squatter removal and relocation. It is a clear case of the use of the myths of marginality as ideological justification to carry out upper-

251

sector policy at the expense of the lower sectors. What this chapter shows is that the squatters were quite astute in recognizing their interests and acting on their own behalf. When they attempted to participate through organizing against squatter removal, they were arrested, shot at, burned out, dumped outside the city, and eventually coopted into helping with the plan for their own removal.

Perversely, the "success" of this removal program is creating the same type of marginalized population it was designed to eliminate. It isolated people from the very jobs and urban amenities that had attracted them to the city in the first place, broke down their survival mechanisms and the social cohesion of their communities, and created anger and animosity toward the government, which had previously been regarded as benign if not benevolent.

The study was carried out in Rio de Janeiro in two time periods: the first in 1968-1969 while the squatter removal policies were being formulated and attempts were being made to modify or challenge them; and the second in 1973 after massive removal had occurred and the former squatters were resettled in public housing projects. It focused originally on three communities: 1) *Catacumba*, a favela in the centrally located upper-class residential and commercial area; 2) *Nova Brasilia*, a favela in the industrial periphery and working-class residential area; and 3) *Duque de Caxias*, a "suburbio" or dormitory city with few urban amenities, located in the far outlying area of the Rio lowlands.[2] In each of these communities, 250 people were interviewed, of which 200 were chosen at random among men and women 16-65 years of age. The remaining fifty were community leaders chosen on the basis of positional and reputational sampling techniques. Catacumba was removed in late 1969. The follow-up study located the residents of Catacumba in the public housing projects and revisited Nova Brasilia and Caxias to examine how they had fared without government intervention in the interim.

THE CASE FOR FAVELAS

The possibility of being expelled from their homes and com-

[2] For a detailed presentation of research method, cf. J. Perlman, "Methodological Notes on Complex Survey Research Involving Life History Data" (Berkeley: Institute of Urban and Regional Development Monograph No. 18, University of California, Berkeley, October 1974).

munities fills most favela residents with dread. Their attitude toward removal can only be understood if it is realized that, given the economic constraints under which they operate, the favela is a functional solution to many of their major problems. The central location of the favela generally puts its residents within close range of the best job markets and affords multiple opportunities for acquiring odd jobs in time of unemployment or financial stress. It also places them at the very center of a wide variety of urban services and benefits: free medical clinics, social services, and sometimes even schools. It gives them a sense of "being where the action is," which figures highly both in their motivations for migration and their satisfaction with urban life.

The favela provides a community where friends and neighbors can be counted on for mutual favors: there is always someone to leave the children with; an accommodating neighbor with a refrigerator where the baby's milk can be kept fresh in the summer heat; someone whose sewing machine can be borrowed for repair work. Also, food and staples can be purchased on credit from local merchants (albeit at higher prices) so that even when there is no income, families can be fed. This level of sharing may seem trivial, but it is of absolute importance to those living on the margin of subsistence. In the absence of government attention, the favela provides a minimal, community-sponsored social security and family welfare system.

Furthermore, because it is the outcome of many incremental decisions based on human needs, the favela is, in fact, well designed. Friends and families live close together; walkways are distributed where the need requires, public spaces emerge and recede according to use; and tacit agreements not to develop certain areas are obeyed. A degree of pride is derived from the fact that most of the families built the homes they live in and that most public amenities are the result of communal efforts. Despite the insecurity of tenure on the favela lands, many families have invested in their homes, creating spacious, solid, and well-serviced houses from what were once simple shacks.

Most critical of all, the favela is *free*. No monthly rents must be taken out of meager family incomes.[3] Although in the older favelas, like Catacumba, the favelado often has to pay the former tenant anywhere from a few dollars to a few hundred dollars for

---

[3] About 10 percent rent their "barracos" (shacks), but the rates are very low, about $10 per month.

253

the privilege of succeeding him, once this is paid, there are no further expenses. Some purchase price was paid by 55 percent of the present residents of Catacumba, 50 percent of Nova Brasilia, and 19 percent of Caxias. Most of the remainder in each case built their own shacks. This self-built housing, along with cooperatively built community facilities, represents the creation of significant capital through the use of labor. It was estimated in 1966 that the value of houses, schools, churches, and cooperatively built electricity and water networks in 185 Rio favelas was fifty million dollars.[4]

With all these benefits, it is small wonder that the favelados resist efforts to relocate them in government housing projects. Hostility to relocation emerged strongly in the interviews. In spite of the image the authorities give relocation in the mass media—the advantages of "modern living," legal home ownership, a healthy new environment for the children—less than a quarter of favelados accepted removal as desirable (see Table 10-1).

It is interesting to note that the residents of Catacumba, most cognizant of the imminence of removal, seem to have adapted somewhat more to it than those in other areas—or perhaps were more afraid to take a stand against it. Even there, however, about twice as many respondents are opposed as are in favor of removal. Almost 50 percent (more than in any other place) gave distance from work as the main reason for not wanting to leave. In Caxias, where most residents work far from their homes to begin with, this factor plays a less important role, while responsiveness of the community to personal needs and the social factors of proximity to friends and relatives emerge as more important. The figures for Nova Brasilia on these specifics fall in between, but the level of general opposition is greater there than anywhere else.

Among individuals in the favelas, those with housing of relatively high quality are more likely to be against relocation than those with housing of lower quality (see Table 10-2). Further, those people who are more highly integrated into their favela community show a greater reluctance to leave than those who are less integrated (see Table 10-3).[5] While there are obviously many

[4] *The New York Times*, August 12, 1966, p. 12.

[5] Although good housing quality and a high level of integration correlate with opposition to removal, other potential factors such as income level and the exact amount of time presently travelled to work, did *not* show significant relationships.

TABLE 10-1

ATTITUDES TOWARD FAVELA REMOVAL

	Catacumba %	Nova Brasilia %	Caxias[a] %
A. In favor of relocation[b]			
1. Yes, because it is urbanized there, the houses are better, and they will be legally ours.	24	14	23
2. Yes, because the atmosphere is better.	8	7	5
Total favoring relocation	32	21	28
B. No opinion			
3. If it's obligatory you have to go, there's no use having an opinion if it's a government order.	6	1	5
C. Against relocation			
4. No, because I've become accustomed to where I am, I have everything here that I like and need including my friends and relatives.	6	21	30
5. No, because it will simply become an urbanized favela worse than this one and without any of the activity or diversity.	2	4	4
6. No, because you have to pay rent.	5	8	10
7. No, because there are no schools, hospitals, stores, churches, or other conveniences.	3	7	5
8. No, because it's too far from work and transportation is too expensive and inconvenient.	47	38	18
Total against relocation	63	78	67
Total	100	100	100

[a] This refers only to the 100 favelados of Caxias; homeowners in the five neighborhoods were not asked the question.

[b] The actual question was, "Would you like to leave here to live in Cidade de Deus, Vila Kennedy, Cordivil, etc.? Why? or Why Not?

features of favela life that could be improved, the data indicate that from the point of view of the favelados, the advantages of favela life far outweigh the disadvantages of removal to publicly provided housing.[6]

TABLE 10-2
RELATIONSHIP BETWEEN HOUSING QUALITY AND ATTITUDE TO RELOCATION

Housing Quality[a]	% Wanting to Relocate	% Not Wanting to Relocate	N
Low	33	67	231
High	23	77	216

[a] Index of housing quality includes the number of rooms, the quality of construction material, the number of stories, and the type of water, sewerage, electrical, and bathroom services.

TABLE 10-3
RELATIONSHIP BETWEEN COMMUNITY INTEGRATION AND ATTITUDE TO RELOCATION

Community Integration[a]	% Wanting to Relocate	% Not Wanting to Relocate	N
Not integrated	34	66	102
Somewhat integrated	28	72	223
Very integrated	23	77	141

[a] Index of community integration includes the location of friends and family, the frequency of visiting them, to whom they go in times of need, and their feelings about the unity of their community.

GOVERNMENT POLICY TOWARD THE FAVELA

From the government's point of view, however, the favelas have always been seen as the problem rather than the solution. From the very first appearance of favelas in the 1930s and early 1940s, official policy has been to prevent their birth, stunt their growth, and hasten their death. Even under Getulio Vargas, erstwhile hero of the underclass, there was an official call to eradicate the favelas in the *Codigo de Obras* of 1937.[7] The Brazilian "red scare," beginning in 1947 when the National Communist party won its first big vote, added a new dimension to fear of the favela. To the upper

[6] J. Turner convincingly discusses the misplaced priorities among urban planners in "Barriers and Channels for Housing Development in Modernizing Countries," *Journal of the American Institute of Planners*, 33, No. 3 (May 1967), 167-181.

[7] The following discussion draws upon A. Leeds and E. Leeds, "Brazil in the 1960s: Favela and Policy, the Continuity of the Structure of Social Control," in R. Roett, ed., *Brazil in the 1960s* (Nashville, Tenn.: Vanderbilt University Press, 1972).

256

sector's abhorrence of visible poverty and the fundamental affront of squatting to the ethic of private property was added an imagined threat to the entire political and social order. It was thus that in 1947 an official "Commission for the Eradication of the Favelas" was created. Its intent, according to those who helped establish its policies, included "returning favela residents to their states of origin, committing favela residents over the age of 60 to State Institutions, and expelling from the favela all families whose incomes exceeded a set minimum."[8]

The main reason these measures were never fully implemented was lack of sufficient power and resources to do so. Official policy toward the favelas was humanized only briefly, from 1960 to 1962, when José Artur Rios was the director of Guanabara's Coordinated Social Services. Most of the residents' associations were created with strong encouragement from the government during that time—71 new associations in 1961 alone. In 1962, Rios was removed by Carlos Lacerda, then governor of Guanabara, thus ending the only period of open dialogue between the favelados and the government.

Although the general pattern has thus been official opposition to squatters, only since the military takeover in 1964 has the Brazilian government had the power, centralization, and resources to implement full-scale eradication. The main body through which this power is channeled is the National Housing Bank (BNH). It was created in August 1964 to "direct, discipline, and control the financial housing system which aimed at promoting home ownership for Brazilian families, especially among low income groups."[9] Financing for the National Housing Bank comes from two sources —one forced and one voluntary. The first is the Guaranteed Employment Fund, a form of mandatory savings to which all employers contribute eight percent of the wages earned by their employees into personalized accounts to be drawn upon in times of illness, disability, or unemployment, or for the purchase of a BNH house. The second is voluntary saving from the sale of housing bonds and from the savings deposited through passbook accounts in the savings and loan system.[10] From these sources,

[8] Quoted in Leeds and Leeds, "Brazil in the 1960s," p. 12.

[9] National Housing Bank, *National Housing Bank—A Brazilian Solution to Brazilian Problems* (Rio de Janeiro, n.d.), p. 14.

[10] BNH, *Economic Development and Urban Growth in Brazil* (Rio de Janeiro, 1972), p. 39.

BNH has control over assets estimated at $5.7 billion in 1973, roughly six percent of the gross domestic product.[11]

In financing housing construction, BNH acts through various state agencies, according to the economic level of the housing. The agency concerned with housing for low-income families is COHAB (Popular Housing Company), which is responsible for the planning, building, and administration of low-cost housing. Funds for this are lent by BNH, later to be repaid by the monthly payments of purchasers of COHAB housing. For families in the next income level, the same function is performed by the cooperatives. For the upper-income brackets, the savings and loan associations perform this function.

In the case of Rio, a special agency, the Coordinating Agency for Housing in the Rio Area (CHISAM), was created in 1968 specifically to deal with the lack of coordination that existed between the COHAB organizations in the neighboring states of Guanabara and Rio. CHISAM was charged with ensuring that there would be "no more people living in the slums of Rio de Janeiro by 1976."[12] Although CHISAM could choose to either upgrade and urbanize favelas or remove them, it concentrated only on removal. Favela removal was justified as integrating the favelado into society and increasing his purchasing power. This was expressed in the official function of the CHISAM program.

> The first objective is the economic, social, moral, and hygienic reclaiming of the slum families. Likewise the program aims at changing the slum-dwelling family's position as squatters on other people's property with all of the insecurity that goes with it, to that of owners of their own home. These families then become completely integrated in the community, especially in the way that they live and think.[13]

CHISAM's basic objective was "to help low income families acquire their own homes and develop a sense of ownership in them as well as confidence in the authorities; to take them out of their

[11] L. Salmen, "Urbanization and Development," in H. Rosenbaum and W. Tyler, eds., *Contemporary Brazil: Issues in Economic and Political Development* (New York: Praeger, 1972), p. 428.

[12] CHISAM, "Coordenação de Habitação de Interesse Social da Area Metropolitana do Grande Rio" (Rio de Janeiro: Ministry of the Interior, 1971), p. 78.

[13] CHISAM, "Coordinação de Habitação," p. 79.

surroundings and give them new horizons and opportunities; and to reclaim them socially and economically so that they can take part in constituted society."[14]

In the early 1970s, with funding from BNH, COHAB began a massive building program in Rio by allowing CHISAM to begin eradicating favelas in earnest. It set itself the goal of removing 100 families a day. By the summer of 1973, a total of 62 favelas or parts of favelas had been destroyed, and the 35,157 families (175,785 people) were moved into public housing projects or, if they were unable to afford these, into provisional housing called *triagem*.[15]

RESISTANCE TO IMPLEMENTING REMOVAL

With the threat of mass favela eradication and forced removal to housing projects constantly hanging over them, the residents' associations in several favelas joined together to form FAFEG (the Federation of Associations of Favelas in the State of Guanabara) in March 1963. The aim of FAFEG was to represent the interests of all favelados, to make known their reasons for opposing eradication, to take a strong political stance on the issue, and at the same time, to help organize the favela dwellers for mutual aid.[16]

The first action of FAFEG members to receive public attention was their support of the residents of the Morro do Pasmado favela in resisting removal in 1964. As reported in the newspapers at the time, this resistance was met by soldiers armed with machine guns, who forced the residents to abandon their homes.[17]

In the following year, strong political opposition to removal was demonstrated electorally in the gubernatorial race. Lacerda, the governor of Guanabara until 1965 and a committed supporter of favela eradication, put forward his son-in-law, Flexa Ribeiro, as a candidate. Ribeiro was defeated, largely by the votes of those

[14] Ibid., p. 101.

[15] B. Wagner, D. McVoy, and G. Edwards, *Guanabara Housing and Urban Development Program*, AID Housing and Urban Development Team, July 18, 1966, mimeo, p. 103.

[16] Information on FAFEG comes from Leeds and Leeds, "Brazil in the 1960s," pp. 48-49, and from personal interviews with Sr. Souza, president of FAFEG, on August 10th and 17th, 1973.

[17] Leeds and Leeds, "Brazil in the 1960s," p. 49.

in the working-class districts, including favelas, and by favelados relocated in project housing.

Eradication continued, however. On May 25, 1966, in Favela Jardim America, the police arrived at 7 a.m. to confront about 2,000 terrified individuals, many of them children, who had received word on the previous day that their homes were to be eradicated. To speed up the process and discourage any possible protest or revolt, gunshots were fired randomly into the crowd, and those who seemed to resist were beaten.[18]

In 1968, FAFEG, which by then had about 100 member favelas, held a congress in which it was resolved to oppose forcefully implementation of the government's policy of eradication. The official report of the congress explicitly stated the FAFEG position as the "rejection of any removal, condemnation of the human and financial waste, and the social problems resulting from removal."[19] In accordance with this position, the federation's membership mobilized to prevent action against the very first favela that the newly created CHISAM had designated for removal, Ilha das Pragas. Almost immediately afterward, FAFEG leaders were arrested by police, held incommunicado for days, and threatened with severe consequences if there were any further attempts at opposition.[20] From then on, open protest by FAFEG was effectively ended.

The following year, however, the 7,000 residents of Praia do Pinto (a favela situated on a choice piece of level terrain in the middle of the upper-class neighborhood of Leblon) refused—on their own initiative—to evacuate the favela and be relocated. During that night, the favela "accidentally" caught fire, and although many alarmed residents and neighbors called the fire department, orders had evidently been issued that no help was to come. By morning, almost everything had been destroyed. Most families were unable to salvage the few meager possessions they had, and the leaders of the "passive resistance" disappeared altogether, leaving their families in desperation. Subsidized high-rise housing for the military was constructed in the place of favela Ilha das Pragas.

[18] *Jornal do Brasil*, May 26, 1966.
[19] FAFEG, "Ralatonis final do 11° Congresso Estadual das Associacoas de Moradores das Favelas a Morres do Estado da Guanabara," Rio de Janeiro, mimeo.
[20] *Jornal do Brasil*, March 14, 1969, p. 18.

These incidents contrast dramatically with the experiences many favelas had during the pre-1964 period. The settlement of Nova Brasilia, for example, had been threatened with removal in 1962. In protest, its residents' association rented eight buses, and men, women, and children from the favela were packed into them in order to stage a sit-in in front of the governor's palace. The association also notified the major radio, television, and newspaper reporters to be on hand, and then presented the governor with a petition demanding that they be allowed to stay in their neighborhood. The governor, unwilling to alienate the hundreds of thousands of squatters in the city—and potential voters—signed the petition.[21]

After the coup, with the end of direct elections, the squatters lost the one bargaining base they had had. The centralization of housing policy and authority through the National Housing Bank, COHAB, and CHISAM, and the explicitly sanctioned use of the armed forces for implementing housing programs, cast the entire situation in a different light. The fact that the favelados themselves recognized their increased vulnerability and powerlessness was clearly demonstrated in many ways.

At the time of the initial study in 1968-1969, most of the favelados interviewed had been confronted with threats of removal at one time or another and had struggled and bargained to preserve their existence. The threat was always more immediate in the South Zone than in the North, and was felt least of all in the Baixada Fluminense, following decreasing land values. In Catacumba, 81 percent of residents were aware that the favela had been threatened with removal, contrasting with only 52 percent in Nova Brasilia and 32 percent in Caxias.

Two open-ended questions were asked in the interview, one regarding what was done in the past removal incidents, and the other asking what would be done in a similar situation today. Table 10-4 shows the responses for the random samples from

[21] In a similar manner, the squatters were able to use their numbers for bargaining power at election time. When a candidate came around to campaign, the leaders of the residents' association would promise all of the favela votes if he would provide water pipes. Then the favela leader would tell the next contender that so-and-so had promised to supply water pipes, but if *he* would supply water pipes and cement for stairways as well, the favela's votes would go to him. Furthermore, favela leaders were astute enough at this bargaining procedure to say that they didn't trust politicians and that they wanted the "goods" delivered before the election.

Catacumba, Nova Brasilia, and the three favelas of Caxias, and for the leaders as a group. In each case, responses to the question about past actions are contrasted to those about contemplated future action, and the responses are divided into active and passive categories.

While the modal response in each of the three places is a cautious "don't know," the main, systematic difference between responses referring to the past and those concerning the future is a general decrease in responses mentioning active protest measures, especially the use of "pull" (pistalão), and an enormous

TABLE 10-4

PAST AND PRESENT RESPONSES TO REMOVAL THREAT[a]

	Catacumba		Nova Brasilia		Favelas of Caxias		Combined Leaders	
	Then %	Now	Then %	Now	Then %	Now	Then %	Now
Active responses								
—Got all the residents together and protested, made up a petition, etc.	12	5	7	5	2	3	21	4
—Went to the government and asked for intervention	17	16	21	17	8	17	40	18
—Solved the problem through the pull (*pistalão*) of an influential friend	6	0	5	1	2	3	19	1
Total active	35	21	33	23	12	23	80	23
Passive responses								
—Did nothing due to lack of access to the government	16	11	9	10	14	15	9	14
—Collaborated with the government	0	29	0	11	0	12	0	25
—Don't know	39	29	57	51	64	46	8	31
Total passive	65	79	69	77	90	77	20	78
Total	100	100	102	100	102	100	100	101[b]

[a] Questions: 1) Then: "What did the residents do when the favela was threatened with removal?" 2) Now: "What do you think could be done now concerning the problem of removal?"

[b] Percentages differ from 100 percent due to rounding off.

increase in the proportion of respondents saying they would "collaborate with the government." The intensification of repression is evident in the decrease of active opposition measures and the large increase in the proportion of favelados spontaneously indicating they would collaborate were removal to become a reality.

Trends are even more visible among leaders whose behavior is subject to closer scrutiny from above. Regarding past efforts, leaders appear to have been far more active than the residents at large, but all active responses declined substantially in this group from past to present: collective protest from 21 percent to 4 percent; governmental intervention from 40 percent to 10 percent; and use of patron-client relationships from 19 to 1 percent. Concomitantly, all "passive" responses doubled, "don't knows" tripled, and "collaborate" moved from zero to the preferred alternative of one quarter of the sample.

The Case of Catacumba

The story of attempts to change the government's removal policy by residents of the favela of Catacumba illustrates well how little influence or autonomy the favelados had. As early as 1968, Waldevino, the president of the Catacumba Residents' Association, and his fellow members were so disturbed by rumors of eradication that they drew up a plan for the on-site "urbanization" (installation of urban infrastructure, services, and buildings) of the favela. The plan was presented to various state agencies, and it appeared in the September 15, 1969 edition of *O Dia*, a Rio newspaper, bearing the caption, "The Project of Urbanization presented by the residents of Catacumba and for which they ask the attention of the authorities." The plan proposed two rows of high-rise apartment buildings and a row of two-family houses at the top of the hill. The favelados hoped to construct the buildings and pay the cost themselves if permitted to remain in their locations.

In an accompanying article, the residents made a plea for the attention of the authorities. "There isn't a single resident of Catacumba in agreement with the possible forced move to "Cidade de Deus" or any other place far from the site of our jobs where we work to support our families. . . . This favela can be sanitized and urbanized. We do not want alms, charity, or hand-outs. With the approval of the public owners, we will construct and pay for our own houses." When Waldevino was interviewed early in 1968,

263

he said that the situation had become increasingly serious in recent times since none of the former recourses to action were open. He cited examples of other favelas and the fate of other FAFEG leaders. Referring to the decree suspending the civil rights of anyone deemed dangerous by the military government, he cautioned that the Fifth Institutional Act "did not stop at the foot of the favela."[22]

The study confirmed that these threats were felt by people at large in Catacumba. The vast majority of residents said that although they did not want to leave, fear of reprisal would make them cooperate with government orders. Waldevino described at length the disadvantages of the government-sponsored housing, much of it two and a half hours away. He showed the urbanization plan for Catacumba, adding regretfully that he no longer hoped to accomplish much since favelados were generally too apathetic and their leaders fearful of the risk of "being sent to jail, deprived of their political rights, and even being tortured." He also pointed out the paucity of channels of influence now that FAFEG had been disbanded, direct elections suspended, the state's powers replaced by federal jurisdiction, and now that the president had become inaccessible and probably unsympathetic to the favelados.

In August 1969, shortly after the burning of a nearby favela and the disappearance of its leaders, the secretary of social services started to organize a house-to-house census in Catacumba. The favela was evidently next on CHISAM's removal list. Newspapers were full of stories about plans for eradication, and the people quickly learned that the purpose of the census was to determine who would be sent where.[23] Ability to pay was to be the sole criterion of the decision, regardless of kinship ties.

While plans for implementing the eradication proceeded, favela leadership in Catacumba was completely coopted. Waldevino, who had drawn up and presented the plan for urbanization of the

[22] The Fifth Institutional Act, enacted on December 13, 1968, was the turning point in the government's move towards a hard-line position. It was considered "a revolution within the revolution," because of the radicalization of authority and ultimate repression of all civil liberties. It closed the National Congress and legislative assemblies, authorized the executive to legislate in all matters of national policy, to intervene in the states and in the municipalities, to suspend individual political rights, to require compulsory retirement from public office, and to initiate investigations that might lead to the confiscation of private property.

[23] See *Jornal do Brasil*, September-December 1969.

264

area just one year before, surrendered the residents' association headquarters to social service agents, donned the uniform of a state guardsman, and assumed leadership of the local vigilante committee mandated to "maintain order in the favela." He and his fellow association officers, as well as many who had figured prominently in previous battles against removal, were "appointed" to positions of leadership and status by the social service authorities. Leadership was thus completely denatured in a classic example of cooptation. The government's action was legitimized by local leadership, which provided the "vehicle of administrative accessibility" for the removal agencies.[24]

According to official reports, 2,158 dwellings were removed from Catacumba. Of these, 1,420 families were sent north to Guaporé-Quitungo, 350 to the older and cheaper housing of Cidade de Deus to the west, 87 to Vila Kennedy, and 350 to *triagem*. This meant that families could be on opposite edges of Rio, separated from each other by as much as a four- to five-hour bus journey.

Resistance to the government's policy of eradication and relocation had been possible to some extent in the competitive pre-coup political context, when votes could be bargained for, and when patron-client alliances could be mobilized. After the coup, however, with the installation of a repressive and closed military regime, there was little reason to take the interests of favela residents into consideration, and their capacity to acquire favorable decisions from the government decreased dramatically. Recognizing both the futility and the danger involved in protest activities, favela residents became fatalistic about their futures. Their leaders cooperated with the government, facilitated removal, and then disappeared. Most have not been heard from since.

[24] Selznick defines the process of cooptation as "absorbing new elements into the leadership or policy-determining structure of an organization as a means of averting threats to its stability or existence." He states: "To develop the needed sense of legitimacy, it may not be necessary actually to share power; the creation of a 'front' or the open incorporation of accepted elements into the structure of the organization may suffice. . . . In this way, an aura of respectability will be gradually transferred from the co-opted elements to the organization as a whole, and at the same time a vehicle of administrative accessibility may be established." See P. Selznick, *TVA and the Grass Roots: A Study in the Sociology of Formal Organization* (Berkeley: University of California Press, 1949), pp. 259-260.

THE PROCESS AND THE OUTCOME OF RELOCATION

According to CHISAM, the process of implementing the removal of a favela is a smooth operation.[25] The first notification about relocation comes via public news media, later followed by official communication with the residents' association. Interviewers arrive in the favela to carry out a socioeconomic survey of the residents, seeking information on family size, income, and location of workplace which forms the basis for the allocation of new housing units. Information about the new housing is made available and the favelados are invited to visit the projects. A few days before being removed, each family is told when it will leave and where it will be taken. On the morning of removal each family loads its possessions into trucks, leaving behind all building materials which are destroyed to prevent their reuse in a future favela home. In CHISAM's words, when the moving trucks arrive, "He [the favelado] and his family show joy and confidence. This attitude on the auspicious start of a new life marks the moving from the slum to the coordination offices' apartment."[26]

From direct conversations in 1973 with some of the favelados who had been removed by CHISAM, a very different account of the removal process emerged. All evidence indicated that the program had been carried out in an impersonal, arbitrary, and bureaucratic manner that degraded the favelados and helped insure the ultimate failure of the program. Most people complained that although there were several different types of housing, ranging from houses to apartments and from no bedrooms to three, the choice was made by CHISAM and forced upon the families without consulting them. No preparation was offered, no meetings held, no information was made available as to the total cost and time period involved, and those few who were taken to visit new housing were disappointed and angry because the places to which they were finally sent were quite inferior to those they had been shown. A notice would arrive a day before removal telling the family to pack its possessions and be ready at dawn the following day for removal to an unspecified destination.

When the families arrived at the project, they were assigned an apartment or house without regard to location near friends or relatives, and the keys distributed turned out to be the same for

[25] CHISAM, "Coordinação de Habitação," pp. 85 ff.
[26] Ibid., p. 95.

the entire building. With the loss of home and community still fresh in their minds, and with the feeling of having been cheated by the removal agency, favela families began life in their new housing environment and began to experience some of the consequences of their removal. The present case reinforces a growing body of findings from Brazil and other developing countries that have documented widespread dissatisfaction with such relocation efforts and devastating economic, social and cultural, political, and physical repercussions.[27]

Economic Repercussions of Removal

A consistent finding of relocation studies in Brazil and elsewhere is that the distance to work for the ex-squatter increases significantly and causes severe hardship. This happens because low-income people, who can ill afford the cost of transportation, generally locate themselves by preference close to their labor market near the city center. Relocation areas, however, tend to be placed on the outskirts of the city where land is relatively cheap. The first

[27] Studies of the effects of relocation in Brazil include CENPHA (Centro National de Pesquisas Habitacionais), "Condições de Vida em Conjuntos Habitacionais de Interesse Social: Cidade de Deus e Cidade Alta" (Rio de Janeiro: Banco Nacional de Habitação, 1970); A. Fortuna et al., "Habitação Popular: O Caso de Cidade Alta" (Rio de Janeiro: March 1973); L. Salmen, "A Perspective in the Resettlement of Squatters in Brazil," *América Latina*, Ano 12, No. 1 (January-March 1969); and B. Rush, "From Favela to Conjunto: The Experience of Squatters Removed to Low-Cost Housing in Rio de Janeiro, Brazil," B.A. thesis, Harvard College, March 1974.

Studies of the effects of relocation in other Third World countries include, R. Bryce-Laporte, "Urban Relocation and Family Adaptation in Puerto Rico: A Case Study in Urban Ethnography," in W. Mangin, ed., *Peasants in Cities* (Boston: Houghton & Mifflin Co., 1970), pp. 85-97; M. Hollnsteiner, "Urban Planning: A Curbside View," paper prepared for the SEADAG Urban Development Panel on "Urban and Regional Planning: Southeast Asian Experience," Bali, Indonesia, April 15-18, 1974; K. Hopkins, "Housing the Poor," in K. Hopkins, ed., *Hong Kong: The Industrial Colony* (London: Oxford University Press, 1971), pp. 271-335; O. Lewis, "Cruz Moves to a Housing Project," *La Vida* (New York: Vintage Books, 1968), pp. 661-669; A. Portes, "The Urban Slum in Chile: Types and Correlates," *Ekistics*, 202 (September 1972), 175-180; H. Safa, "Puerto Rican Adaptation to the Urban Milieu," in P. Orleans and W. Ellis, Jr., eds., *Race, Change and Urban Society* (Beverly Hills, Ca.: Sage Publications, 1971), pp. 153-190; R. Worth, "Urbanization and Squatter Resettlement as Related to Child Health in Hong Kong," *American Journal of Hygiene*, 78 (1963), 338-348; S. Yeh, *Homes for the People* (Singapore: Statistics and Research Department, Housing and Development Board, 1972).

effect of removal, then, is a long and expensive journey to work on a usually unreliable transportation system.[28] My original study had shown that the vast majority of Catacumba residents (79 percent) took only a half hour or less to arrive at their jobs. Follow-up studies in the relocation projects found that only 13 percent had this ease of access, while almost three-fourths (71 percent) travelled over an hour each way. Apart from the waste of time, an obvious concomitant of these long journeys is the increased cost: Barney Rush found that more than half of former Catacumbans now spend at least 10 percent or more of their total family income on transportation for the head of household alone, and many spend as much as a fourth.

Apart from cost in time and money, the isolation of the apartment complexes leads to a feeling of separation from the center of urban life and activities, and to a very acute isolation from the job market. This has seriously affected working women who depend on service jobs for the upper classes such as washing clothes, sewing, or working as baby-sitters or maids. The pay from these jobs is barely enough to cover transportation costs, and since the jobs can no longer be done at home, arrangements must be made for a baby-sitter, this being more difficult with the dissolution of mutual favor networks after removal. As the complexes are generally located on peripheral low-value land far from wealthy families, many women are forced to give up their jobs entirely after removal. One study indicated that whereas 46 percent of women from South Zone favelas and 30 percent of women from North Zone favelas had worked before removal, only 32 percent and 20 percent from the two areas, respectively, were still able

[28] In his 1966 study of Vila Kennedy, Salmen found that people travelling to the center of Rio would have to travel two hours each way and spend about one-third of their minimum salary on fares. Several men reported to him that because of the unreliability of the service, they had lost their jobs from coming to work late. The CENPHA study of Cidade Alta and Cidade de Deus in 1970 reported that only about 20 percent of the people took half an hour or less to go to work, and that about 50 percent had to travel more than an hour and a half each way. Rush found in a 1973 study of 100 people in five Rio housing projects that before removal, 79 percent of favelados from the South Zone took less than half an hour to reach work and only 4 percent took an hour or more; after removal, fully 65 percent had to travel for over an hour each way. See Salmen, "A Perspective," p. 86; CENPHA, "Condições de vida," pp. 33, 38; Rush, "From Favela to Conjunto," pp. 44-48.

to work after removal.[29] And a similar decline is evidenced for children whose odd jobs after school and on weekends were a welcome contribution to family incomes.

For men, there is a strong tendency to continue working at the same job, and to learn to tolerate the long daily commute.[30] Three years after relocation, 59 percent of the people from Catacumba still worked either in Rio's South Zone, or in the city center. BNH and COHAB had assumed an open and flexible job market whereby the favelados could quickly find new jobs nearer to their homes. Quite to the contrary, a 1973 study found that most people believed job opportunities in the new area to be worse than before, and the the number of people doing odd jobs and the number of working wives had dropped considerably.

One group whose livelihood is critically affected by removal is favela merchants, who are almost universally bankrupted by loss of clientele, costs of new licenses, prohibitions against using part of their new homes for business, plus exhorbitant rent for new store premises. The merchants were not given any assistance in moving their stores or compensation for trade lost during the process of removal. In addition, the stores they were provided in the new area are costly—3,000 cruzeiros down payment (about $740 in 1969) and monthly payments of 300 cruzeiros (about $74 in 1969)—and are located at the back of apartments, away from the main thoroughfare. Nobody took the new stores, which still remain empty, and most of Catacumba's storekeepers were simply forced out of business.

Besides the financial cost of transportation and the income lost because of inaccessibility to jobs, the favelados must accept the loss of all their investment in their favela homes without being indemnified, and pay a high proportion of their monthly income as mortgage repayment for their new housing. CHISAM guidelines for the amount of the installations state that it should not exceed 25 percent of the family income.[31] Considering the fact that favela housing was virtually free and favelados still had to struggle to

[29] Rush, "From Favela to Conjunto," p. 53.

[30] Salmen relates the not uncommon story of men who find the cost and time of the daily commute so burdensome that they arrange for a place to stay in the city, returning to their families only on weekends. Eventually they stop returning home at all, meet other women in the city, and begin second families, thus creating the social disintegration and family breakdown they were accused of in the favela. See Salmen, "A Perspective," pp. 82-83.

[31] CHISAM, "Coordination of Housing," p. 95.

feed and clothe their children adequately, the demand of one quarter of the family income is a change of disastrous dimensions. Nor is that all, because additional charges must also be met for water, gas, electricity, and "condominium" (an amount paid for the upkeep of the apartment), as well as for the bus or train fares that are indirect housing costs. In many cases, these costs are well above one quarter of family earnings, and are often close to 75 or 80 percent.[32]

It has been shown in many studies that people who have been moved to projects express resentment over the payments for the new housing because they never wished to incur the payments, because the cost keeps rising due to adjustments for inflation, and because the length of time for repayment of the loan is continually extended. While expenses for food, clothes, transportation, and services cannot be delayed, inhabitants of the new housing have, in vast numbers, defaulted on their mortgages.[33] In my follow-up study, only 20 percent of the people from Catacumba were up to date with their mortgage payments, and at least 46 percent were more than six months behind. Many people, faced with severely reduced incomes and higher expenses caused by the move, had a choice between feeding their families or making their payments. Although they feared reprisal and dreaded being expelled to *triagem*, they had no choice but to default.

Once in a position of defaulting, the inhabitants of apartment complexes are concerned that they will soon be evicted from their new homes and be given an even less desirable home, or simply be forced to begin life again in some other favela. Some people, finding the situation intolerable, have left the projects of their own

[32] To make matters worse, in attempting to be relocated in a better or closer project, many families reported their incomes as higher than they actually were, while others included income from grown children who subsequently moved into their own homes or were relocated elsewhere. Still others were counting on earnings of the wife and younger children, along with the husband's extra jobs.

[33] See Salmen, "A Perspective," p. 79; CENPHA, "Condicoes de vida," pp. 76, 78; Rush, "From Favela to Conjunto," pp. 60-63. In 1966, Salmen reported that Vilas Kennedy and Esperanca had 60 percent and 40 percent of their families, respectively, behind in payments, and BNH figures for four years later show that the same relocation zones have default rates of 74 and 85 percent. For 1970, BNH figures for eight different complexes show an average default rate of 77 percent. The Rush study found the average default rate in five complexes to be 74 percent, which was explained by most people as due to their shrunken incomes and their lack of desire to pay.

accord, leaving the vacant apartments and houses prone to invasion or to takeover by families of moderate income.[34] Others have been forced to move to the *triagem*, long barrack-like buildings with one family per room located even farther from the center of the city than the apartments. The *triagem* are, in effect, a type of punishment for poverty, like debtors' prison, in which the indigent is supposed to remain until he mends his ways and becomes affluent enough to move out. However, the *triagem* provide no opportunity for moving out.

Social and Cultural Repercussions of Removal

The sociocultural effects of removal can be understood in relation to the advantages of the favela as a functional community. Because individuals are scattered throughout new districts on the basis of income level rather than on the basis of their social and familial ties, the support structure of the favela does not survive relocation.

In their new setting, the favelados are separated from the urban services on which they had relied in the favelas. Shops are less convenient and more expensive, and do not provide the informal social welfare services of allowing purchases on credit or in very small quantities; and schools and medical services are often inaccessible and of lower quality. The favelados are also cut off from most of the "urban use" factors that enriched their lives, gave them experience with a diverse range of peoples and institutions, and integrated them into the city at large. It was often for just such advantages that the people migrated to the city in the first place. Movies, beaches, markets, spectator sports, and hangouts are inaccessible, or nearly so; even newspapers and magazines may be unavailable in the new districts. And without community solidarity or trusted leadership, the sports clubs, youth groups, samba schools, and church groups of the favela were never recreated.

Suspicion and distrust seem to rise in the new districts as does the crime rate. Aspirations remain high for a time, but with decreased probabilities for fulfillment, people grow more passive, fatalistic, and resigned. Although there has been little empirical research on these issues, popular opinion is unanimous. People

---

[34] Langston found that one and a half years after removal, 11 percent of his study sample had left the Cordovil Conjunto. See R. Langston, "Remoção: A Study of the Rehousing of Urban Squatters in Rio de Janeiro," draft, June 1973, p. 23.

who live in the projects repeatedly say there is more violence there than in the favela, more street fights, more child abuse, and less concern for others. They say they are afraid to go out on the streets at night. Meanwhile the government procrastinates in installing streetlights.[35] Whether or not the crime rate in the complexes is actually higher than in the favelas remains to be documented. However, the widespread feeling of residents attests to their own uneasiness in living in that environment, and it seems likely that high unemployment, difficult living circumstances, and lack of recreational outlets contribute to antisocial expressions of inner frustration.

Political Repercussions of Removal

The political consequences of removal follow a similar trend. The local favela leaders who initially formed resident associations for the specific purpose of fighting against removal, and for coordinating efforts towards favela improvement, were the first to be removed. They have either disappeared or been sent to housing projects distant from each other and their constituencies. Those who have tried to create new resident associations or organizations find apathy and distrust among their neighbors, and such great fear and despair that it is impossible even to get people to attend a meeting.

Sr. Souza, for example, founder of the residents' association in Catacumba, lived in the favela for 22 years until being moved to a project in 1970. He admitted that, even though nobody wanted to leave the favela, he and other association leaders eventually were coopted into helping the government carry out the removal, distributing evacuation notices, and aiding with the house-to-house census. He said that the association couldn't fight the state order, and in any case, there was always a government agent in the organization. Souza was one of the two leaders allowed to live in the projects. He tried to set up an association of residents, and even registered the association and worked out a written constitution for it. But people were afraid to come—afraid of being visible either to the government or their unknown neighbors.

[35] Salmen reports that even after three years, Vila Kennedy still has no streetlights, and I found the same to be true of Quitungo in August 1973. See Salmen, "A Perspective," p. 82. On delinquency, the *Jornal do Brasil*, December 16, 1973, reported that "Cruzado Sao Sebastao is responsible for 70 percent of crimes in the South Zone."

The other kinds of political involvement which link the favela to the larger system suffered as well. The process of gerrymandering the new settlements out of independent representation is already under way. Now that the "dangerous elements" are concentrated in isolated districts, all important local officials are appointed, not elected. Direct-action politics such as petitioning and demonstrating have diminished, partly because of reduced access to authorities and partly because of increased fear of repression. In addition, the implicit threat of violence to the upper classes is less real now with the favelados removed to distant locales. They can no longer play upon the fear of those in the city that they would—if pushed too far—*descer do morro* (come down from the hills) to loot and riot.

Finally, the most immediately detrimental political consequence of removal has been the disruption of administrative political activity. In the absence of effective action on the favela's behalf by interest groups, it has always been possible for the favelas to pursue their interests on their own through the labyrinthine bureaucracy of government. Although they have never been highly successful in these efforts, the potential of such action is even further reduced in the relocated settlements. Of major importance is the sheer physical difficulty of getting to agencies in the center of the city. The traditional bureaucratic "runaround" is even more devastating when sandwiched between long, expensive trips to and from home.

These factors may have serious effects on the favelados' political orientation. All of our indicators of conformism were positively related to socioeconomic status and power within the system —that is, to the degree of integration. It is reasonable to expect, therefore, that if this integration is seriously disrupted, increasing disaffection from the system might be the result. It is my impression that this is going on. The normally optimistic favelados are now voicing strong discontent with their situation, and for the first time their anger is linked directly to actions the government imposed on them. After their experience of removal, it is no longer so easy for them to see the system as benign.

Physical Repercussions of Removal

While the economic, social, and political ramifications of removal have tended to be mostly negative, the physical effects of the new housing have been mixed. Water, bathrooms, and sewage

273

services in the projects are major improvements over those in the favelas, and this reportedly results in improved health of children, as well as greater convenience. Electricity services are usually cheaper than in the favelas, and for some people the new housing is more spacious than where they formerly resided. There is also less fear of disastrous consequences from fire or landslide. However, despite potential gains in comfort, the poor quality of construction in the new housing is the subject of numerous complaints. Typically, after only a few years the apartments are extremely run-down, the walls are badly chipped, and there are constant leaks in the plumbing system, leaving all apartments damp except for those on the top floor. Maintenance by COHAB is blatantly inadequate; for example, it is not unusual for a project to be without water for months at a time and have backed up sewage drains and frequent blackouts.

Many complaints are also voiced over the spatial organization of the new apartments and houses. They are often cramped closely together in monotonous, simplistic rows. The buildings themselves are identical, and the favelados miss the variety of their former owner-built houses. In contrast to the favelas, where doors were always open during the day, the doors of the new apartment units are always kept closed. The layout and scale of the housing projects is not conducive to the sense of spatial and social intimacy that is so much a part of favela life.

Finally, where the new units were intended as permanent and secure homes owned by the favelados, the inability or unwillingness of the residents to pay for them has made the people as insecure in the new housing as they were in the old. In the new housing they await the day of eviction to an even less satisfactory environment.

OVERALL OUTCOME

What has been described in the case of U.S. urban renewal as "grieving for a lost home"[36] is an apt summary of the sense of loss and longing experienced by the displaced favelados of Rio. Study after study revealed profound dissatisfaction and a desire

[36] Cf. M. Fried, "Grieving for a Lost Home," in L. Dube, ed., *The Urban Condition* (New York: Bane Books, 1969); and H. Gans, "The Effect of Community Upon Its Residents," Urban Sociology Colloquium, Rutgers University, 1961.

274

on the part of the favelados to return to their former communities, or similar ones. Among people from Catacumba, sixty-nine percent said they would prefer to return, and eighty-two percent said they'd go to any urbanized favela rather than remain in the housing projects.[37] Common opinions expressed by the former Catacumbans were: "I'd go back and build a new shack the same day if they'd let me"; "If I could go to any favela in the South Zone, I would"; "We were fooled—they told us that we'd come to beautiful places with direct and cheap transportation, and that the payments would be minimal"; "They only removed the favelas so that the rich could earn more money."

Lack of choice was one of the most critical factors in the dissatisfaction. Those families who had voluntarily sought out apartments in the projects, rather than been forcibly relocated, were much more content and had a much lower default rate on the monthly payments.[38] The other big factor was the element of absurdity and waste. The favela's removal had unleashed such bitter legal disputes over land ownership that after four years the site remained totally unused and overgrown with vegetation. To prevent further squatting, a huge barbed wire fence surrounded the area, ironically bedecked with billboards advertising Kodak cameras, Ben-Gay, automatic dishwasher detergents, and American cosmetics. The former favelados said it would have been easier to accept leaving their homes had the land been put to public use, but to see it simply unused while the battle of the speculators dragged on was too much pain.

While the policy of removal has been ruinous for the favelados, the original aim of BNH to stimulate the construction industry has been partially fulfilled. In addition, the visual scars of the favelas have been removed from the landscape, especially in the elite south section of the city. However, the original intention of reinvesting the monthly mortgage payments in additional housing has had to be altered because of the massive default rates. The aim of providing housing for low-income people has been shifting slightly as the poor abandon the new housing because it is too

[37] The Rush study showed 70 percent of project residents would have preferred favela upgrading and would be willing to go to an urbanized favela, even if it weren't their own.

[38] Rush, "From Favela to Conjunto," p. 60. Yeh, *Homes for the People*, p. 195, reports consistent findings for housing in Singapore. Twice as many people living on housing estates not of their own choice wished to move as compared to those who were living where they wished to be.

275

expensive, leaving it open to those in a higher income bracket who are delighted with the low interest terms of BNH. However, as of 1974-1975, many apartment complexes had been totally abandoned and others had to be destroyed or completely remodeled to attract any population at all.[39]

The aim of integrating the favelado into middle-class life has not been achieved. Rather, alienation and despair have taken over. Sr. Joya, the storekeeper, said many of his friends have actually died from sadness at leaving their homes. "Everyone who had a little sickness got worse and died." Using misguided notions about the favelados, the government has unwittingly created exactly the sort of marginalized, unintegrated people it wrongly presumed to reside in the squatter settlements in the first place.

CONCLUSION

BNH, with its vast sources of funds for the improvement of housing in Brazil, was lauded by the United Nations Committee on Housing, Building, and Planning as "the most advanced system of housing finance in Latin America at the present time."[40] In the first eight years of its operations, from 1964 until the end of 1972, a total of 875,000 housing units were financed by the bank throughout Brazil, providing a considerable stimulus to the construction industry, to employment, and hence to Brazil's economic development. The cost of the relocation from favelas was $80-100 million and it was estimated that the entire project would cost $350 million. Theoretically, this cost was to have been borne at least in part by the former favelados as they paid off the cost of their new apartments or houses. Thus far, however, the default rates have been startlingly high, so the removal has not paid for itself. Worse still, the social welfare goal of creating housing for low-income groups has not been achieved and a disproportionate share of the resources has been used to benefit middle- and upper-income groups.

The first reason for the failure of the bank to create better housing conditions for the poor is that the bank is interested in profit in order to increase the future supply of housing finances. It therefore has a strong disincentive to provide low interest fund-

[39] *Jornal do Brasil*, January 1975.
[40] United Nations Committee on Housing, Building, and Planning, *World Housing Survey*, January 31, 1974.

ing for low-income housing, although it continues to draw 80 percent of its capital from the working class through the guaranteed employment fund and from the savings of low-income workers.[41] The second reason for the failure is that the housing that has been financed by BNH for low-income people has been built in such a way that it actually decreases the welfare of those forced to live there.

Both BNH and CHISAM have been generally insensitive to the needs of the favelados; they have instead served their own interests as a bank and a removal agency respectively, and have provided benefits mainly to already privileged groups. As expressed by Anthony and Elizabeth Leeds,

> The creation of CHISAM . . . reflects an institutionalization on a national level of economic and social policies and an ideology operating to intensify control by the elites, to serve their economic and political interests, to concentrate wealth in fewer hands—and to control and repress any agent seeking to prevent these developments. Favela policy is a mirror of all these institutionalizations, operations, controllings and repressions; in the Rio area, CHISAM is the agent of the national hierarchy as the BNH is for the country at large.[42]

The Rio de Janeiro relocation experience I have described was by far the greatest failure of BNH, both in terms of meeting the needs of the people and of being economically viable. This occurred partly because it was done in such a hurry and on such a massive scale in order to be used as a "showcase" for international as well as national prestige. Despite all of the evidence against favela removal and in favor of on-site urbanization, the government still intends to eliminate the favelas of Rio by the target date of 1983.[43] As the government policies persist, it is increasingly difficult to see the startling default rates on public housing as a result only of economic pressures on the poor. Even now defaulting on payments is partly a political expression of deep frustration

[41] R. Carpenter, *Brazil's Housing Finance System: Social Inequity in a Dynamic Mechanism of Savings Mobilization*, Stanford University Food Research Institute, working copy, 1974. Carpenter concludes that Brazil's Housing Finance System views low-income groups as "an excellent place to seek funds, but not a particularly desirable place to apply them," p. 22.

[42] Leeds and Leeds, "Brazil in the 1960s," p. 48.

[43] C. Nelson, "The Bras de Pina Experience," Cambridge, Mass., MIT, mimeo.

and resentment. This is perhaps the only politically viable means former favelados have to protest their treatment by the government.

Since it seems that the present military regime in Brazil is unlikely to be overthrown from without or undergo radical changes from within in the foreseeable future, the poor will doubtless continue to be subjected to policies that sacrifice their interests to protect the power, wealth, and privilege of the upper sectors. Although their discontent and bitterness may grow, their position of powerlessness is sufficiently evident that it is unlikely they will take any futile risks.

Under these circumstances, the most rational response is not to protest or demonstrate, but to follow the familiar Brazilian adage: "Deixe como está pra ver como è que fica" (Leave things as they are to see how they'll turn out).

Conclusion

ELEVEN · *Implementation Amidst Scarcity and Apathy: Political Power and Policy Design*

PETER S. CLEAVES

WHAT are the conditions for a policy or program to be successfully implemented in the Third World? Each of the case studies in this volume has reiterated two central ideas in response to this question. First, political and administrative actors need to mobilize sufficient power to execute a policy design, and their ability to do so depends on the influence and predilections of others in the political environment. Second, because of their content, some policies or programs themselves can be more or less difficult to implement. Thus, the scope of political power available to implementors and what I would call the policy's *problématique* are two broad categories of variables that need to be considered by analysts when they evaluate the potential of various programs to be carried to completion. The specific examples of policy execution in this book present a number of operational lessons of how policymakers, bureaucrats, and political activists may be able to manipulate these variables to facilitate the implementation of reform programs. Briefly, they may be able to do so either by mobilizing additional political resources to achieve their goals or by making policies less complex and more responsive to the interests of affected populations.

It should be clear, however, that the "success" of program implementation depends upon the perspective of the observer. Implementation involves a process of moving toward a policy objective by means of administrative and political steps. To the degree that these steps approximate the desired end, the program is be-

Note: This chapter was written while the author was a visiting fellow at Yale University. He is currently Ford Foundation representative for Mexico and Central America. The ideas expressed herein are his and do not necessarily represent those of either of these institutions.

ing implemented and the policymaker is pleased. When the policy itself, however, contains features that are contrary to the interests of the target populations, successful implementation will not cause them to rejoice. Indeed, the failure of such a program may be a source of relief. Thus, when the words "successful implementation" have been used in this book, they refer to the outlook of those groups that favor the respective policy objectives.

In this summary chapter, I draw on the case studies to explore broadly the nature of the policy context in terms of the political power available to different actors in the society, including the government, and to analyze how the problématique of a policy affects its implementation. Also, I attempt to join these two elements schematically as a means of explaining why some policies are implemented and others are not. The chapter concludes with a number of recommendations for how implementors can proceed under unpropitious conditions, either by altering the correlation of forces mobilized around a policy or by modifying its content, to bring about change in their societies. Thus, while most of the previous chapters have dealt with failures in implementation, my task here is to try to suggest how things "might have been different."

POLITICAL POWER AND POLICY PROBLÉMATIQUE

Political power can be understood as a variable that directly affects implementation because the amount of resources that can be mobilized in favor of or in opposition to a specific policy is vital to estimating its chances for implementation.[1] But the resources available to policy actors are not uniform in all societies. Power is divided differently in various types of political systems, and implementors need to be aware that its distribution influences both the content of policy and the success with which policy is executed. Although it is difficult to classify specific systems into rigidly defined ideal types, it is possible to make at least three distinctions among regimes depending on the amount of power vested in the government and the structural arrangements linking the bureaucratic apparatus to groups, classes, and individuals in the society at large. Systems approaching each type—open, closed,

---

[1] By resources I refer to the differentiated definition of power developed by W. Ilchman and N. Uphoff in *The Political Economy of Change* (Berkeley: University of California Press, 1969), pp. 49-91.

and intermediate—have been included in this volume, and each type calls forth different tasks for policy implementors and analysts to address.[2]

Open political systems are characterized by a large number of relatively autonomous interest associations, political organizations, and governmental agencies. These diverse actors generally have competing ideas about what the government should do in response to public problems and the scope and direction of change to be sought in the society. In such a context, classes and groups that join alliances or maneuver skillfully can tilt the content of policy in their favor or undermine policies that are contrary to their interests. In fact, it is often misleading to consider policies in these systems as being simply "public" or "governmental." Quite frequently, important private groups also pursue policies that have an affect on the public domain. Moreover, as soon as public policies elicit an organized response from nonofficial sources, they may generate counterproposals and activities that change the intentions and perceptions of the original policymakers in governmental circles. This sort of pluralism can enhance policy implementation when public and private resources eventually support compatible goals, but it can also entail costs. For instance, when

[2] It is venturesome to utilize all-encompassing labels for contemporary political systems, and this nomenclature is a compromise that applies generally to the cases in this book and to many other Third World countries. The "open" type refers to systems that might also be called liberal, democratic, pluralistic, or multiparty. Characteristic features of the open system are manifest in works following upon D. Truman's *The Governmental Process* (New York: Alfred A. Knopf, 1965). "Closed" systems would include most authoritarian, totalitarian, centralist, or single-party dominant governments. One type is described by V. Lenin, *State and Revolution* (New York: International Publishers, 1932), but such systems are not confined to the left of the political spectrum, as G. O'Donnell spells out in *Modernization and Bureaucratic-Authoritarianism* (Berkeley: University of California, Institute of International Studies, 1973). "Intermediate" systems are those that have sectoral or communal subsystems with relatively little autonomy, and are alternatively labelled neocorporatist, consociational, or premobilized. The corporatist type is described in Philippe Schmitter, "Still the Century of Corporatism?" *The Review of Politics*, 36, No. 1 (January 1974), 85-131. For useful attempts at systems comparisons across geographic and cultural regions, see G. Almond and B. Powell, Jr., *Comparative Politics: A Developmental Approach* (Boston: Little, Brown & Co., 1966); D. Apter, *The Politics of Modernization* (Chicago: University of Chicago Press, 1965); and J. Linz, "Totalitarian and Authoritarian Regimes," in F. Greenstein and N. Polsby, eds., *Handbook of Political Science*, 3 (Reading, Mass.: Addison-Wesley, 1975), 175-411.

power is widely distributed in a policy arena, there is less chance for the implementation of a policy connoting significant change. The case of housing programs in Cali, Colombia, documented in this volume by Irene Fraser Rothenberg, is an example of the pathological effect of severe power fragmentation on policy implementation. In this case, stalemate and failure were the consequences of a multiplicity of actors seeking incongruent objectives, not compromise and subsequent collaboration. In open systems like the cases of Colombia and India discussed in this volume, the basic issue for the analyst often is not the degree to which a public agency achieves its original goals but what mix of interested-party objectives appears to be most consolidated in response to the policy initiative. There is a need, in such a situation, to ask how this alliance of forces has affected the ability of the government to approximate its goals. Government programs in such systems are most likely to be revamped (or discarded) during their execution when officials have set their original priorities with little regard for the preferences of influential opponents or potential supporters in the society at large.

When the state apparatus itself monopolizes economic and social power in the society and retains full discretion over policy initiatives, the system can be labelled closed. Its policies generally respond to the institutional interests of the group that dominates the government machinery. Commonly in such systems, national elites conclude that their goals for the society, such as economic development or national security, are prejudiced by the social and economic patterns characterizing "marginal" populations. The chapter by Janice Perlman provides an example of how this type of regime—Brazil in her case—may embark on programs to coordinate the behavior of the poor with national plans. She is also able to suggest reasons why these policies are usually inconclusive, pointing to the tendency of the regimes to be unresponsive and to misperceive the factors that in actuality determine the behavior of the underclasses. Interestingly, although a unified core may dominate organized political activity in the country, such a system may not have sufficient power to force compliance from disorganized but wary people who are well aware that the government's policies do not respond to their particular needs. In this case, the subdued antipathy of Brazilian *favelados* toward their new dwellings sabotaged the government's stated intentions and actually exacerbated many of the problems that relocation was to resolve. Thus, although these sectors did not articulate overt hostility toward the policy during execution, and indeed were incapable of opposition on a group basis, they could withhold their individual cooperation to a point of representing a barrier to implementation that surpassed the resources of the political leadership and bureaucracy. In closed systems, negative sanctions are usually more frequently employed than positive inducements because of the difficulty of reconciling the logic of ideologically inspired policy with the economic and social interests of affected populations. The task for the analyst here is to question how much coercion the regime will employ to achieve its goals, the impact that this will have on the responses of the affected population, and whether the goals actually are a viable solution to the problem, given the aloofness of policy planners from the interests and life styles of the poor.

The situation is somewhat different in intermediate systems, where power is less centrally concentrated. Policy content corresponds partially to the interests of national elites and of popular sectors who, theoretically, are harmoniously integrated into the state via nationalism (or an organicist ideology) and special political structures are managed vertically. In Africa, Asia, and Latin America, such systems are usually found in countries with long-standing corporate or communal structures (church, army, tribe, village), and where large portions of the population are parochial in outlook, living at close to subsistence levels, and unorganized for collective political action. Classes and privileged groups in the "modern" sector of these countries typically behave in ways that are similar to those in open societies. They generate demands, form coalitions, and may even share the reins of power on a rotational basis. The existence of large unmobilized populations, however, distorts many aspects of "normal" political life, including public policy. Although traditional groups do not generate policy alternatives nor determine their outcome, their very numbers have an important effect on elites' perspectives, as Merilee Grindle points out in her discussion of agriculture and food policy in Mexico. In this case, the government provided positive incentives to integrate potentially unruly groups into the distributional network and attempted to design a policy that would forestall violence or public dissent. Similarly, in Kenya, the Temples indicate that housing policy became a tool to be used in clientelist fashion to help allocate rewards in the political system. When assessing implementation problems in cas such as these, the

285

analyst needs to be sensitive to the extent to which policies serve as symbols rather than designs for execution, and side bargains or payoffs are tolerated as a means of system preservation despite the negative effect they may have on achieving stated policy goals.

The political leadership makes periodic decisions about the priority of each sector of the population, and these choices tend to be supportive of the type of political system that the elite hopes to sustain. Given the limits on the government's capability, resources allocated to one sector obviously cannot be invested in another, even though the regime may announce uniformly high priority for most of its economic, political, and social goals. Implementors often find that even an initial, formalized allocation plan, such as a yearly budget or a five-year plan, may be altered during the course of its execution because of an underestimate of program needs, general resource shortfalls, or new priorities announced at mid-stream. System-threatening disturbances in some sectors may draw a sudden influx of resources to attend to the crisis, draining them from other programs. Also, the failure of certain sectors to provide outputs crucial for the success of a coordinated plan will deprive other policy areas of the means for achieving their objectives.

These introductory remarks, which will be amplified later in the chapter, should be sufficient to demonstrate that the kinds of power underlying implementation attempts are conditioned by varying state-society relations. They should not be interpreted to mean, however, that the only factor weighing on policy implementation is the distribution of power among implementors, their allies, and their opponents, measured along some scale. If so, ideologically convinced or intensely goal-oriented political actors would have no compunction about "shooting for the stars" in terms of policy objectives whenever they perceived a favorable political advantage, however slight. Similarly, more prudent political or bureaucratic leaders might hesitate to implement even modest changes if their power was on the decline. The policies that these actors pursue can vary significantly in terms of how difficult they are to implement.

There are at least six intrinsic aspects of any policy that affect its chances for successful implementation (see Table 11-1). First, there is the complexity of the change mechanism itself. When innovative organizational forms, untried technology, extensive coordination, or complicated methodologies are prerequisites, the chances for successful implementation are reduced, as Jeffrey Pressman and Aaron Wildavsky have pointed out.[3] In Chapter Five, David Pyle argues that these factors of complicated organization, staging, and supply lines were crucial in determining the outcome of the nutrition project in India. Likewise, one of the findings of the community development pilot project that Gerald Sussman discusses was "keep it simple," but the lesson was not applied in subsequent efforts. A second aspect of policy content to consider is that, as Charles Lindblom has argued, when the change sought is incremental in comparison with the prepolicy status quo, the possibilities for execution are greater because the risks of error and the amount of information required are both smaller.[4] It is conceivable that an incremental approach might have resulted in more positive results in the case of the cooperative organizations in Zambia that are analyzed in Chapter Two. Certainly the rapid and extensive attempt to spread the program nationally for maximum visibility and impact discouraged policy planners from paying much attention to the concrete details of the effort or to the amount of change realistically possible through the program.

TABLE 11-1
CHARACTERISTICS OF POLICY AFFECTING ITS IMPLEMENTATION

Less Problematic	More Problematic
1. Simple technical features	Complex technical features
2. Marginal change from status quo	Comprehensive change from status quo
3. One-actor target	Multi-actor targets
4. One-goal objective	Multi-goal objectives
5. Clearly stated goals	Ambiguous or unclear goals
6. Short duration	Long duration

Implementation is also affected by the number of actors involved and the variety of goals that each espouses vis-à-vis the policy in question. In the simplest case, a unified set of policymakers with a single goal confronts a target group with a similar preference regarding the same issue area. Such two-actor, limited-goal interfaces are rare, however, and when the number of actors increases, the incidence of trade-offs generally increases as does

[3] J. Pressman and A. Wildavsky, *Implementation* (Berkeley: University of California Press, 1973), pp. 6, 93, 100-101.
[4] C. Lindblom, *The Intelligence of Democracy* (New York: Free Press, 1965).

the cost of competence. Cynthia McClintock shows that peasants in Peru attempted to maximize the agrarian reform's positive elements while minimizing its negative aspects in terms of their own goals, and in so doing significantly altered the feasibility of the policy. Such activities may not oblige a public reformulation of policy objectives but can result in sufficiently severe alterations in the original guidelines to force the conclusion that the plan being carried out is no longer the one originally designed.

Implementation and its measurement are complicated by the existence of the multiple goals a policy may incorporate. A policy to increase expenditures in health care for the urban poor, for example, may derive from a variety of interests, many of them difficult to pin down, ranging from the stated objectives to tend to the sick to a desire to promote the hospital construction industry or give greater visibility to the newly appointed minister of health. N. Roos points out that goal definition may vary because people disagree about the objectives of a given program or because "no one is willing or has given time to defining them," often because it is not to their advantage to do so.[5] Certainly McClintock, Quick, and Pyle, in their separate chapters, emphasize the ramifications of goals not agreed upon or not clearly stated for the outcome of implementation activities. Indeed, clarity of objectives is one of the most important factors singled out by Susan Hadden in determining the utility of the strategy of controlled decentralization for successful policy execution.

On other occasions, the policymaker simply *assumes* he knows the aims of the groups whose situation he is attempting to ameliorate. This is a persistent cause of failure of social policies directed toward nonmobilized populations, as Perlman's Brazilian case illustrates. Consequently, the researcher often must deduce inherent policy goals from the behavior of participating actors over time, rather than from their stated preferences. Frederick and Nelle Temple utilize this approach astutely to learn that the real purpose of public housing in Nairobi was not to build shelter for the poor, but to respond to nationalist sentiments and to provide status and income property for the middle and upper-middle classes. If all other factors are equal, when many goals are pursued at once, or when goals are unclear, a policy has less of a

[5] N. Roos, "Proposed Guidelines for Evaluation Research," *Policy Studies Journal*, 3, No. 7 (Autumn 1974), 107-111.

chance for successful execution than when its goals are limited, explicit, and mutually reinforcing.

The final element of a policy's problématique is the length of time programmed for its implementation. If the policy lends itself to rapid execution, the policymaker can reduce uncertainty to a minimum. On the other hand, the greater the duration of sequential steps involved in the implementation stage, the greater the possibilities for existing actors to alter their goals, for leadership to turn over, for new actors to enter the scene, or for unintentional consequences to take their toll.[6] Gerald Sussman points to such factors of timing in considering why the original pattern for community development was abandoned and a new model adopted in India. Since it is unlikely that policymakers can foresee the exact mixture of these contingencies and compensate for them in the original plan, the longer the duration of implementation, the slimmer the possibility that the original policy will prevail, even if relative power factors have not altered significantly.

This discussion of the resources of political power available to a regime and the problematic aspects of a policy suggests that both factors need to be taken into consideration by implementors and policymakers in gauging chances for successful execution. Table 11-2 postulates four possible outcomes of implementation activities depending upon whether the regime has more or fewer resources to apply and whether the policy itself is more or less problematic, based on a composite reading of the six continua in Table 11-1. This table presents a number of basic hypotheses. It suggests, for example, that the more problematic the intrinsic features of the reform, the greater the amount of power that will be required for implementation. The kind of policy and political context conforming to Box I in the figure are the most absorbing and difficult. The policies in question are technically complicated, comprehensive, with many actors seeking multiple goals; they imply long-term horizons, and require a large amount of physical and material resources for implementation. This type of policy is exemplified by the Peruvian agrarian reform in the McClintock chapter. Box IV suggests the corresponding hypothesis that the less problematic the policy, the less power required. As a consequence,

[6] D. R. Bunker makes a similar point and presents a three-dimensional figure to illustrate his argument in "Policy Science Perspectives on Implementation Processes," *Policy Sciences*, 3, No. 7 (March 1973), 75-77.

when policy actors have reduced power they are well advised to deal in less problematic policies, as I will discuss in the next section. In addition, Table 11-2 indicates that a policymaker could expect to face defeat if he attempted to implement an extremely complicated policy with very few resources, a situation corresponding to Box II. Nutrition policy in India clearly faced this problem, as David Pyle reported. Likewise, the policymaker would be foolish to engage in overkill in Box III, which besides squandering resources might engender exaggerated unintended consequences, such as Perlman foresees as a possible outcome of the favela relocation project in Brazil.

TABLE 11-2
COORDINATES AFFECTING POLICY IMPLEMENTATION

	Policy Features	
Policy Actor	More Problematic	Less Problematic
More resources	I	III
Fewer resources	II	IV

These statements on the problématique of a reform policy and the power generated by different parties during its execution indicate that reformers may be able to manipulate some aspects of the policy or its environment in order to bring about changes in a society. The main lessons to be drawn from the preceding chapters relate to this observation. But not all factors that impinge on an implementation outcome can be controlled or even predicted. One such factor is the "historical moment" of the reform attempt. This term is less esoteric than it sounds, referring simply to the coincidence of events, many of them seemingly insignificant by other standards, that appear to play an important role at a particular point in time with respect to a policy outcome. The fact that these variables often cannot be systematically classified analytically does not diminish their importance. The arrival of a reform leader with deeply felt commitments or animosities, the emergence of an outside threat bringing together erstwhile enemies in a coalition of convenience, or the partial breakdown of a political system may generate sufficient momentum for reformers to overcome normal resistance. The importance of historical moment is exemplified by attempts at land reform. In Mexico, China, Japan, Cuba, Algeria, and Peru, severe disjunctions occurred in the national political systems that fixed attention on the rural sector and provided reformers with considerable impetus to push their policies forward.[7] Similarly, national independence and anticolonialism in Zambia, India, and Kenya were important forces behind the policies described by Quick, Sussman, and the Temples.

These structural breaks are not explicitly linked to theoretical propositions about implementation because they occur earlier in the policy process. When they occur, however, they do affect the ideological predispositions of both policymakers and those affected by policy in their perceptions of what can and should be accomplished. They often result in simultaneous policy initiatives in other sectors, which modify the environment for implementation. They may change the total political power in the system as a whole (by means of force or additional budget, for instance), and imply a new relationship with unintegrated or only marginally participant sectors of the population.

Another factor weighing on implementation not fully apparent in Table 11-2 is *non*opposition to reform. The table suggests that were implementors to face no resistance, the chances for successful implementation would be greater. Such is not always true, however. Stephen Quick refers to this point by arguing that bureaucratic adversaries can have a salubrious effect on policy implementation by obliging program advocates to specify their goals and procedures in advance. Nonopposition to reform may also camouflage public apathy. This issue pops up frequently in the case of social or economic policies (such as "basic needs") ostensibly favorable for, but foisted upon, unmobilized groups. Policymakers often design such legislation by themeslves, justify the measures on ethical grounds, and create the necessary infrastructure for their implementation, counting on few if any allies and facing no visible opponents. When the implementors leave, the beneficiaries feel little attachment or gratitude for the services rendered. The whole operation may be counterproductive because it deprives the recipients of the practical experience of having demanded and obtained these public goods through their own pressure and initiative. Since the "cheap" goods of the basic infrastructure have already been granted, the next level of ostensible demand on the government (such as greater employment opportunities, rent laws, progressive tax policies) requires more negotiating skill than these groups can

---

[7] See Hung-Chao Tai, *Land Reform and Politics: A Comparative Analysis* (Berkeley: University of California Press, 1974).

muster. Thus, over the long term, implementation is abetted when initial policy suggestions (even "basic needs") are questioned by doubting beneficiaries, and the resulting compromise obtains support from all sides. An important challenge facing reformist leadership is the development of policies with the capability of generating, during the stage of implementation, wide popular participation that can later be directed toward *other* objectives benefiting these classes.

IMPLEMENTATION ALTERNATIVES IN LOW-RESOURCE ENVIRONMENTS

Many policies formulated in Third World countries are highly problematic and count on few resources for execution, a situation graphically represented by Box II in Table 11-2. Indeed, the failures of policies documented in this volume correspond mainly to Box II, while those that succeeded are in either I or IV. In attempts to design implementable policies, then, the issue for policymakers is how to avoid Box II, or to move from there to I or IV, either of which engenders greater chances for success. This observation is particularly relevant when considering objectives that involve ameliorating economic and social conditions that afflict the poorest segments of the population in Third World countries.

The enormous gap in understanding between policymakers with ambitious national plans and target groups with particular lifestyles underlines the paradox of policies that fit into Box II. The term "policy," as an entry in the planners' and politicians' lexicon, connotes the rational achievement of collective good and long-term material benefit. Frequently, the use of the term also implies that a more acceptable set of social and economic relationships *can* be achieved by means of short-term sacrifice. Many groups that are asked to change their behavior for implementors to succeed, however, have quite distinct outlooks. Like the Peruvian peasants who choose to cultivate small individual plots rather than cooperative tracts, or the Brazilian favelados who prefer shanties to concrete apartment buildings, these target populations have a clear understanding of what is and is not in their interests. In the past two decades, academicians, policymakers, and political activists have discovered that groups they once called marginal ascribe to norms that are short-term, not long-term; individual rather than collective; and material, not idealistic. These values are engendered

292

by a situation of poverty and resource scarcity over centuries that conditions family attitudes, religion, and status norms. It has become a truism that "traditional behavior" has an internal logic that maximizes short-term security and tends to reject new behavioral patterns that are inconsistent with it. Conversely, it is also true that policy initiatives that respond to this combination of factors have greater possibilities for implementation.

Changing Policy Content: Farsighted "Shortsightedness"

One possibility for manipulating an implementation process to take such factors into consideration would be to hold power constant while making policies less problematic—that is, attempting to move from Box II to IV. A glance at Table 11-1 reveals what is required: technically simple, clearly defined, marginal, short-term projects of limited scope. While such policies might seem myopic from a revolutionary perspective, they represent a way of conceiving problem solving among unmobilized populations that is more farsighted and requires a more careful review of details than at first might be suspected. The point would be to adapt policy contents and incentives to the interests of those who are to be benefited by the program.

To apply this perspective to the housing field, the policymaker or the political activist would not promise the construction of fully equipped neighborhoods to shelter urban poor, but would provide plots, water, and sewage facilities on vacant urban land where families could construct their own dwellings. In agriculture, large-scale reservoirs and colonization schemes would give way to small-scale irrigation canals to help small farmers increase their food output for marketing. In population, rather than wait for economic development to create market incentives for decelerating the birthrate, concerned officials would provide direct material incentives to limit family size or, in the case of national underpopulation, eschew nationalist exhortations to heads of households in favor of direct compensation for increasing family size. In education, instead of designing advanced curricula purporting to transform, after twelve years of schooling, children of poor families into literati, educators would rather focus on instructing essential functional skills during the early years; this, combined with material rewards for teachers to accept appointments in outlying districts, and perhaps special privileges to families who keep their children in school. In health, a more problematic policy would

293

call for the integration of all doctors into a national health plan, and simultaneous research on and treatment of malnutrition, infant mortality, and local diseases. In a situation of low resources, more realistic approaches would be mass publication of medical guides; special training of folk healers, pharmacists, and paramedics; the provision of cheap basic drugs; and limited obligatory public service for medical school graduates. The suggested programs are less complicated and require less behavioral change than what might be desirable, but they do have the advantage of resulting in some immediate and visible benefits to target populations. Similar programs, adjusted according to local circumstances, have met with success in various settings around the world and merit broader application.

What guidelines exist for making a policy less problematic? In earlier years a combination of influences militated against even trying to do so. Global planning with quantitative methodologies was promoted in international circles, and this tended to confuse the ultimate benefactors of policy innovations—people—with numbers. The rate of European recovery after 1945 imbued the international development community with the impression that it could raise the standard of living in the Third World in similar fashion. Widespread optimism about man's ability to achieve economic development in the most unpromising situations, as well as a belief that such growth would be a cure-all for social and political ills, led to a condescending attitude toward gradual, grassroots solutions. For many countries, the exhilaration of political independence engendered false images of short-order change that could be achieved on economic and social fronts.

Some leaders, aware of the complexity of the development task, use their rhetorical skills to sweep away many problematic aspects of policy. They collapse contradictory goals into one objective such as national dignity or development, obfuscate the significance of deep social cleavages through repeated references to *the* nation or *the* people, and imply that comprehensive change is just around the corner. In an analysis of policies dressed in nationalist rhetoric in Zambia, Stephen Quick labelled these policies "ideological." Certainly, charismatic leaders can jostle many of their followers into desires for new standards of living, but their regimes generally have difficulty following up with practical policies to attend to real material needs. Ironically, as the Temples lament, noble exhortations may serve to legitimize bureaucratic behavior

294

that ignores social reform and entrenches the status quo. In situations such as these, disillusionment with policy outcomes may intensify the apathy or resistance among groups who were convinced that they were to be the beneficiaries of public action.

Policymakers concerned with the lot of the poor can take certain precautions to design and implement less problematic reform. One step that can be encouraged is greater utilization of *social science* and *technical investigation* before policies are made concrete. Anthropological, economic, and sociological research into the goals and motivations of unmobilized sectors of the population, with careful attention to the internal logic of prevailing behavior patterns, can indicate the types of projects and inventions that would be most easily embraced, yet still represent a step forward in terms of collective betterment. In many societies, important subjects for investigation are questions such as what constitutes tolerable margins of risk among the poor, what desires for social mobility exist, and what long-standing authority patterns motivate group or individual activity. Answers to such questions can very usefully be integrated into the design of incentives and instruments of policies aimed at producing change. They can result not only in greater acceptance of innovation among the target population but also in more energetic participation in achieving the goals of the policy. Elsewhere, for instance, Perlman has discussed an attempt by Brazilian planners to deal with housing problems in the favelas by capitalizing on the goals that the inhabitants themselves considered to be of greatest importance.[8] Not surprisingly, the policy —later abandoned by the government—met with considerably more success than the coercive relocation projects discussed in this volume. If such an approach had guided the formulation of housing policy in Cali, cooperatives in Zambia, and nutrition programs in India, the content of the measures would have been different. Certainly, the cases of rural electrification and the pilot phase of community development activities in India incorporated such careful and insightful planning, and both seem to have met with considerable success.

A second precaution is *experimentation*, or the process of evaluating different approaches under varying conditions to determine which policies are indeed less problematic and most operational. Here, however, policymakers need to recognize that experimenta-

[8] See J. Perlman, *The Myth of Marginality: Urban Poverty and Politics in Rio de Janeiro* (Berkeley: University of California Press, 1976).

tion is not the same as showcasing. Model projects are susceptible to the Hawthorne effect, whereby the participants change their normal behavior because of the extra attention focused upon their activities. Social experiments often benefit from management expertise, funding, and institutional backing that are not generally replicated on a national basis. Pilot projects must absorb no more resources than would be available if the program were deployed throughout the policy arena. The Etawah project, for example, as described in Chapter Four of this volume, was faithful to these and other criteria typical of a well-designed social experiment. The lessons that Sussman enumerates about such experiments might usefully be applied elsewhere. Third, once new approaches are instituted, *continuity* is essential. The first year or two of a reform may simply inform relevant populations that the project exists. Given the understandable hesitancy of traditional groups to upset existing relationships, patience and perserverance are preconditions for the policy to take hold. Steady rather than momentous change is sufficient proof that nonproblematic policies are effective. This precaution might have enhanced the viability of the cooperatives stimulated by the government of Zambia. Unfortunately, by the time policy directors no longer demanded immediate results, participants and political supporters alike had become largely disillusioned with the entire program because of the erratic way in which it had previously been pursued.

Fourth, national leaders and policymakers must change their frame of reference as to the *definition of personal and policy success* and reward policy implementors accordingly. When money is limited, quality personnel in outlying districts scarce, and possibilities for change marginal, administrators who undertake these assignments must be recompensed, in terms of both remuneration and prestige, for handling small budgets, working in difficult terrains, and accomplishing small, gradual, and continuous change. The policy must contain self-evident measures of social improvement so that administrators and supervisors can record their progress. While appeals for altruism are legitimate ways to build motivation, they cannot completely substitute for direct compensation, especially when implementors sense that they are bearing the brunt of the responsibility for national development. In cases of doubt or alienation, they are likely to seek advantage from their working environments, which could vitiate policy objectives, a subject of concern in Grindle's discussion of Mexico. The contact points between implementors and clients, and implementors and the central bureaucracy, must be monitored closely to assure that inducements and sanctions motivate behavior consistent with policy goals.

Instructively, David Pyle attributes the failure of the Poshak nutrition policy in India to each of these factors and to all of them acting together. It is clear in this case that thoughful analysis of the policy context was absent prior to implementation. The food supplement, Instant Corn-Soya-Milk, was a sophisticated import chosen instead of an effective product developed locally. Promoted by CARE, the pilot project was a showcase requiring substantial financial resources and administrative resources that clearly were unavailable on a large scale. Continuity suffered when only part of the project extended for more than one year. And the lower echelon health workers, on whose shoulders the success of the intervention rested, were demoralized because the project added responsibilities to their jobs without increasing their prestige or salaries.

Contrarily, Susan Hadden's case study of rural electrification in India exhibited quite opposite features, which she summarizes under the heading of "controlled decentralization." Policymakers thoroughly examined the state's electrification needs beforehand, including the relative capacity of electricity to raise the agricultural productivity and income of village farmers. The technology utilized was easily available and maintained. Policymakers accurately calculated the cost of the project, and established criteria for extending electricity to villages that were based primarily on economic factors. The administration of the project was rather simple, because cost was measurable along a single scale. Widespread knowledge of operating rules allowed engineers and accountants to resist political and social pressures for inorganic electricity growth. The program's long duration did not trigger goal distortion because its continuity had a soothing effect on popular expectations. Villages denied one year knew that their position on the eligibility list would rise. Finally, implementors worked earnestly in their jobs partially because of their belief that they were participating in the dramatic modernization of rural India and because their status as engineers and "scientists" was protected and enhanced throughout the program.

These are a few general suggestions for manipulating the content of various policies to ensure more successful implementation of reformist policies. Nevertheless, even though problematic policies are thus reduced in scale, it is still important that the bureaucratic and environmental contexts be sensitively nurtured by policy promoters to further enhance the possibilities for success. If not, it is unlikely that policy actors will be able to take best advantage of the small amount of resources that are available to them. In the following section, various strategies for affecting the policy environment to encourage successful implementation are discussed.

Changing the Power Balance

Many policymakers and political activists refuse to abandon the notion that comprehensive or highly problematic policies can indeed be implemented, and rightly so. A question then arises: Is it possible to mobilize sufficient resources in a policy arena to overcome the inherent constraints of technically complicated, comprehensive, multiactored and multigoaled, long-term policies?

There are, of course, several ways to do so, and all are difficult. The first is by means of revolution, or a total modification in the structure of power in a society which displaces dominant elites and incorporates previously powerless groups and their articulated preferences into the decision-making structure. The occurrence of such upheaval is linked to the concept of historical moment discussed earlier. "Revolution" is possible only at specific moments of social disjunction, and is not often an event that can be planned in detail beforehand. Even when such drastic change occurs and progressive political leadership takes advantage of it, problems emerge concerning how to direct the energies that are unleashed. Attending to short-term, individualistic, or material values that motivate many popular sectors may help sweep away the defenders of a pernicious system, but may also result in a new set of relationships that is little more economically or socially advantageous to the poor and, more importantly, has no effect on consolidating their power for future initiatives. Spontaneous redress of deep grievances, such as land invasions in rural areas or vengeance against an alien commercial class, can have the effect of weakening the class power of the perpetrators, because once the political act is complete, the threat of its occurrence in the future disappears.

One practice proposed to solve this problem is the "mass line." As developed in Maoist ideology, the concept involves abstracting particular aspirations of the masses into an awareness of total interrelations and corollaries for action. The leaders who abide by

298

the mass line are also the followers of the popular sectors. The responsibility of the government is to gather the ideas of the masses, which are scattered and inconsistent, merge them into a consensus, and then discuss them with the masses so that the ideas can be incorporated as their own.[9] While there is debate as to the precise nature of Chinese revolutionary praxis, and whether it can be repeated in less extraordinary historical circumstances, the general objective is sound, especially if policies are to be comprehensive, not incremental, and their implementation to depend on the internalization of their goals by the populations and leaders affected by them.

A frequent occurrence in revolutionary situations, however, is that one elite is displaced by another, but the masses do not take part; or, if they do participate, they disaggregate soon afterwards and continue to reflect defensive, short-term, security-maximizing attitudes toward new initiatives. In such instances, it is clear that no significant change occurs in the total amount of power generated that can be used to underwrite various policies for change. Soon the revolutionary government is faced with the same set of hurdles in implementing problematic policies affecting poorer constituencies, and the latter have no means of proposing systematic alternatives. More seriously, because the new regime does not rest solidly on the organized backing of previously nondominant groups, opponents not eradicated by the revolutionary thrust can rear up and undermine its progressive intent.

In summary, revolutions are not commonplace because their necessary preconditions occur infrequently, and often revolutionaries are incapable of seizing the moment. Even when revolutions topple the elite in power, this does not guarantee that comprehensive policies can be implemented to benefit the country's poorer sectors, because transforming the society's unintegrated population into a new power bloc is far from simple. When revolutionary leadership fails to do so, or abandons the task, a possibility exists for counterrevolutionary forces to fill the void.

A second means of generating extraordinary resources for problematic policies (though not of the magnitude potentially available in a revolutionary situation) is through bureaucratic mechanisms, both within and among reigning national institutions and in association with various social classes. This tactic, however, is

[9] See S. Schram, *The Political Thought of Mao Tse-Tung* (New York: Praeger Publishers, 1963), pp. 315-317.

delicate, requires political acumen, and runs some risks. Bureaucratic response to social demands is related to the type of political system in which the policy actors are embedded. When an open, modern sector is differentiated among various political parties, social institutions, and relatively autonomous public agencies, power contenders claiming to represent the masses can promise revolutionary programs in the hopes of changing the power balance in their favor. Especially when accompanied by isolated outbursts of dissatisfaction among these sectors, the result can be a realignment of national priorities, investment of funds in social programs, and the integration of affected groups into a new relationship in which they have a stake.

The risks inherent in this sequence, however, can escalate rapidly. If the manifesters do not succeed in changing the government's outlook, the state may endeavor to change theirs. Dominant social classes perceiving popular agitation to be a threat may commission the state's repressive arm to quiet the turmoil. Extreme leftists and/or anarchists, denouncing policymakers as exploiters, reactionaries, and elitists, may provoke the government into further repression on the notion that coercion is preferable to reform because repression aggravates misery and alienation. The paradox is that liberal politicians must tolerate and encourage political organization of target groups for implementation to succeed, yet the creation of that power is often perceived as threatening to the system and may bolster the position of reform opponents.

In closed systems, on the other hand, the state concentrates enormous relative power within its boundaries, but it tends to become blind to the society of which it is a part. The public institutions of these regimes have difficulty tapping the resources of the poor because the poor's most effective resource lies in numbers, and mass pressure is inconsistent with bureaucratic norms of deliberation, procedure, and control. Typically, the norms for promotion and recognition make administrators respond to superiors' aspirations for the image of success, rather than client satisfaction. In addition, power concentration may in reality be somewhat illusionary because the overall poverty of the society places absolute limits on the regime's capabilities to execute far-reaching change. A frequent occurrence is that leadership, exhilarated by the reflection of its own power, sponsors highly problematic policies that fail spectacularly.

Implementation in such systems can be enhanced when internal control is translated into disciplined monitoring of policies of intermediate levels of complexity. To compensate for the rigidity spawned by control and discipline, bureaucratic organizations in these systems need to devise means to assimilate new information at the project site and to learn from program beneficiaries. In this system, but in others as well, administrators often decry the lack of participation in myriad organizations created by supposedly innovative policies. The invocation, "Participate," is confusing because groups not organized on a national basis have roles and obligations that they fulfill quite actively locally. Animated by criteria formulated by political superiors, reform implementors refuse to participate in *their* systems. And if policies do not reach some sort of compromise with these short-term, material, and individualistic orientations, successful implementation is unlikely. The challenge for reformers therefore lies in utilizing the discipline inherent in a closed system to loosen the structure and thus to permit the system to adapt and learn rather than remain persistently sealed from the social forces in its midst. When this task is accomplished, the resources available for policy implementation are recombined and increased.

In an intermediate state-society power relationship, the potential power of unmobilized groups is implicitly acknowledged and the regime caters clientelistically to some of their demands while assuring that these pressures do not reach a level requiring more severe structural reform. Dispensing valued services on a selective basis creates an image of resource distribution that is more symbolic than real. The positive aspect of corporatist or communal structures is that their local agents do tend to maintain close touch with the mood and preferences of traditional sectors, and the goods distributed, while insufficient in quantity to serve the whole population, at least are suited to their immediate needs. On the other hand, stability is dependent on steady economic growth and an ideology that creates a mystical barrier between the popular sector's awareness of its relative impoverishment and of the operations of the overall system. Corporatist structures tend to foment competition within the same class over valued goods, defusing popular agitation but at an ever increasing cost.

In these systems, Grindle and the Temples agree separately that the most promising means of increasing the ability of the popular sectors to receive benefits from public policies is through direct organization. Historically, political activists who have been most successful mobilizing power among potential benefactors of social policy operate outside of the government machinery and define their followers' interests in class terms. Since this type of system can move toward either a more closed or open mode, however, these activists are well advised to proceed gingerly. Their tactics generally involve a mixture of incentives, including a close attention to their constituencies' material aspirations and need for short-term results. In some situations, building voting strength is an alternative. In others, rural land invasions, workers' strikes, and urban squatting are feasible tactics because they operate on the margin of the poor's tolerance for risk taking. Furthermore, they provide an opportunity for popular leaders to demonstrate that collective action can bear fruits.

It is in the interests of the bureaucracy to establish links with the most organized of these groups, if only to absorb them into national structures and make them dependent on government largesse. The combination of popular mobilization and official concern in intermediate systems results in an uneven and staggered distribution of political goods. The gradual implementation of social policies is in the interests of the regime and the populace until the magnitude of the operation outdistances the government's resources. At that point, the integrating ideology may be challenged, and deep transformations may take place. If popular groups have remained organized, they may be in a position to help define the nature of the new system.

CONCLUSION

In brief, drawing on the preceding chapters, I have tried to indicate how the content of policies and the resources available to political leaders in various kinds of political systems might be changed to enhance the possibilities for successful implementation. Conditions in Third World countries will occasionally emerge that are favorable to a revolutionary breakthrough. In usual cases, however, the situation will be one in which only less problematic change can be implemented. In the past, opportunities for gradual change have been scorned, poorly analyzed, and rarely seized, meaning that for all the development rhetoric, little improvement has occurred in the living standards of vast sectors of Third World peoples. The implementation of workable policies in situations of low economic resources and low to intermediate political mobilization is not as difficult as complete social transformation, but elusive nonetheless.

Identifying the most pertinent lessons from the preceding chapters depends on the vantage point and goals of the observer. Whether inside or outside of government, however, the implementor should have a general idea of how power is distributed in the society, and the margin of change that can be realistically accomplished at that particular moment. In normal times, policies and programs should be explicit in their objectives and procedures, and modest in their pretensions. For best results, the content of the policy should reinforce many of the propensities of the target populations so that their support is likely to abet the implementation process. Determining those propensities, however, requires sensitivity and insight on the part of policy advocates and administrative personnel. Implementation itself requires bureaucratic responsiveness even if, as in the case of closed political systems, it must be artificially manufactured. In general, it appears that the tolerance of relatively autonomous political organization among the poorest sections of the population is an essential feature of the implementation of both gradual and large-scale policies for change. In cases where the politically dominant groups are unable or unwilling to carry out this assignment, or even actively oppose it, the way is left open for antisystem advocates to try to fill the breach.

Contributors

MERILEE S. GRINDLE is Assistant Professor of Political Science at Wellesley College. She received a B.A. from Wellesley (1967), an M.A. from Brown University (1973), and a Ph.D. from the Massachusetts Institute of Technology (1976). She is the author of *Bureaucrats, Politicians, and Peasants in Mexico: A Case Study in Public Policy* and a variety of articles in professional journals dealing with bureaucracy and public policy. Her current research interests include agricultural development policies and their implementation.

PETER S. CLEAVES is Ford Foundation representative for Mexico and Central America. He received a B.A. from Dartmouth College (1966), an M.A. from Vanderbilt University (1968), and a Ph.D. from the University of California at Berkeley (1972). He has spent academic years at the University of Grenoble, France, and at Yale University, and has carried out research in Argentina, Chile, Peru, and Mexico. His writings include *Bureaucratic Politics and Administration in Chile* and *Agriculture, Bureaucracy, and Military Government in Peru*.

SUSAN G. HADDEN is Research Associate and Assistant Professor at the Southern Center for Studies in Public Policy at Clark College in Atlanta, Georgia. She received a B.A. from Radcliffe College (1966) and a Ph.D. from the University of Chicago (1972). Her publications include a forthcoming textbook on public policy and articles concerning U.S. aid programs, policy cycles, and the use of technical expertise in policymaking.

CYNTHIA MCCLINTOCK is Assistant Professor of Political Science at George Washington University. She received a B.A. from Radcliffe College (1967) and a Ph.D. from the Massachusetts Institute of Technology (1976). She spent a year in Peru during 1973 and 1974, and has returned several times thereafter. Her publications include *Self-Management and Political Participation in Peru, 1969-1975: The Corporatist Illusion*, a Sage Professional Paper in Contemporary Political Sociology.

JANICE PERLMAN is Associate Professor of City and Regional Planning at the University of California, Berkeley. She received a B.A. from Cornell University (1965), and a Ph.D. from the Massachusetts Institute of Technology (1971). Her book, *The Myth of Marginality: Urban Politics and Poverty in Rio de Janeiro* recently won the C. Wright Mills Award for the most important work of the year in public policy. At present she is involved in research on grass-roots groups and urban neighborhood revitalization in the United States and Europe.

DAVID F. PYLE is a candidate for a Ph.D. in Political Science/International Nutrition Planning at the Massachusetts Institute of Technology. He served with CARE in India from 1970 to 1973 and in Turkey from 1973 to 1975. His research interests focus on the delivery of integrated health, nutrition, and family planning services at the community level in the Third World.

STEPHEN A. QUICK is Assistant Professor of Political Science at Holy Cross College. He received a B.A. from Antioch College (1969), a Ph.D. from Stanford University (1975), and was research associate at the Institute for African Studies in Lusaka (1972-1973). He has published articles on Zambian rural development in the *Journal of Modern African Studies* and in the *Zambia Papers* monograph series.

IRENE FRASER ROTHENBERG is Associate Professor of Political Science and Director of the Public Administration Program at Barat College. She received a B.A. from Chatham College (1966), and an M.A. (1966) and Ph.D. (1973) from the University of Illinois-Urbana. She is coauthor, with Peter Bock, of *Internal Migration Policy and New Towns: The Mexican Experience*, and she has published articles and book reviews in the *Journal of Ethnic Studies*, the *Hispanic American Historical Review*, and the *Revista Latinoamericana de Administración Pública*.

GERALD E. SUSSMAN is Assistant Professor of Public Health Administration at the School of Public Health, University of Texas, Health Science Center at Houston. He received a B.S.s.s. and LL.B. at Georgetown University (1959 and 1962), an M.A. at Johns Hopkins (1964), and a Ph.D. at University of Michigan (1975). He has published a number of articles and studies concerning public administration, especially with regard to rural development, in professional journals. Currently, he is involved in a project for regional delivery of health services in rural underserved areas.

FREDERICK T. TEMPLE currently works for the World Bank's Urban Projects Department. He received a B.A. from Yale University (1968) and a Ph.D. in Political Science from the Massachusetts Institute of Technology (1973). In addition to his research and practical experience with urban development in Africa and Asia, he has studied the administration of HUD-sponsored housing programs while working with Abt Associates from 1974 to 1976.

NELLE W. TEMPLE was Special Assistant to a U.S. member of the Independent Commission on International Development Issues (the Brandt Commission) in 1978 and 1979. She received a B.A. from Smith College (1968) and a Ph.D. in Political Science from the Massachusetts Institute of Technology (1979). She has taught at the University of Maine at Portland-Gorham, lectured at the Johns Hopkins School of Advanced International Studies, and consulted for Abt Associates.

Index

Africa, 5, 15, 30, 44, 285
Agency for International Development, *see* USAID
agrarian reform, *see* rural development
agricultural development, *see* rural development
Algeria, 290
allocation decisions, 10-11, 13, 18-19, 20, 26, 30-31, 47, 119, 133, 195, 197, 201-23, 224-49, 286
Asia, 5, 15, 30, 120, 285
authoritarian governments, 30, 31, 250-78. *See also* military regimes

beneficiaries, 17, 42, 67, 75-97, 124-25, 151, 170, 172-74, 177, 182, 189, 195, 197, 201-209, 219, 242, 282, 288, 291-92, 293-98; definition of, 38, 187; isolation from, 55, 175, 285; low income, 12, 20, 24, 30-33, 34, 128
Bolivia, 65, 95n, 96n
Brazil, 19, 30, 32-33, 196, 224, 250-78, 284, 295
bribes, *see* corruption
bureaucracy, 3-4, 10, 13-14, 18, 25-26, 42-43, 45, 53, 95-97, 101-102, 105, 109, 115, 118-20, 139, 201-208, 221, 241, 285, 299-302
bureaucratic politics, 94
bureaucrats, 3-4, 9, 12-13, 17, 19, 24, 30-32, 37-38, 47, 61, 66, 101, 121, 142, 171, 196, 246, 249, 281

CARE, 126, 130-31, 132, 135-36, 137, 140, 297
Chile, 65, 96
China, 290, 299
civil service, *see* bureaucrats

clienteles, *see* beneficiaries
Colombia, 19, 20, 28-29, 102, 147-69, 284
colonialism, 22, 55, 102, 108, 171, 225-26, 232, 235-36, 248
community development, 27, 103-22, 289, 295
compliance, 11-14, 24, 33, 52, 95, 188, 195, 203, 207-208, 284
conflict, *see* implementation, politics of
Congress Party, 116-17, 120, 174, 180-82, 184
constituency, 119, 134, 136, 148, 177, 181, 188, 201, 244-45, 250, 272, 299, 302. *See also* beneficiaries
controlled decentralization, *see* decentralization
cooperative policy, 19-20, 23, 44-63, 64-97, 295, 296
cooptation, 203, 265, 272
corruption, 15n, 206, 213, 249
Cuba, 95-96, 290

decentralization, 14, 28-30, 65, 94, 95, 145-69, 170-91, 288, 297
demonstration project, 132-33, 139
Deutsch, Karl, 55
development administration, 26n
district officer, 105. *See also* field staff

Echeverría, Luís, 208-12, 220
economic planning, 38
education policy, 9, 10, 293
elections, 14, 33, 244-45
elites, 12, 22, 24, 30, 32, 41-43, 48-49, 55, 58, 61, 66, 71, 143-44, 198-208, 221-22, 224, 233-35,

307

elites (*cont.*)
  242, 244-46, 249, 276, 284-86,
  288, 298, 299; attitudes of, 235-37
Etawah Project, 108, 109-14, 115,
  120, 121, 123, 296
ethnic ties, 18, 243, 246
expatriates, 60n, 240-41
expertise, 54, 60, 61

factionalism, 18, 158, 160, 161-64,
  165, 167, 191
family planning, 128, 134, 144, 293
favelas, see squatter settlements
feedback, 8, 23, 52-56, 57, 59, 196
field staff, 45n, 49, 52-54, 55, 60,
  77-78, 84, 111-12, 117, 138-39,
  197-223. *See also* bureaucrats
Frank, André Gunder, 51

Gandhi, Mohandas, 107, 117, 118,
  171
goals, 37, 46, 54, 57, 173-74, 184-
  88, 195, 201, 222, 281, 287-88;
  achievement of, 103, 207, 217,
  221, 288; ambiguous, 37-38, 42,
  46, 48-52, 57, 59, 65, 173, 288;
  clarification of, 59, 83-84, 141,
  182; conflict over, 64, 70-97;
  multitude of, 42, 46, 48-52, 57,
  59, 65; subversion of, 249

Hawthorne effect, 296
health policy, 9, 19, 124-44, 288,
  293-94. *See also* nutrition policy
high-income groups, *see* elites
housing policy, 9, 20, 28-29, 32-33,
  147-69, 196, 224-29, 250-278,
  285, 293, 295

ideology, 42, 44, 55, 61, 64, 70, 76,
  83, 117, 286, 302
implementation; actors involved in,
  10-11, 17-18, 37, 197-209, 287-
  88; choices about, 20, 25-30, 45,
  48, 101-102, 115-16, 118-22,
  129-33; content of policy and, 5,
  8-10, 11, 14, 19, 27, 28, 31, 33-
  34, 37-39, 196, 281-82, 286-92,

293-98, 303; context of policy
  and, 10-15, 21, 23, 26, 33, 34,
  59, 102, 146, 173, 196, 201-208,
  247-49, 281-86, 289-92, 298-303;
  continuity and, 296-97; criteria
  for, 49, 59, 172-74, 177-91, 297;
  decentralization and, 14, 28-30,
  145-69, 170-91; definition of, 5-8,
  10, 20; efficiency of, 54, 143, 170-
  74, 183; ideological programs
  and, 40-63, 285, 294; local agencies and, 145-69; paralysis of, 165-
  67; participation in, 17, 119, 295;
  political power and, 4, 281-92;
  politics of, 3-4, 8-9, 10, 13, 15,
  17-19, 30, 48-52, 248; rationality
  and, 59, 63; reform governments
  and, 64-97; reform policies and,
  281, 290-91, 298, 301; regime
  characteristics and, 12, 14, 30-31,
  33, 34, 222, 250, 282-84, 289-92,
  298-303; site of, 9-10, 65, 195-96;
  strategies for, 25-30, 103-22, 123-
  44, 145-69, 170-91; studies of,
  3-5, 6, 14, 19-34, 40-41; success
  and failure, 6-8, 25, 27-29, 33-
  34, 37, 40, 61-62, 64-68, 83, 88-
  89, 102, 104, 110-11, 127, 128,
  169, 172, 173, 198, 225, 252,
  281-303; timing and, 129, 140-41,
  289, 290; variables affecting, 3-4,
  8-10, 20-21, 93-97, 101, 108-109,
  140-41, 142. *See also* pilot project;
  feedback
India, 19, 27, 29, 102, 103-22, 123-
  44, 170-91, 284, 287, 289, 290,
  291, 295, 297
influence, *see* allocation decisions
institutionalization, 123
interest groups, *see* voluntary
  associations

Japan, 290

Kaufman, Herbert, 55-56
Kaunda, Kenneth, 44-63
Kenya, 19, 20, 30, 32, 196, 224-49,
  285, 291

Library of Congress Cataloging in Publication Data

Main entry under title:

Politics and policy implementation in the Third World.

  Includes index.
    1. Underdeveloped areas—Politics and government—
Addresses, essays, lectures.   2. Underdeveloped areas
—Economic policy—Addresses, essays, lectures.
3. Underdeveloped areas—Social conditions—Addresses,
essays, lectures.   I. Grindle, Merilee Serrill.
JF60.P66   351.007'09172'4   79-3213
ISBN 0-691-07617-0
ISBN 0-691-02195-3 pbk.